Red Velvet

Red Velvet

Memoirs of a Working Girl

Lisa Lou

NEW HOLLAND

First published in Australia in 2006 by
New Holland Publishers (Australia) Pty Ltd
Sydney • Auckland • London • Cape Town

14 Aquatic Drive Frenchs Forest NSW 2086 Australia
218 Lake Road Northcote Auckland New Zealand
86 Edgware Road London W2 2EA United Kingdom
80 McKenzie Street Cape Town 8001 South Africa

A record of this book is available from the National Library of Australia.
ISBN: 1741104130

Publisher: Fiona Shultz
Project Editor: Lliane Clarke
Copy Editor: Jenny Scepanovic
Design: Leigh Nancurvis
Cover Design: Greg Lamont
Production: Linda Bottari
Printed in McPherson's Printing Group, Maryborough, Victoria

10 9 8 7 6 5 4 3

About the Author

Lisa Lou was born in Devon in the 1960s. She studied English literature in Exeter and moved to Australia in the 1980s to escape crippling poverty in London. She has lived the life of a gypsy in England, Germany, Denmark, Perth, Melbourne and Sydney. She has been a wife, a witch, a lover and a mother.

Lisa has lived with prostitutes, transsexuals, drug-users, bisexuals, gay people and fetishists—on the periphery of the underground and the underworld.

As well as a working girl, she has been a beauty consultant, make-up artist, fashion designer and retailer, and promotions and entertainment coordinator.

Lisa began writing to deal with her bipolar affective disorder, which makes real-life experience acute and a life of fantasy more comfortable. She practises Buddhism and aestheticism.

Contents

I live in red rooms
dim lights
all night
water washes my skin
but doesn't clean me

hands rip my flesh
sweat doesn't touch me
words are distant sighs
but the dream is real

my friends laugh their questions
knives cut my clothes
cut my body

you can touch me, tell me, ask me
understand the words
speak them
intrude with your noises
keep me awake
demand more
laugh, entertain, pretend

you can never
dig in the dirt of my knowledge

I'm paid for but never owned.

Preface

Melbourne at the end of the 1980s.

I had given up my three children to their father because I was at the end of my rope.

I knew that the day I hit my son.

I'd never hit him before.

I had almost run out of options, but I had two options left:

Option One: Become a prostitute.

Option Two: Suicide.

I thought about suicide a lot.

My father had abused me to the point where I hated myself, and my husband to the point of despair but not *quite* to self-destruction.

This was to be my journey to empowerment.

Throughout my marriage I was inexperienced and so inhibited that my husband never saw me naked. One night, towards the end of our marriage, after a particularly mediocre session of sex, he said to me that if I had to rely on fucking to make a living I would starve to death.

I laughed about that later.

I wanted to prove him wrong, about everything he'd ever accused me of. I wanted revenge. At the time I wanted revenge on men. But, more importantly, I just needed to survive.

Prostitution was to become an enlightening and often educational career.

I had a creative mind. I survived. I flourished.

I felt special living a glamorous, sensual existence, far better than the lives that 'ordinary people' had. I did it with style. I became an actress, a dancer—part entertainer, part psychoanalyst. A mental acrobat, a seductress creating one fantasy after another.

I became *the* fantasy for many men—and a few women.

The men I saw treated me like a princess. They valued me more because they were paying for me. They valued me more than their wives. They certainly treated me better than they treated their wives.

I knew that other people saw me as living in some sort of moral twilight, visiting five star hotels, working in brothels and losing myself in nightclubs, sleepwalking in a drug-induced haze.

I survived all this—without permanent damage.

This is a story about me, how I became a whore, how I sold myself and what I did to earn a living. But it's important that you know that at the time my clients were not with *me,* they were with *their fantasy,* and it is this detachment that allows us, the women who work in 'the industry' to give so much of ourselves night after night after night.

I want you to see my clients the way I saw them—as damaged children. I always felt compassion, even tenderness, for them and I am eternally grateful to them for their support, financially and emotionally.

Well, most of them anyway.

Many women not only survive this profession, they thrive. The skills they learn to deal with people empower them in their relationships, in business and in all aspects of their lives. I've known women who started in the world's oldest profession with nothing and ended up property owners, directors of companies, starting new careers, and entering into happy marriages *and* having well-adjusted children.

I was fortunate. I was one of the lucky ones.

Let's be alone together now. Follow me. Come with me.

1
Preparation:
building the fantasy

They liked me to look artificial, it contributed to the fantasy: the 'slut' image. After all, I was an insatiable slut who 'loved it'. The mask of carefully applied make-up helped me assume my role in this, my private theatre.

As I moved with the languid grace of a cat, diffracted light from nine candles of varying sizes and a side lamp threw off a golden glow as though a bed of daffodils had burst into bloom around me.

My delicate floral perfume moved through waves of a haunting Arabian love song, mingling with thin trails of grey smoke from the candles of varying sizes placed on the dresser and windowsill.

I bent to the old dresser to light the wick of an oil burner scented with geranium and rose.

Sitting with my legs spread wide, I pulled a tangle of lingerie onto a thinning Persian rug. From the large, wooden bottom drawer of an old dresser I sorted coordinating pieces; separating a dark-grape-coloured lace G-string and bra with a plain satin suspender belt and black lace-top stay-up stockings.

I liked dressing up.

A plump grey and white cat, who I'd named Miss Piggy, sauntered in arrogantly and made herself comfortable in front of the bar heater. She licked her dainty white paws and gazed at me with a blissful, contented look, from half-closed eyes.

I let her stay for a while, recognising a kindred spirit.

I fastened the school gym skirt that just covered the tops of my stockings and buttoned a short, white cotton school shirt; left open at the top to show my bra and the creamy curve of an uplifted breast.

I tied my hair in two pigtails, high on each side of my head, fastening them with black satin bows. I dragged a pair of shiny black stilettos from under the bed, ready to slip on at the last minute.

Kneeling on the floor next to the bed I peered into a small silver mirror propped against a pillow. I applied plenty of thick, pale concealer to cover faint dark shadows beneath my eyes, that gave my face the look of a Japanese doll. I outlined my lips with a pencil and applied dark-red, matte lipstick that stayed on well. I gave my eyes a smoky outline, smiling at my reflection, pleased with the overall effect.

Studying the sheet on the bed, to make sure it still *looked* clean; I pulled it tightly, hastily pushing my doona into the bottom of the wardrobe that smelt of dust and old ladies.

I hurriedly pulled three towels from a cupboard, laying one across the bed, pinching it in the centre so that it resembled butterfly wings. I placed a tightly rolled bolster across the centre to form a fat butterfly body. I had learnt this in a brothel. Different brothels have their own towel etiquette, varying in intricacy. The last towel I placed in the bathroom.

I put a video on: '*Teenage Fantasy*'. Some overly made-up, blonde 'office worker' being seduced during a job interview. As if.

I couldn't see many clients at home: it was too risky, although no-one seemed to notice during the week, since most people were at work.

I charged a hundred and fifty dollars for an hour of straight sex and an extra one hundred and fifty dollars for anal. Occasionally I went to hotels. This was fun but the journey there and back was too time-consuming.

I tried to keep my condom use down to three a booking; they were expensive and I was a businesswoman.

As I prepared, I spoke to myself gaily: 'Good girls go to heaven, bad girls go everywhere. Here for a good time not a long time. Live fast, die young; leave a beautiful corpse.'

My mother said money doesn't grow on trees, but I sure as hell have a bush it grows on.

I made sure everything was close at hand; it was better not to expose the condoms and lube to my clients, they liked to think I got wet just *looking* at them.

I hid my 'accessories' under one side of the bed and sat the vibrator in the middle. A rotating purple penis with little pearl beads sat in the centre of the bed like a child's toy—a very expensive one that had to be replaced every three to six months. They don't come with a warranty.

It looked slightly ridiculous in its colourful rubber glory.

It reminded me of a Japanese pearl diver from Broome I once serviced, who had pearls pushed under his foreskin. They formed a row down the shaft of his cock, which made it difficult to suck.

I think it was some sort of status thing, or to 'pleasure' his women.

Yuk!, was all I remember thinking at the time.

Verdi swaggered into the small apartment. He nodded to me without speaking. As I shut the door I turned away from him and leaned forwards. I pushed my arse into his groin, swaying from side to side slightly, rubbing his cock between the cheeks of my arse. I gave him an arch look over my shoulder then turned slowly. Reaching up, I hooked my hands around his neck, twining my fingers through the short wavy hairs. I pulled my face up to kiss him lingeringly on the lips.

Taking him by one hand I slowly moved towards the bed and sat him down on the edge. Kneeling before him I undid his shoelaces and pulled off his shoes one by one, pushing his socks into them.

I leant my face towards his groin. I could smell his distinctive fishy scent as I placed my mouth over the bulge in his trousers. I breathed hot air into the fabric. I looked up at him and gave him one of my sleazier smiles as I slowly eased down his zipper. I slid the belt open and undid the top button, then raised myself to sit on his lap, straddling his shaft, rolling over it with my arse.

When my legs began to ache I dismounted.

While he sat on the bed I knelt in front of him and undid the buttons of his shirt. I draped it over the back of a chair next to the bed. He leant forward. I pulled his singlet over his head.

Then, together, we eased his pants off—clumsily. I folded them at the creases and hung them over the chair back.

He knew the way to the bathroom and headed there in his silky red boxer shorts, which he discarded on the bathroom floor. He helped himself to a shower, fiddling constantly with the taps.

I followed him into the bathroom. I sat on the cold, smooth edge of the old bath with the plastic shower curtain pulled halfway across. I chattered gaily, trying my best to keep him in the shower for as long as possible.

'How's work?'

'Great, yeah.'

'How's your girlfriend, family?'

'Great, yeah.'

Verdi stepped out of the bath. I was already holding the towel ready. I slowly rubbed the droplets of water from his back, legs and groin, bending over to expose my round cheeks to their best advantage as I dried his feet one at a time with the care of a mother.

'Mustn't forget the cracks,' I said, to be amusing.

I knew Verdi well; probably better than he knew himself. I certainly knew what turned him on. He was, like most straight men, boringly predictable. He liked to fantasise about two girls together and about anal sex: the allure of the forbidden perhaps?

He had one of those melodious names that reminded me romantically of the Sistine Chapel, the Borgias, Venetian glass and tradition. He was ridiculously open, all surface, boasting and ego. I wondered if his life was as romantic as the 1930s gangster movies I'd seen, or if the stories that he told me were invented out of crippling mediocrity trying to make itself more interesting.

I watched his face. I thought it shiningly insincere. He was acceptably attractive with arrogant dark eyes and Roman features. He emanated power by proxy of his family connections: born into a life of paranoia. The sub-strata between classes that facilitate greed: drug dealers, debt collectors and hit men. They had their own morality—more expedient than the law (and, as I thought, occasionally more honest).

Verdi was more credible since his cousin had been shot in his suburban laundry in a well-publicised 'hit'. Stupidity is dangerous, and I wondered idly how he had survived.

He removed a plastic bag containing a sizeable white rock from his jacket on the chair.

Verdi darling, you are almost attractive.

I smiled slightly to myself.

His phone rang endlessly.

I looked into the mirror of the dresser next to my bed, and saw a stranger looking out at me: a Sex Kitten.

Prrrrrrrrrr.

'Lee, yeah brother, call John, I'll give you his number,' Verdi was saying.

'Yeah! Call Maserelli!'

'Call Ginarelli.'

I listened to his conversations. *Elli Alli, Ferrari,* I thought, *he's obviously a referral service for gangster-land.*

'Chop me a line, baby!' he called out to me, while still in mid-conversation.

I loved being paid to sit around in my underwear snorting cocaine while he talked on the phone. The busty blonde on the porno looked a little stupid with her head hanging upside down over the edge of the bed and an enormous cock thrusting in and out of her mouth. Her facial expressions were vaguely annoying.

I hope she gets the job.

My head was thick with cocaine as I lay back on the bed, slowly moving the vibrator in and out of my pussy. I held my left breast up to my mouth and slowly moved my tongue around the nipple. I had long sensitive nipples and laughed involuntarily to myself.

Muffled noises from the television provided sound effects: 'Ooohh, aaagh, aaagh.' Panting, bad music and a phoney voice-over saying 'Oooh baby' followed by more monotonous music.

Verdi switched his mobile phone off; his cock was only semi-erect. This wasn't surprising since he'd probably been using cocaine for days. He lay down on the bed. I turned him over for a massage, rubbing oil into his hairy back and buttocks and threw some trivial remarks around the room.

'How's Sydney?' I asked.

'A lot warmer,' he said.

'How've you been? I've missed you,' I said.

'I've got a new Harley Davidson. I keep it in the lounge room. Do you watch Westerns? I really like Westerns. I'll bring you some,' he said.

'Have you got still got your girlfriend?' I asked.

'Viridis? Yeah.'

I used my best girlie voice—'Would you like me to lick her pussy one day? I could make her come in my mouth and then you could fuck us both.'

'She'd love that. I'll ask her,' he said.

I was amazed that it seemed perfectly reasonable to this sweet little muffin that he should suggest it to his girlfriend later. I wished I could be a fly on the wall.

Oil coagulated around the dead skin and hairs on his back. The wiry, tough hairs scratched the palms of my hands. I massaged the nodules of his spine up and down with the tips of my fingers. I pummelled his arse and rubbed the inside of his thighs, moving down over the muscular legs to his feet.

'Feet are the most sensitive and under-appreciated body part, don't you think?' I asked, as I lingered over them, feigning appreciation. I bent his leg up and slid his big toe into my mouth, rolling my tongue around it slowly, suggestive of sucking a penis, until it relaxed in my mouth, and then took the other toes one at a time in the same manner. I prolonged foreplay for as long as possible to minimise wear and tear on my body.

Tickling his hard balls with one hand I slid up over his limp body, resting my bare breasts on him. I used my chin to massage his back, sliding up and down and over his body rhythmically.

I am a snake, sensuous and gleaming with a dangerous untouchable pride lingering in the light behind my eyes, small, yet sure of my power.

We are capable of many disguises in the jungle of life.

He moved suddenly, interrupting my reverie. He lolloped into the small kitchen where, on the bench top, I'd laid out the cocaine for him in thick lines. The sound of snorting filled the room.

'The good thing about cocaine is that you can never have too much,' I said. 'It's much better than food, isn't it?'

My various ploys to avoid fucking him were working. His need for cocaine had overcome his need for sex—almost.

'I'm just going to the toilet. Don't start without me,' I said.

Sitting on the toilet my mind wandered without direction over banal issues like paying the rent and shopping. I felt tired and tense as I leant forward clutching the warm bare folds of my stomach as it churned and emptied. I thought, ironically, how good drugs were.

I slinked back to the bed, cupping my breasts in my hands self-consciously and hovered, waiting for Verdi to position himself comfortably. I sensed that he was impatient to come. The only way I was going to help him to achieve that was using my ingenious mind over his reluctant matter.

Throwing a leg over his cock with my arse facing him, I took the limp member in my hand and squeezed it hard at the base, which made it swell. Holding it against the crack above my arse I squeezed my cheeks together, trapping it firmly between them so that he could watch the head of his penis open and close as it appeared at the top of my arse and then disappeared in the cushions of flesh. I slowly moved myself up and down to stimulate the shaft.

'It's *soooooo* big,' I said appreciatively.

16

'I bet your girlfriend would like me to lick her clit while you fuck me. I like licking pussy. I could make her come with my tongue while you fuck her from behind,' I said.

I repressed a sudden urge to dry retch.

'I love dry fucking. Oh, your cock feels so good, I can feel it rubbing against my clit. I'm going to come against your shaft.' I made several moans.

'Oh! My God,' I said.

I emitted some satisfied sounding moans.

His warm gluey cum shot up onto my back. I wondered how anyone fell for that crap.

'Are you going to have another shower?' I asked.

'Na, I'll get going,' he said. He dressed hurriedly, pushed the scrunched-up notes into my hand and left.

I pondered Verdi's life. I wondered whether he would be killed in the gang-land war that raged. I doubted he was important enough. As far as I knew he was just a small time drug-dealer. Someone would probably just shoot him because he was annoying.

After they came my clients must have felt guilty because they were usually out of the door at the speed of light leaving me poring over sticky notes and feeling restless.

Alone at last, I slid my hand under the pillow and pulled the vibrator towards me. Flicking it on, I held it against my clit.

I closed my eyes.

In my mind I was pushing a submissive dike between my legs.

2
Initiation:
the first time

My imaginary sex slave was wearing a leather harness and mini-skirt and a studded leather cap over her cropped dark hair. She had a pretty face and kissable plump pink lips. I imagined her warm tongue on my clitoris. As I pushed the lilac plastic phallus up into my vagina so that it hit my G-spot, in my mind I was being fucked hard from behind with a strap on.

My fingers were gentler and well practised, and I finished by stroking my clit quickly in a circular motion.

I came in delicious warm waves.

Sex had warmed the room. The lube, rubber and musk in the air were dense and moist as rainforest.

I showered quickly.

I tended to get rashes from constant showering and looking like you have a venereal disease is bad for business so I used as little soap as possible.

Here I am, suspended between day and night, between this world and the next, where A Midsummer Night's Dream *is as real as the taxation department, which is not at all real to me.* I had welcomed the freedom of becoming a prostitute. My father had called me a slut when I was thirteen and the notion stuck.

I was merely fulfilling my programming.

When I was a little girl my mother used to say: 'Little girls should be seen and not heard.' By the time I was thirteen I was angry enough to retaliate. I screamed back at her in an uncontrollable rage, at the top of my lungs where it tore at the lining.

'I hate you. You're more interested in going out drinking with your friends than listening to me. You don't love me. You haven't got time for me.' And all of the other vile things I normally pushed back into my heart, until it pumped heavily, bloated and sluggish from depression. This caused me to purge over the toilet bowl after a frenzy of feeding. I struggled with bulimia. It ruled my life. I obsessed about being fat and unlovable. If my mother stopped loving my father when he got fat she would surely stop loving me too. If she ever did, that is—it was hard to tell.

I slammed the glass door to my bedroom so hard the glass shattered. I threw chairs against the wall. I broke windows. I drank rough cider in the park and vomited over myself. I truanted from school, threw things at teachers. I behaved as badly as I could because I knew no-one cared what I did anyway.

She never responded. Her weapon was silence. She wouldn't speak to me for days, not that she was home much. She worked long hours and spent the evenings with one of the two men she was dating or her friends.

One day I was so angry I threw a handful of coins in her face, just to see if I could get a reaction.

She let me know I was just a nuisance with little digs like: 'If I hadn't had you I could have had a nice home and more money. I wasn't cut out for motherhood.'

She could barely afford to feed us both on her wage as a secretary.

I guess that wasn't her fault—she did the best she could. I felt guilty about the way I punished her. I felt guilty about a lot of things.

That was why I moved to the other side of the world: to get as far away from my mother as possible.

I married an Australian tourist I met in London and had three children with him. It probably would have helped if I'd got to know him first. I was only nineteen when I met him. I'd always wanted children. I thought having a family would give me love and security. Hah!

I don't know how I found the strength to leave him. Thank God I did or I think the misery would have killed me.

I tried to look after the children on my own but I couldn't manage. My ex wouldn't pay child support. He gave up working so he wouldn't have to pay me. I think it was his revenge because I left him.

I tried to get by on Social Security payments and give the children the things they needed, but I just got further into debt until one day I realised I wouldn't be able to catch up. I didn't even know how I was going to feed myself let alone them. My stress was affecting them badly.

I called my ex-husband to tell him I was dropping them off with him at the apartment he was sharing with his friend in the city. He seemed happy with my decision. It would have been a victory for him.

Afterwards, I went back to the house I was about to be evicted from.

I closed the blinds and howled. I cried for three days. I barely ate. I thought I was going to die from the pain. Two days later I pulled myself together enough to pack my things into boxes and have them put in storage.

I scoured the papers for jobs. There were very few; it was 1989. Being destitute was the most frightening thing that ever happened to me. The fear was overwhelming, it's like drowning—the moment of panic when your lungs fill with water and you can no longer breathe.

I will never forget the first time.

I found an ad at the back of the local paper. There were very few employment vacancies. It was 1991. The recession had hit Melbourne harder than the other states. Company directors were driving taxis and a number of corporate heavyweights had committed suicide rather than face bankruptcy. The top end of the real estate market had been affected dramatically. There were mansions for sale for a third of their previous value. Investment property was hard to sell and in some cases almost worthless. It was a desperate time.

I had almost no money and nowhere to live. I was sleeping on the floor of a friend's house for a week until his flat-mate returned from a short holiday.

I wrote down the phone number of the most appealing advertisement. It said 'Earn up to two thousand dollars a week'. I took the number to a payphone and called. A charming, well-spoken woman answered.

'Why don't you come in for an interview? You don't have to stay. Just come and have a look around,' she said in a warm, friendly voice. She gave me the address and I wrote it down with a shaky hand.

As I walked towards the entrance I looked around nervously to see if anyone was watching.

I walked through the discreet, tinted glass door from bright sunlight into a dim reception.

I couldn't see the interior at first, but felt it pressing heavily against my skin.

Red velvet was all around me, scented with an unfamiliar musky mixture. I later learned its composition—sweat, perfume, rubber, baby oil and Windex.

The attractive, young receptionist wore blonde and gold. Her blonde hair was bobbed, neat and respectable. She was soothing and professional.

I saw her mouth moving but couldn't process the words, so I shoved them somewhere all jumbled up, to be sorted out later.

I was shaking violently. A tentacle of fear had wrapped its way slowly around my heart, constricting the beats, making them faster.

My heartbeat caused my ribs to reverberate inside the hollow cavity of my chest. My throat was dry and dusty. My words were choked and would not come.

My oily palms clenched on their own perspiration in an effort to squeeze out feeling.

Half of me still wanted to turn and run out, to preserve the truths of my upbringing, of society, the church— to safeguard my need for approval. The other half, the pragmatic, desperate half, won out and I stayed.

'We'll find you a really nice client for your first time. You'll find it easy, you'll be surprised. If you work here for a short time you can save a lot of money. You'll be back on your feet in no time,' the receptionist purred. I got the impression she had seduced many women with the same words.

She showed me around the three-storey building. The rooms were small, in order to be less threatening to clients and to women like me who came in to see if they could cross the line and become prostitutes. Of course, once you'd walked through that door you'd already crossed a very big line.

The red velvet interior gave the impression of a giant vulva.

This was the world of eternal night, hushed, waiting and padded like a giant, succulent, flesh-eating flower. The sort that snaps shut suddenly, swallowing its victim whole, yet pleasantly, into its dank depths.

In the lounge room the faces of three young women shone out of the gloom. They were painted like burlesque flowers. One was an iris, one a pansy, and perhaps the other was a bluebell, although you couldn't be sure in the dark. I was definitely a wallflower.

The women were dressed in voile skirts and sequinned bras to look as though they were in a harem and not an office building in middle-class Melbourne.

I was fitted with a costume and led back to the lounge area.

I sat with three girls on the imitation, red velvet lounge-chair that circled the room. I felt dazed, naked and silly in my borrowed gold harem outfit that comprised a sequinned bra, and decorated G-string and a voile skirt. I wondered how marketable I was going to be. At five feet three and a half I was petite. (The half an inch is very important when you're my height.) Sometimes I felt big and heavy even though I knew I was really slim.

My body was toned and athletic looking. I didn't exercise, I was just lucky to have good genetics. My breasts were small and firm, my skin soft and smooth. My arse had the pleasing curves of a peach. I hated the curves at the top of my thighs.

My bone structure was typically Anglo-Irish with high cheekbones and a small mouth. I had shoulder-length, chestnut-brown hair and turquoise-grey eyes. I'd always been told I was pretty but my feminine mannerisms made me seem more attractive than I was, that and my wit. I wouldn't call it intelligence. I wasn't sensible enough to be called smart.

My head felt like it was full of cotton wool.

I chanted over and over in my head my new name, which was Morgan. I didn't feel like a Morgan, which is an old car, probably Welsh. I realised then what was wrong … I needed a wig—all the other girls wore a wig!

I hadn't been sure what to expect when I'd walked through the door on that first day. At the time I had only thought about my desperate need for money.

Looking back, the brothel was exactly as I might have expected it to be.

Maybe, as I thought later, this was my destiny. A fortune-teller told me once that I had been a Japanese Geisha in a past life.

He was white-haired, about fifty. The sort of man you wouldn't remember or notice in a crowd: clean, neat and of average height, build and weight, with a middle-income occupation.

He must have deliberately suntanned his skin, and probably felt happy as he looked in the mirror that morning. As he tied his dark-blue tie over his carefully selected, pale-blue pinstriped shirt with a white contrasting collar, he would have turned sideways to admire his profile, using vocabulary conversant with his day, like 'nifty', 'jaunty' or 'debonair'.

He would have thought himself good-looking, and thought what a favour he would be doing by bestowing himself on womankind that day.

You would have hoped then that I could have stopped myself shaking when he chose me from the line-up of girls in his lunch -break.

Floundering is done at night in the shallows of the seashore with a torch. When the torchlight reflects off the phosphorescent eyes of the fish, it freezes with fear, expressionless and stupid.

My first 'John' had caught himself a flounder for lunch that day.

I took him by the hand up a flight of narrow stairs to a large room with a spa bath.

In the centre of the room, dominating the space, was a circular bed. The fitted bedspread was nylon, imitation zebra print: faux. You couldn't describe it as skin, as it bore no resemblance to anything except what it was, which was fake.

The nylon tufts had conspired together in circular patterns suggestive of multiple usage.

Two towels folded on the end of the bed were thin and red—probably washed through with the blood of virgins.

Cold white tiles stared clinically from the corner of the room. The red carpet underfoot was thicker for thousands of hair follicles and skin cells.

I had never perspired so much from the palms of my hands.

My voice had become high-pitched. I trilled like a demented budgerigar. Normal platitudes sounded obscure and inappropriate.

I was suddenly acutely aware of double entendre.

'You'll have to excuse me, I'm not sure where everything is. I mean I *know* where everything is, of course, you know, I just don't know where to *put* things. Oh no. You're so nice and clean, not that I thought you were dirty. I mean you can be as dirty as you like. Oh God, I think I'll keep my mouth shut, or perhaps I'll put something in it *other* than my feet.'

I giggled nervously.

He didn't respond to my prattling. He smiled at me indulgently and proceeded to place his mouth over mine. Old men have a particular way of kissing. They have thin, hard lips and tend to kiss quickly, as though they're stealing something that they're not entitled to. It felt as though he didn't really mean the kiss.

I sure as hell didn't!

He was wearing so much aftershave it burnt the back of my throat as I breathed it in.

He undressed himself calmly and helped me out of my scant clothing.

With his old grey flesh beneath my hands and his flaccid body over mine, whether his penis was inside me or not seemed irrelevant.

He lay over me. He entered me moving gently at first and then picked up momentum.

His manner was apologetic and shy.

I flinched as he touched my clit with soft fingers. He was trying to turn me on.

He was trying to be kind. It was touching and sad.

I cared that he felt uncomfortable.

I imagined his lonely life devoid of love and meaning. Just the same repetitive routine every day, the dead-end job and lonely nights. His featureless retirement; waiting for death. I shuddered.

I realised how few people write stimulating details in the script of their lives. *He must be here with me looking for excitement, maybe even emotional fulfilment.*

How bizarre!

I began to feel more confident and sat on his cock. I realised I should just pretend he was my ex-husband. Thank God I'd had all that practice at fucking when I didn't feel like it.

I bounced up and down on top of him, making what I assumed were realistic sounds of enjoyment. I admonished myself for being nervous. *Hell, this shouldn't be too hard for me. Haven't I been faking it for years?*

They play techno music in brothels because it has a perfect, mindlessly repetitive beat to keep rhythm with.

The beat seemed endless in that very long hour.

It was a shock to me that I could objectify the experience so effectively. I felt nothing, just a cold empty feeling in the pit of my stomach.

My limbs were reluctant but my mind was numb and detached, hanging somewhere above myself, commenting on the proceedings with humour.

He came into the condom and withdrew. He wrapped the condom in tissues carefully and placed it on the bedside table and lay down with me. I lay next to him with my head against his chest silently, thinking.

We're only at the top of the evolutionary ladder—we're just animals.

It had been easier than I could have imagined. After all, this was just like being married to a man you didn't love. Except, *thank God!* You didn't usually have to put up with them for more than an hour *and* you got to go home alone at the end of a shift.

My marriage had been torture. My husband had been cruel and he'd hit me. This was much easier.

It may not have been one of my most shining moments but it was certainly pivotal.

As innocence left me, I felt sad. I would never think of sex as sacred again. It was just a man emptying his semen into a woman because his animal instincts were programming him.

Love and romance were just tricks of nature.

In that first week I realised that each intimate encounter with a client was a distillation of their life; a clownish paradox of their perceptions: a blink of their fateful whole.

All the stuff I'd been brought up to believe about sex went out of the window. At school it was uncool to be a virgin. This contradicted the message from my parents who told me to wait for the 'right one', preferably my husband.

Mine, and most of my friends' parents seemed pretty confused; they were all having extra-marital sex and getting divorced. Not particularly good role models.

During the long shifts in the first few months I fucked dozens of men. At times hatred towards men in general tumbled from my subconscious and resonated off the walls, vibrating around the room. Mostly I just felt bored with the repetition.

I could meet their physical needs, it seemed, but they could not meet mine, only my need for money.

The owner of the brothel came in several times a week. She introduced herself to me in a regal manner. She was a tall, slim woman with waist-length, shimmering black hair that floated on her back. She was probably in her late forties—it was hard to tell—she'd had plastic surgery.

She wore expensive flowing cream clothes. She was impeccably groomed—a snow queen in her domain.

She wafted ethereally through the lounge area, barely touching the coarse carpet with her small feet. Sitting with us, she took time to advise us on our professional performance and tried to inspire us with elegant words and assumed kindness.

'Make sure you save your money. Some of the girls have saved as much as ten thousand dollars after working for just six months. You have to work hard so you can make a better life for yourself. If you don't trust yourself I can save your money for you in my safe,' she said.

Although it sounded patronising it was good advice. I smiled at her appreciatively.

Most of the girls who worked in the brothel were intelligent, pretty, charming and manipulative. Some were married or had boyfriends who they told they were manicurists or receptionists. Most were young and beautiful and saving to buy properties or finance businesses.

They were adept at their profession. Money is an effective motivator.

The girls helped me with advice. We were bound together by our outcast status. It was like belonging to a secret club.

At the very beginning I learned several useful things: to cut a sea-sponge in half, moisten it under the tap and push it high inside my vagina under the cervix to stem the flow of menstrual blood. It had to be taken out and washed in between clients.

Drunks tended to fuck hard.

I was told to lube the palms of my hands and hold their cock tightly in one hand behind my buttocks. I was surprised that men couldn't tell the difference. The tight grip helped them come.

'Nicth tight cuunnt,' they'd say appreciatively.

Men really are stupid.

I'd had my suspicions and now they were confirmed.

There were some unusual bookings, Bacchanalian orgies with six girls and six men all swapping partners. In the interests of safety this was a nightmare of condom swapping and avoiding saliva.

Some of the bisexual doubles with other girls were exciting. Most would pretend to lick me, putting their hand over my vagina, miming the actions. I'd take their cue and do the same. Occasionally I'd feel a hot tongue on my clit and feel a thrill of pleasure.

Some of the situations were hilarious.

I was wearing my new wig of long red hair. During a tiring session with a man who insisted on fucking me vigorously in missionary position for the better part of an hour, I lay on my back thinking of England, trying not to imagine ways of murdering him. Unbeknownst to me, my wig had detached itself from my head.

As the mattress bounced up and down, the hair moved across the bed away from me, like a furry animal hopping away. I looked up and caught sight of it with horror, aware that my own hair was frizzy and ugly from being squashed under the wig all night. I reached up with one hand and pulled it back and tucked it underneath me.

I wonder if he had nightmares afterwards, about women losing body parts or going bald when he fucked them.

⌒

Another of my early bookings was memorable.

We introduced ourselves to him one by one in the small entrance foyer, emerging one at a time from behind the red velvet curtain that cordoned off the lounge area.

I observed that people often look like what they are. This man looked like an accountant and he looked like a pervert. He was around forty-five, balding and obviously married.

We greeted him with our best seductive smiles and posturing until he selected two girls. I was one of them and the other was a tall, wide-hipped blonde called Cherise. Cherise took his hand and I followed them upstairs.

In the dimly lit room he removed his clothes and folded them fastidiously. He had brought his own strap-on vibrator and a bag of lingerie and toys that he laid out on the bed.

While he showered, Cherise and I walked down the narrow red-carpeted stairway together to the receptionist with his credit card.

Cherise hurriedly explained to me that she had seen him before and that he paid forty dollars extra to each of us for a fantasy booking to each of us.

She said nonchalantly, 'He's not too bad.'

I wondered nervously what 'bad' was.

Cherise was nice, she seemed as though nothing would faze her.

We stripped to our G-strings and stockings whilst he dried himself.

Cherise put on the strap-on vibrator and fastened it around her waist.

He wore only his pale, ginger-freckled skin.

We began the pantomime.

He barked orders at us quickly, one after another, like gunfire.

'Bend over in front of the mirror with your arse near it. Take off your panties. Put your finger in your pussy. You, walk around the room. Put the cock in her. Rub it over my arse. Smile. Now, stick your tongue out. Further!'

He pulled at his cock slowly, licking his lips and concentrating intensely.

'Stick your tongue in and out quickly. Right out. Bend over in front of the mirror, facing away from it. Rub your pussy. That's it!'

I was the one doing the in and out tongue thing, while following the other instructions. All Cherise had to do was walk around the room wearing the strap-on.

My brain was getting tired from following the instructions and my tongue hurt. I tried not to think about how ridiculous I looked.

'Now come over here and lick my arse.'

He bent over expectantly. My brain screamed, *no way!*

But I couldn't seem to find an answer for myself.

I looked at Cherise imploringly. She pointed to the condom and to my tongue. I could have read braille at that moment and thankfully understood her. I grabbed a condom from the side table and put it over my tongue so that I could lick his arse without touching it.

He must have had his arse licked a lot because it was shiny and clean.

It was my turn to wear the strap-on.

'Fuck me with it!' he barked at me.

Here it comes, *Ouch!* But he didn't seem to mind. It wasn't a big vibrator and he'd put plenty of lube on himself. He was obviously a pro.

I changed the condom on the vibrator and fucked Cherise with it, in between walking around the room and sticking my tongue in and out like a gecko.

The time passed as quickly as wet sand passing through an hourglass.

He wouldn't have got that service for that price from some of the more experienced girls.

Being a new girl meant I scored all of the good bookings.

During the first two weeks I had sex with an odd variety of misfits.

The dwarf was a nice guy. He owned a car yard and spoke intelligently about his business and his family. His wife and daughters were all normal height. Sex with him felt normal. It was only his legs that were short. I kept wanting to baby-talk to him.

I saw a young severely handicapped guy. His carer and the bus driver helped him up to the room in his wheelchair.

'He's been bathed,' the middle-aged woman said.

'Great, thanks,' I said as she left the room. It was silly of me to feel embarrassed and nervous in front of him. I'd never been this close to a handicapped person before.

'Hi, sexy,' I said. He dribbled a little and his head bobbed on his chest. I laughed nervously.

I stripped slowly and threw my clothes on the floor. I touched my genitals, positioning them close to his face, for him to watch. He was smiling and nodding to show his appreciation. I undid his fly and pulled his trousers back as much as I could. I eased his flaccid cock out and pushed my arse against it.

I wondered if this was a government sponsored programme and how they got funding for it. What did they write on the forms?

I knelt in front of him, rolled the condom onto his cock and began to suck it slowly. Gradually it came to life in my mouth. I sucked and sucked and sucked and sucked. My jaw was aching. There wasn't much chance of a conversation to fill in some of the hour.

Poor bastard.

I stood up and let him have a long look at my genitals while I rubbed myself with my fingers and then sat on his lap rubbing my pussy over him. I managed to push myself down over his cock by holding onto the sides of his chair and bracing one leg against the footrest. With one leg up on the side of the bed I fucked him. It was a good job I did gymnastics when I was at school.

Flushed with exertion I eased myself off him and knelt down and sucked his cock again. I was getting tired.

I discarded the condom and squeezed lube onto the shaft of his cock. I gave him a sleazy smile and milked his cock as hard as I could. His body jerked as he came in my hand. Relieved, I grabbed a handful of tissues from the box next to me and wiped up the milky residue. I went to the sink in the corner of the room and ran warm water onto a face washer. I gave him a thorough wipe and kissed him on the cheek. I guessed he was only about sixteen. I hoped he would get a service of this kind for the rest of his life and not be the victim of a budget cut.

'Wait there, sweetie,' I said, a little unnecessarily.

I showered and dressed myself and rang reception to tell them he was ready.

The man in uniform, who I'd guessed was the driver of the bus, collected him and slowly eased his wheelchair down the stairs. A wry smile lingered on my face.

At least I was performing an important social service.

My next client was an alcoholic who stank of urine. The other girls were deliberately unfriendly so he chose me. *Just my luck!*

I helped him into the shower and handed him the soap.

'Wash yourself nice and properly for me,' I begged.

He staggered out unsteadily. I helped him dry himself. The overwhelming stench of urine that seemed to ooze through the pores of his skin was still hard to cope with. Some smells just don't wash off.

I wondered where he got the money to pay for sex. Luckily, he was a happy drunk. He lay nice and still while I massaged him. The smell from his arse reminded me of meatballs or rotten cabbage. I pushed his side hard so that he rolled over. I fondled his limp cock.

Siting on top of him and fucking him became exhausting and my thighs were aching. My 'yeeh hah' became more of an 'ow ouch'. I dismounted and decided to use my hands to stimulate him.

'Come all over my stomach,' I breathed, in my Marilyn Monroe voice.

'Yeah alright,' he said. He smiled stupidly. His cock winked at me lazily. *Spineless wonder that it is.*

I forced myself not to think of the smell.

I deserve a medal for my service to humanity.

I yanked and tugged and pulled and eventually he spilled come onto his thin white stomach.

I've really done it all now.

I shouldn't have thought that, I was throwing a challenge out to the universe.

When we filed out to introduce ourselves to the enormously obese man seated in the waiting area, I just knew he was going to pick me. Two of the young girls looked at me sideways. They knew I was on a roll. I was hot property. They definitely weren't jealous.

Of course, I thought, as I was summonsed by the receptionist to lead my client upstairs by the hand.

I undressed him with the usual ridiculous lines.

'You're so gorgeous,' I said.

'Really, girls don't like me,' he said.

'No, why wouldn't they?' I said in disbelief.

'I'm a bit overweight,' he said.

'That's good, there's more of you to love. You gorgeous hunk,' I cooed.

He was so big I had to lift up a large white roll of fat to find his small dick and position myself over him at an uncomfortable right angle to get near it. Maybe it was a very large penis and it only seemed small because half of it was lost in the rancid mass of fat. Perhaps his body was eating its own appendages, perhaps his mass would devour me.

As I caught the tram home, I felt vaguely disgusted with myself – dirty – the kind that doesn't wash off. I rationalised that it was better than starving, far better than the hardship and fear of not being able to pay the bills. I loved having my own money far more than I hated working. I would never be trapped in an abusive marriage again. I pushed the children out of my mind. Every time I thought of them I felt as though I was being stabbed in the heart.

Earning money was my freedom. I smiled to myself and gave the old man opposite me a filthy look. Perhaps he wasn't looking at me and thinking about sex—maybe I was becoming a bit neurotic.

I had been at the brothel for about nine months, it was nearly the end of my first year as a hooker. My first year without my children. At the back of my mind always, was the guilt and the pain of missing them, of worrying about them, of feeling as though I was failing them in so many ways. They were living on a farm with their father and his girlfriend and although they seemed okay I was sure it was hard for them without their mother.

I saw them every second weekend. Thank God I could now afford to take them out and spoil them. It helped me cope with my heartache.

The shifts were getting longer and more tedious. I was averaging about four clients a day and working the standard four shifts a week.

After paying two hundred dollars a week in shift fees, which was pretty normal by industry standards, I had become used to earning about $1500 a week. Greed was the only enjoyment I had and it had become an all-consuming monster in my life.

I had learnt to spend money. I lived in a small, reasonably priced apartment that I paid two hundred dollars a week for. I had bought some new furniture. I had lilac contact lenses, waist-length, honey-blonde hair extensions and thousands of dollars worth of clothes and lingerie.

My shoe collection would have been the envy of Imelda Marcos or of any self-respecting drag- queen. I sent money to the children every week.

I woke up one morning in a bad mood. I had to be at work at ten in the morning. There were fines for being late. There were more regulations at the brothel than in the army and hefty fines for breaking any of them.

The girls were very competitive and some of them could be bitchy, especially if you made more money than they did.

One girl called Sharon hated me. She also hated most people.

She was tall and big-boned and claimed to be a gym instructor.

If the attributes that they laid claim to were true, I was probably working with some of the most talented women in the country.

Sharon must have sensed that I was in a bad mood on this day and she seemed to be picking on me more than usual.

I could feel steam building inside me like a kettle coming to the boil.

I finally blew up when Sharon put her arm in front of me to stop me walking past her into the kitchenette where the girls ate lunch.

Up until that moment I had seemed sweet, polite and meek.

The other girls watched in stunned disbelief as my head did a three-sixty-degree turn, turned green and grew horns.

I screamed like a fishwife.

'You fucking bitch! I've had enough of you! You think you can bully me, do you?! Well, I think it's about time someone taught you a lesson! Just one word, just say one word and I'll grab you by the hair and smash that ugly head of yours against the mirror!'

I sounded as though I meant every word, and looked disappointed that Sharon didn't rise to the challenge.

I turned, adjusted my face to its normal appearance and said calmly, 'I don't think I'll work today, I'm going home.'

I got changed, grabbed my bag and left for the last time.

I shook violently for the rest of the day. I really wasn't that big or that brave! And I had just lost my only source of income.

In the brooding weather my block of apartments was dark and forbidding. The windows facing mine were watching eyes. Crickets or cicadas were chirruping from the viscid, nether regions of the under-garden.

Why does old cooking always smell like cabbage? I wondered. *I hate cabbage.*

I put on a Portishead CD at high volume, kicked off my shoes and danced. Music filled the empty room. Volume brought the sound to life, the layering of rhythms, the ethnic influences, the instruments and sampling. For a short while everything was forgotten as my arms flailed the air. My bare feet followed a pattern on the soft, acknowledging floorboards as I hugged the rhythm, feeling it in my hips.

I gyrated and rolled my spine. My shoulders and muscles embraced the sound.

An elderly man walking past in the rain watched me from the street for a few moments. The expression of my body spoke of my sensual, gypsy passion.

I was demented and alone, naked, like an animal running free in the woods.

The sense of freedom was marred by my rising panic. I had to find somewhere else to work.

I'd heard the girls talking; most of them had worked in other brothels. Some had worked all over the country and even overseas.

My friend Apple was seeing men at home during the day while while her daughters were at school. Apple was a pretty, petite, vivacious Italian-Australian with a flamboyant dress sense. I admired her for her 'fuck you' attitude. I thought she was beautiful.

I had met Apple at the brothel just before she left. She was warm, motherly and generous. It was unusual to make friends at work for a number of reasons. Partly because the women like to keep their personal lives separate; they don't want it to be known in the wider community that they're prostitutes. And partly because so many of the women have big problems from the stress in their personal lives and are often a nightmare. Apple and I were as close as I ever got to another 'working girl'.

Apple had offered to book me for bisexual doubles. She could charge up to double the price for each of us for these bookings. I called her for advice.

'Hi, Apple. I've left the brothel. I'm thinking of working from home. I'm a bit worried that someone will notice the coming and goings,' I said.

'It's fine, really. I always meet them outside and walk in with them. Always get their number and don't tell them anything until you've called them back. Make sure you take the money before anything happens though. I haven't had a single problem. The clients are much nicer. They're married professional men who want a discreet service. They don't like going to brothels in case someone sees them there.

'Look, if you like I'll divert my phone to yours tomorrow. I'm not working this week while the girls are on school holidays. I can't answer the work phone anyway,' she said. 'Thank you, you're an angel. I'm changing my working name to Ruby. I can't stand Morgan, it's ugly,' I said.

In the first few months that I worked, I vowed I wouldn't become a cliché—a prostitute *and* a drug addict but after all it was the only way to escape from reality and boredom. I'd had cocaine because it had been offered to me by clients. I liked it. I could afford it and it was fun. I was already part of an elite group of degenerates, or as I saw it, left-of-centre rebels. I identified with gays, drag queens, artists: the bohemians. I suffered from a complete lack of responsibility. I didn't even have to be at work in the mornings anymore.

I had been sleeping with one of my friends, Forrest, for a month. I knew he was gay but I hoped he would change his mind. He'd only had one gay relationship and he said he was still confused.

Forrest had been introduced to a celebrity hairdresser who'd invited him to a birthday party. Forrest asked me to go with him.

In the dusk, multitudes of fairy lights lit the pale trunks of plane trees. As Forrest and I walked up a path through rhododendrons and azaleas into warm light curving up a small stairway at the front of the house, a seated ensemble of classical musicians were playing Mozart on the patio.

A waiter in a black tuxedo, with satin lapels and tails and an elaborate pin-tucked shirt with a black bow tie, smiled charmingly, and offered us a silver tray of glasses. Forrest and I took champagne flutes half-filled with dusky pink Billie-Cart-Salmon champagne.

Thirty or so people had already gathered—mainly gay men. They were as decorative as brocade, dressed in their evening finery. Forrest wore a self-conscious facade of self-importance that passed for confidence in the candlelight.

He had a charm that played around his mouth. His face was lovely, like brandy in milk, surprisingly potent and heady.

The atmosphere was deliciously tinged with sexual undertones. A vibration, perhaps purple in colour, thickened the air. It caused my mouth to water involuntarily.

I looked at the few glamorous women who were obviously A-list—wealthy socialites and models. I whispered to Forrest, 'If there was a Crufts for breasts, this would be it. They're all sitting up and begging.'

Light tumbled in a cascade from a crystal chandelier. Dancing rainbows frolicked inside giant, tubular, mauve and white striped lilies that emitted a languid perfume. Rich umber powder dripped onto a circular glass table in the centre of the lounge-room.

Retro green bottles of champagne were circled with a haughty French label.

I was beginning to feel slightly drunk. I could feel the warmth in my rose-petal cheeks. My eyes shone because I was pissed, as usual. Forrest curled easily through the celluloid party like a movie star. I watched him sparkle.

'Lisa, this is Mr Green. It's his birthday,' said Forrest.

'Hello, happy birthday. It's very elegant.' I waved an arm unsteadily around the room.

'Charmed,' he said. He extended his arm to me. I wondered if I should kiss it or curtsey. He turned his attention to Forrest.

'Where did you come from?' Mr Green asked, letting the words trail off seductively at the end.

'New Zealand originally but I've lived in Melbourne for five years,' Forrest said.

'Your English is excellent,' joked Mr Green.

'Thank you. You'd be surprised, most people speak English at home as well,' Forrest said. His eyes were shining. Mr Green whispered to me loudly so that Forrest could hear.

'He's gorgeous.'

I smiled. His eyes looked like a rabbit's eyes.

Goodbye Forrest.

Mr Green sat down imperiously on the edge of a silk sofa with a straight back. He smiled into Forrest's eyes as if he was beaming himself into their light, pulling Forrest down beside him. I watched the interaction between Forrest and Mr Green, the play of hand on the seat of Forrest's pants. Forrest accepted the touch greedily.

The room got fuller, the perfume and warmth intensified.

I held onto the table of lilies, alone, feeling awkward.

'Hello. I'm Rouge and this is my partner Jade. We're in Melbourne visiting,' said a slight man next to me.

'How lovely, where are you from?' I asked.

'Sydney, not far,' said Jade.

'I love Sydney,' I said enthusiastically.

'I don't know anyone here. My boyfriend is more interested in the men here than me. I'm thinking of doing what any girl would do. Getting very drunk,' I said.

The two men laughed with me. I smiled at them. They were nice.

Jade pushed a pill into my mouth. I washed it down with champagne. I knew about ecstasy but I'd never tried it. I was long past caring.

The next thing I knew I was dancing and laughing and happy. I propositioned every gay man in the room and asked Jade if he'd like to have babies with me.

'I'd love to,' he said politely, 'but I'm gay and I'm HIV positive.' He said it in such a sweet British manner. I knew I loved him, and him over there, and well, all of them.

I even loved the man who sold me a felafel on the way home that was stuck to my belly when I woke up early the next afternoon.

It was the beginning of a fabulous relationship with Rouge and with Jade and with ecstasy. It was also the end of my fling with Forrest.

I woke feeling beautifully decadent. Parts of the night before came back to me. I seemed to remember Jade and Rouge carrying me to a taxi and escorting me home.

Oops.

I turned the phone on and took a one-hour booking for three-thirty.

The client wanted me to go to the Hyatt. He was staying in the penthouse. He told me his name so that I could use it at the hotel.

It was a name I knew well—a name everyone knew well. He was a guru in the music industry. For a short time I'd dated a musician who was signed to his agency.

I was impressed and nervous as I dressed in a long black skirt and expensive black jacket with green appliquéd crosses on the pockets.

I packed my condoms, lube and massage oil into my handbag and wrote down the details on a piece of paper.

3
Penetration:
anal stimulation

I felt sassy and mysterious as I walked up Collins Street past the office workers. *If only they knew how much more interesting I am. I might look like a well-dressed secretary but I'm really a daring sex-kitten.* I felt sexual and free—gorgeous. I was still high.

I always assume a haughty air in hotels.

'I'm here to see Mr R in the penthouse. Could you call him and tell him I'm here please.'

I waited to be collected next to the lift in the marble lobby.

The lift door opened to reveal a tall, dark, middle-aged man in a white towelling dressing-gown and bare feet. He had thinning, slightly ruffled dark hair. He smiled at me and beckoned me in, swiping his card to access the top floor. I pushed my back against him and wriggled.

'Hi, sexy,' I said in a husky voice.

'I like your jacket,' he said.

He seemed surprised and pleased that I was dressed stylishly.

In his large suite, he offered me some cocaine. He had laid lines out on a bureau. He was obviously coked off his head, and admitted he'd been up all night.

I took the condoms and tube of lubricant from my handbag and placed them on the bedside table. He explained to me briefly that he liked kinky sex, but no intercourse.

What the hell does that mean?

He lay on the bed as I stripped to my lingerie slowly, bending right over facing away from him. I slowly slid my finger under my G-string into my pussy, then into my arse.

Moving my hands very slowly up under my breasts, I straightened my back, jutting my arse out towards him. I looked back over my shoulder provocatively and talked about having sex with girls, but felt no response. I changed the subject, 'I love being fucked in the arse.'

There was still no response.

'You're a very naughty boy,' I told him.

Third time lucky.

I registered the glimmer of interest that passed across his face quickly, lighting his features like an electric current.

I slid myself slowly up the brocade bedspread in my lingerie until my mouth was next to his ear.

I proceeded in a husky whisper,

'I'm going to handcuff you over a stool in a public toilet, naked, with your soft, white arse in the air.

'One after another people are going to come into the toilet and fuck you. Some of them will piss on you and make you suck them off. You'll have to do anything they want. There's nothing you can do to stop them and if you protest, *even a little bit*, you'll be spanked *hard* until your arse is raw and red. Some of the men will have huge cocks and women will be allowed to watch you being fucked. If I tell you to drink their piss you'll have to do as you're told.'

'Oh, yes, yes,' he panted.

His cock became hard. I reached for the lube and squeezed a small amount of the clear jelly on to my middle finger. I slid my finger into his arse. Most men like having their arses fingered; this one begged for more. I slid my entire hand into a condom, gradually working his rubbery rim loose until my arm was up to the elbow in his arse. He was obviously used to it. I wondered what else had gotten in that far.

I was surprised how wide the passage became once entered. I could feel the soft membranous wall expand and grow inside him. I reached around and pulled at his cock with my other hand until he came on the bedspread.

Imagine how much semen there is trapped in the fibres of carpets in hotel rooms.

He looked at me with wide eyes and a calm face.

'You're the first woman who has really understood me,' he said softly. He looked younger, relieved.

You probably don't want a woman, buddy, you just don't want to admit it to yourself.

'I'd really like to see you again, Ruby,' he said shyly.

'That can be arranged. I'm all yours, sweetie,' I said. I was patronising him, not in the least bit impressed any longer. His need to be abused and punished meant I could have stood up and spat on him and he would have loved me even more. I wondered what he felt so guilty about. They say you inherit a lot of guilt from your parents.

You poor, fucked-up bunny. You're just a bit of a joke really. I bet there are plenty of people who have a laugh at your expense.

I found out much later from a friend who worked for him that his sexual exploits were well known. I felt sorry for his wife and kids. I'd read an article about him being a family man. He was leading a precarious double life. Maybe it was his guilt and shame about cheating on his wife that he wanted to be punished for. One of my clients knew him well. He said Mr R had been beaten up at school regularly. There was something about him that made the other boys pick on him. Perhaps his sexual needs came from being abused by the other boys. Perhaps he was just gay.

He paid me the *exact* amount of money I'd quoted on the phone, before I'd known that it was going to be a fantasy booking. If I had known what he wanted I would have charged him more.

He's probably fisting the bands who are signed to him. Metaphorically, if not literally.

I left thinking, ironically, *tightarse.*

4
Domination:
torture fantasy

To kill time while my mobile phone was quiet, to stave off the claustrophobia of being trapped in the apartment waiting for the phone to ring, I went for a walk by the sea. It was windy and lonely.

Rain began to fall lightly; it gently tinkled the surface of the water, marking it with quickly merging circles. I thought it sounded like miniature soldiers marching, and then it stopped politely.

The foamy, molten mercury sea swelled, licking the land, threatening to devour it. Fine, cold, white mist rose from the water, blurring the surroundings into a surreal haze. In the guttural ice-tipped crashes I heard the voices of sea gods and whispering mermaids beckoning me. Metallic grey-green hid the subterranean life as I breathed in the particular briny smell of female genitals.

The weight and volume of the sea sat in my mind and washed it with irrational dread. I imagined it rising up and taking me—water flooding my nose and lungs, choking life from me. The sensation of drowning and the fear seemed like a half remembered past.

I took a tram along the Esplanade. Some of the faces on the street were familiar. I had lived in St Kilda for several years, long enough to see the character of the area change. I was attracted by the excitement of the red-light district, the bohemian and dangerous reputation and the village atmosphere.

At the turn of the century it had been an affluent seaside resort and the opulence of the architecture reflected the boom of the gold rush. Now populated by artists and musicians, the bars were full of open-minded conversation and camaraderie. The local community readily embraced the street characters as part of the aesthetic of the culture. They were used in photo shoots for a fashion advertising campaign and several books of photographs, giving them star status.

It was only a short ride to the stop in Inkerman Street. I decided to walk the rest of the way home. A couple of street walking prostitutes passed me, wearing crotch-hugging, obscenely short skirts that exposed wasted, pale legs, and stilettos worn to frayed plastic at the heels. Their unwashed, dry, bleached and brassy dyed hair exposed dark roots. Most of them were obviously heroin addicts. I felt sorry for their depravity.

It was painful to watch one of my own kind lose control of her body. The younger of the two working today would have been a pretty, young girl if her sunken and twisted features hadn't been ravaged by poor nutrition and the look of desperation that she wore.

I felt removed from their reality and yet the gulf that divided us wasn't so wide.

The thought of heroin repelled and attracted me at once.

Occasionally at night an attractive well-dressed girl would work a corner near my home. I wondered if she saw the same clients as I did.

The message bank on my mobile phone was full, mainly with hang-ups. Most of the callers from the small add I'd placed in the local paper, a few I'd picked up in the couple of days I'd worked from Apple's phone number. She didn't care, most of them saw her as well. They did the rounds—sex addicts probably. The odd one or two liked to be faithful to one girl, they never ever strayed.

Most of the callers were either cranks or just curious. The ones that actually made bookings usually became regulars and if not weekly, I would usually see them more than once. There was a message from a 'John' who I remembered because he was so weird. He was a Swedish doctor: Vietnam vets were always fucked-up. He wanted to see me in an old motel near the city. It was a bad hangover from the seventies: built of ugly brown brick with mission brown trim characteristic of the era. I remembered him well.

Nothing in the room was at all interesting. This only drew more attention to the striking icy blue eyes of the tall man sitting on the edge of the bed—eyes that burnt with a cold flame and definite purpose. Even while seated his height was apparent. His large square shoulders emanated power. I imagined the hundreds of men who had slept in this room, stopping here on business trips. The old gold bedspread was kept plump with their skin cells, hair and body secretions.

His voice was cultured, slow and careful, his command of English crumpled at the edges. He looked and thought in his native tongue: Swedish: tight and sculptured.

Blonde is not just a colour; it is a quality.

There was no flattery or softness in his voice as he instructed me, in the way, no doubt, that he instructed his patients and colleagues.

He wished to be scarred for life.

I was to shave off his pubic hair and force him to eat it. I was to force him to drink my urine. I was to abuse him.

He seemed familiar with these practices. I was not. He told me he had killed in the Vietnam War, that he had been tortured in a concentration camp and he seemed to want to purge himself of the experience by translating it into a sexual ritual. For this service he wished to pay as little as possible. I knew I could charge heavily for this type of booking, and he had plenty, I could smell the wealth on his clothes. We finally agreed on seven hundred dollars for an hour and a half.

I insisted that he shower first, even though he pleaded that he didn't want to touch me.

I had an animal cunning in these situations that enabled me to think quickly and clearly.

I peeled off my black stockings, removed my short, grey, pleated skirt and blouse and unhooked my suspender belt, tucking the money carefully into my bag.

I stood in the dim room wearing black satin lingerie, looking out of place and feeling cold. Goosebumps pricked my arms and my nipples contracted.

I had brought lube, condoms, make-up and body lotion. I added the bathroom products and a candle and matches, brought with much prettier thoughts in mind. I had nail scissors in my bag.

I was an empty vessel ready to be filled with a character suited to the needs of this stranger.

As he dried himself, I had a strong image of his wife. An elegant greying blonde woman, tall and supple like a silver birch. With inner strength and a sense of self. It must have blinded her to his perversion. I imagined fancifully that as her beauty slipped from her like water into sand, he slipped further into the dark practices from his past, as though his past became nearer: a whim of time.

I liked to empathise with the needs of my clients, but this man's experience was a depth of trauma too foreign to me.

I exchanged my soft voice for another's and my feminine stance for that of a tyrant. I searched my heart for some anger with which to administer the punishment. The space around me was full of expectation.

His will bore the force of a monarch.

To scar someone for life is not as easy as it sounds. It was my intention to burn the inside of his thighs badly with a lit candle but his cries of pain stopped me short of the desired result. I felt his disappointment at my reluctance. I shifted my focus to shaving his balls with a razor and pissed a little into a glass.

I gathered up the pubic hair into the urine and held the glass to his mouth.

'Drink up,' I said.

He chewed lengthily on his pubic hair and seemed unable to swallow it. With his ankles and wrists tied tightly with my stockings, he had assumed the demeanour of a tortured and slightly pathetic overgrown child. With his intelligence stripped away, a less attractive and smaller man was revealed.

I had become the cruel tormentor, carried along heavily as a semi-trailer towards delivery at its journey's end, feeling compelled to give the best performance that I could.

As a dominatrix I felt taller: a Japanese cartoon character, clad in vinyl and metal armour. My legs astride the invisible steed of my own warrior power, Queen Boadicea of the Britons. The reversal of roles was almost liberating.

As the air fell around us warmer and heavier, a dense wrap filled my nostrils and lungs with ermine.

I, queen to his slave.

My brain congealed with assumed anger as I watched with my sensory instinct for his responses. I rubbed make-up, shampoo, conditioner and body lotion into his chest hair telling him to imagine that it was my shit. His muscles remembered youth but had relaxed at the edges to a tanned elastane.

I growled at him.

'You *excrement*! Don't try to touch your cock or I'll make you sorry.'

His hands were trying to wriggle free. I slapped them sharply. The sound reverberated around the walls.

'You filthy low-life scum, you deserve to be punished'.

My brain felt strung out from the effort of concentrating.

'You deserve to die! Don't cry out, you baby. Lick my cunt.'

I squatted over his face and urinated into his mouth. He drank the urine greedily, with noisy gulps. He could reach his cock, even though his wrists were bound he still had movement in his fingers. One hand rubbed his soft cock slowly.

'I said lick my pussy arse-hole!'

I yanked his thin grey hair, it was fine and soft like cotton. The strands became unwoven from the back of his scalp into my hand. The rubbing of his cock had become more urgent now. I struck his hand hard; the sound rang like a triangle.

'You dirty, worthless pig. I warned you!' I shouted.

'Lick my arse, now! Not like that or I'll cut off your cock!'

It occurred to me that I might be getting a little carried away.

I relit the candle and dripped thick waxy skin onto his chest and thighs, burning red blotches on the vulnerable skin of his pale, freckled, inner-thighs. Drunk with adrenaline I grabbed the nail scissors and quickly stabbed him there. His scream I supposed to be the orgasm of his tortured mind.

The wax had hardened in little white crusty globules, no longer mimicking skin; it had reddened and puckered a little at the edges of the cold, hard, plastic dots.

The scene had become wearisome and a little sickening. My subconscious ticked like a clock, measuring time against experience. The room was narrower and darker, as unseen jurors in the corner whispered amongst themselves. I became a barber now, clipping his pubic hair and pushing the hair into his mouth as he choked and gagged. I let him play with his feeble, semi-erect cock. I sat on top of his mouth again not caring if he could breathe, until with a little spasm he ejaculated on himself.

I had to cut the stockings from him. It was difficult to talk normally now, as I dressed hastily. I thanked him and gathered up my things, leaving hurriedly.

Once outside, I ran down the corridor hugging myself and shuddering, pulling a face to squeeze out the last vestiges of contamination.

'I'm not going there again! No amount of money is worth that,' I said out loud.

I had a moment of panic.

Please, please don't call. Surely he's going home after his conference, Fingers crossed I've missed him. I'll have to see him if he calls back—the money's too good. Thank God I haven't got his number.

I never kept their numbers.

Interlude: Recreation

Nightclubs and casual liaisons

I couldn't sleep. I got up at midnight and got dressed and put on make-up. I caught a taxi; driven out by the wildness that stirred inside me.

'Clubbing' suggests hitting something repeatedly with a large, blunt object as well as the brain damage that results.

I felt privileged to be recognised by the superior beings posted as sentries outside the well-guarded door of the club.

In order to pass through easily I wore clothes that looked like circus costume—an original sparkly, white, very mini, 1960s dress with enormous, white platform shoes and green glitter on my eyelids.

The long, glossy, red room of the club was half full. I ordered a double vodka from the bar and stood leaning on a narrow shelf attached to the long wall. I waited for the E I'd dropped half an hour before to take me away from myself.

Moments later I was rapturously lost, wandering in the luscious garden of my own mind.

I am the Maharani of Jaipur, fleshy, lascivious and insatiable. Sensual, gold-embroidered silks caress my skin, softly rippling against my thighs where the languid afternoon heat has left a moist, satin glide.

As I recline into abundant silken cushions, I inhale deeply the many perfumes from the flowering gardens: jasmine, attar of rose, clove and cinnamon.

The sights that surround me arouse me, filling me with milky glistening warmth. Two nubile young women strut daintily like birds of paradise on the lawn in front of me—innocent houris, eager nymphs.

Crouching animals tense with desire. They await their release.

As they dance in a circle slowly, with linked arms, smiling at each other coyly, I think of them as a nest of soft downy skin. Their perfume further loads the air, overwhelming my ability to think.

The vivid colours of their silken swathes are reflected in the cascading water of a three-tiered fountain. Water rolls over the voluptuous, smooth, white buttocks of a naked marble cherub.

Colours tumble through the water like gemstones: rubies, emeralds, sapphires and diamonds.

I continue to watch the mating dance, of two young plump-breasted houris, dressed in turquoise, purple and gold. Two tall, lissom peacocks, petting and stroking each other with tapered fingers and delicate pink tongues. Slowly teasing in a garden of exotic rustlings.

A beautiful young man seated cross-legged on the lawn, plays sitar with an air of poetic sadness. I wonder who knows what his story might be, what torture his mind must bear to bring forward such sweet music? His taut, golden skin is smooth like the skin of a drum. I watch the muscular ripples of his triceps. They dance and accompany the waves of music.

It was as though I were living in the last ruling days of the British Empire. Days of colour and drama. Here was the advent of majestic steam ship travel, of overly large, luxuriously padded, cream and black motor vehicles. This was the age when women wore mesh veils over stencilled blood-red lips and feather-trimmed felt hats perched to the side of sculpted wavy hair. Fragrant with whisky vapour, they kiss one another in the smoky basements of melancholy jazz clubs.

I am sure I see Paddington Bear standing alone in the corner wearing his own little red felt hat and navy duffle coat and his lonely label, standing amidst the sooty steam-train hustle-bustle among the shouting porters of Victoria Station.

What is the tag that one should wear, that would declare what one is searching for? Is there someone to love and care for each and every misplaced pet? I wonder sadly.

The soot and spilt drinks on the floor beneath my feet have become a shiny visceral swamp, of floating tendons and entrails, a morphing sewer lacking only crocodiles.

My judgement regarding fact of high is marred by the being of high. How high am I? Am I high enough? Not too high? Is there such a state? I think perhaps there might be, having frightened myself, seeing a procession of elderly ladies walk through the centre of the nightclub; each one identical, with blue-rinsed carefully coifed hair, wearing plastic raincoats and pushing shopping trolleys.

I shrugged my shoulders, smiling slightly and fumbled with the tattered plastic bag tucked into my bra to make sure I had more drugs, wondering at my state of divine senselessness.

A strobe of light fell across one side of my face, a sepia glowing frame around my Anglo-Irish features, slightly pointed in profile, illuminating me for a moment against the dank sea of shadows.

In this other world, inky like the underside of the ocean, cavernous and treacle thick, bodies writhed in desire. It was a scene from hell; sucking my mind downward into a subconscious chasm.

I was part of an unscripted film noir. Movement was language and the writhing participants, all feathered and sequinned like exotic animals, worshipped physical perfection.

My thoughts raced in a circular fashion, chasing shadows of feelings that I tried to capture and pin down to milk further for information. I was looking for prompts to satisfy the restlessness growing in my belly.

Desire grew at the base of my spine like a vine growing upwards: to the throat and then down to my urethra, tickling my nerve endings and teasing, until my desire was an overwhelming tide.

Thoughts conspired, cajoling instinct to charm and posture provocatively. My lust had no morality and limitless cunning. I desired strangers without reason. Sometimes attracted to qualities I would like to own myself; sometimes turning the object over with my hands and in my mind, devouring them as art.

My luscious red lips moved; my sparkling eyes swam with meaning as I talked to a guy who I recognised from the scene.

'Hi! Carl, how're you going?' I asked.

'Great!' he shouted.

'How's the café?' I said.

'Not bad, I'm still working for Telstra though.'

'You're looking well!' I said.

I was lying. He looked like shit. *How did he get so pale and so thin? This boy was a good prospect for an anti-drugs campaign: the wan 'after' shot.*

47

I met him at four in the morning. I looked into his liquid chocolate eyes. He was beautiful, but it was his femininity that seduced me.

I didn't usually sleep with guys unless they were paying me.

The rounded edges of his voice soothed and transported my mind to foreign shores, complete with orange sunsets reflected off crumbling, time-eroded walls.

We recognised each other from a life before, one of gentle grace and grapevines maturing on sunny, terraced slopes.

I took him home to my apartment and let him make love to me.

He lay over me with a slow rolling movement. The contours of his abdomen were smooth ripples of ripe, golden corn silk, brushing against my belly.

I gasped for breath as his perfectly shaped manhood filled me again and again, releasing shudders of pleasure at the height of each penetration. My instinctive inner woman supplicated to his powerful rhythm. I arched my back at the intense sensation. I felt the hard muscles of his back working with the earthy power of a plough-horse.

His head bowed backward over his spine, outlining the ridged bones of his throat and his Adams apple as he reached orgasm.

The pearly light of dawn washed over our bodies, falling over us from my tall window. We were two supine young animals crouched together, half asleep.

I was shy as he left and avoided his eyes as I gave him my phone number. After he left, alone with my thoughts, I felt guilty. I didn't want to feel guilty.

No-one owns me! Life is short. I'm a tramp, so what? I'm a whore! Why shouldn't I do something unexpected.

I knew it was the drugs; they made me do things I wouldn't normally think of. I prayed he would call me.

5
Domestication:
working from home

I readied myself as usual in the morning, carefully blow-drying my hair. I applied make-up and tidied the room. I switched on the mobile phone and opened my diary ready to take down appointment times.

The first call was from a crank whose voice I recognised. He called me at least once a day to listen to me describing myself. He wanted to know what I would do to him in a booking. After he'd called me several times I gave him my standard reply, 'But then it wouldn't be a surprise. You'll have to come and see me to find out.'

He never made an appointment.

I always tried to be polite. *In this industry it's better not to upset anyone.*

'I'm sorry I'm not available this week,' I said abruptly and hung up.

The next caller had a mature, educated voice. I had developed an instinct about genuine enquiries. They were usually polite and short, not at all sleazy. They were mature men who made a booking without asking for any details because they knew the drill. I was usually right. I called back on his mobile to confirm an appointment for two-thirty.

'Tooth-hurty, the dentist's hour, sure,' I said brightly. 'I can see you for an hour.'

He arrived exactly on time. Most of my clients did.

He wore a tweed jacket, flecked with green and beige and a trilby hat in a similar herringbone fabric. He was five-foot-ten and fit for a man who was at least fifty.

'Hello, handsome. Come in out of the cold,' I said. I slowly ran my hands over the coarse tweed of his jacket, sliding them under his jacket. I felt his chest and fondled the bulge under the rough wool fabric of his pants.

'Let me make you nice and warm,' I said in a husky drawl, caressing each syllable. I held his hand and led him to the bed.

I took his jacket to hang in the wardrobe and placed his hat on the dressing table. I tussled his fine grey hair affectionately with one hand.

I made the decision not to ask for payment first.

With older, respectable clients it added a touch of class if money wasn't mentioned. Very often they would leave the folded notes discreetly on the dressing table, sometimes with a tip.

I used my discretion.

'Are you English?' I asked.

'No, but I've just returned from a year in Ireland,' he said.

'Really, what do you do?' I asked.

'I'm a judge,' he said.

'My grandmother was Irish,' I said, as though that connected us in some way.

He smiled at me charmingly.

I helped him unbutton his shirt and trousers, hanging his clothes carefully on a coat hanger because I liked him.

He walked to the shower in socks that were pulled up neatly on his calves. I adjusted the water temperature for him.

'There are clean towels on the rail,' I said in a sing-song voice.

I undressed to my G-string and stockings and ripped open three condoms, laying them on a tissue under one pillow. I applied lube to my arse and pussy.

He returned with his socks back on. I stood in front of him smiling up into his eyes.

'I'm very wet,' I said. I took his hand and placed it between my legs.

I rubbed the grey hairs on his chest with both hands and pressed my breasts against his chest.

'I've been very naughty,' I said.

'I daresay,' he said, with a sardonic tilt of his top lip.

He slapped my arse hard. I knelt on the bed with my arse pointing towards him expectedly.

'Are you going to punish me for being bad?' I said. He slapped me again.

'Harder,' I said, 'I like it.' The sound of smacking resounded through the room.

I squealed.

'Tell me what naughty things you've done,' he said.

'I've been licking my girlfriend's pussy,' I said.

I put my face down on the bed as he spanked me again.

I reached my hand up under the pillow and took a condom and put it into my mouth. I turned and pushed my mouth over his erect cock quickly sliding it in place.

He pushed me down on the bed on my stomach, quite roughly and pressed his body on top of mine, thrusting his cock into me as he smacked me again with one hand.

He was breathing heavily. His body was hard and taut. He ejaculated quickly with a short roar and then stood up. I gently removed the condom from him with a tissue

'Can I have another shower?' he asked.

'Wouldn't you like a massage?' I asked.

'I have to get back to work,' he said. I wondered if court was in recess.

I tidied up hastily and wrapped myself in a towel. When he returned from the bathroom to get dressed I plied him with conversation as I handed him his clothes piece by piece.

'Do you enjoy your work as much as I do?' I asked.

'Sometimes,' he said.

'There must be so many sad people. Do you feel sorry for them?' I said

'No, not usually,' he said.

'Is there such a thing as justice? Does the system really work?' I asked.

'Yes, of course,' he said. Although he curled his lip. I didn't feel he was committed to his answer.

He tucked the money neatly under the edge of the massage oil on the dresser. He had paid me for an hour although he had only stayed for half of that time. It was his way of tipping me.

He did up his shoelaces.

I walked him to the door, reaching up to kiss him softly on the lips.

'See you soon. Don't you have any fun until you see me again,' I said, wagging my finger at him, pouting my lips.

'I promise, goodbye dear Ruby,' he said.

You seem really interesting. I'd love to just sit and talk to you. But that's not what you're paying for is it? What a shame. You might like it more if you knew me—if you didn't just want the same old, boring, repetitive crap. If it wasn't just a jabbing of genitals. Maybe friendship or a bit of a connection would be nice for a change. I miss intimacy.

Anyway, at least he kept his promise. I was to see him every week while I worked in Melbourne.

I usually left half an hour in between bookings to tidy up and re-apply my make-up. I dawdled around in my towel and made tea. I had another booking shortly.

From my window I saw a car park in the street outside. It was a vintage ute, beautifully restored in shiny dark green. A stout, casually dressed man walked towards the building. Shortly afterwards there was a knock on my door.

'Hello, Michael,' I said. 'I really like your jacket. It's very funky,' I said, fingering the leather appreciatively.

'That's me,' he said. I laughed. He had a self-deprecating way of speaking that made everything he said sound funny.

He wasn't tall and he was heavily set with a thick neck and wide shoulders. I ran my hand over his smooth scalp.

'It suits you,' I said.

'Just as well, it's mine,' he said.

'Let's get you undressed,' I said

'I had a shower before I left home,' he said.

'Yes, but if you want me to lick your arse I need you to be nice and fresh. Another one won't hurt you. You're waterproof,' I purred, smiling at him.

His brow lifted.

'You've got me. That's an offer I can't refuse,' he said.

'I thought that would get your attention,' I said.

He showered very quickly and returned wrapped in a towel.

'I'm getting cold,' I said, 'You'll have to warm me up.' I hugged him around the waist. I had a blow heater in the room and a bar heater in the bathroom that I left on all day. I was too mean to buy things that didn't give me a feeling of delicious instant gratification, a decent heater wasn't a *fun* purchase.

'Are you local?' I asked.

'Yes I live on the Esplanade. In Robe Street,' he said.

'I used to live there,' I said. 'Are you in that building on the corner that's just been renovated?'

'Yes, at the top,' he said.

'Great view, of course it would have been better if I was still living across the road, you could have watched me walking around naked,' I said. 'Don't be shy.' I removed the towel and dropped it on the floor. I knelt down in front of him, holding onto the sides of his thighs.

I licked the smooth skin on the inside of his thighs and under and around his balls. He had a stiff, pink erection. I put a condom over my tongue and pushed him towards the bed. He put his hands on the edge of the bed. I spread the cheeks of his arse with my hands so that I could push my tongue into his anus. He leant further forward with his face pressed down on the mattress and his arse in the air obligingly.

I removed the condom surreptitiously from my tongue and hid it under the bed. He stood up as I moved around him on my knees so that I could tease the shaft of his cock with the tip of my tongue. I looked up at him and smiled, with my head tilted slightly to one side.

I lay on my back on the bed and let him watch me finger myself. I reached up and took the vibrator and pushed it slowly in and out of my pussy, while I pushed one finger into my arse.

'Do you like it in the arse?' he asked.

'I love it,' I lied. *I love everything, of course.*

'Can I fuck you there?' he said. His voice was strained.

'It's very expensive,' I said. That was usually enough to put them off.

He took his jeans from the chair and took his wallet from his pocket.

'How much?' he asked.

'Double the price for double the holes,' I said in a jolly voice that belied my true feelings on the subject.

He counted out three hundred dollars and placed it on the table.

Oh, shit, I thought.

At least he wasn't big. I wouldn't have entertained the idea if he'd had a big cock.

'Let me massage you first,' I said, stalling for time.

He lay on his stomach on the bed while I massaged the two columns of hard fat at each side of his back. I worked around the nodules of his spine vigorously with my fingers. I cupped the cheeks of his arse with my hands in circular movements that pushed them together comically. His arse looked as though it was pulling faces at me.

'What do you do?' I asked.

'I'm a comedian. I also do a breakfast show on the radio,' he said. He told me which one.

'That's why you're so funny,' I said, slapping his arse.

'Do you listen to me?' he asked.

'No, but I promise I would if I got up that early,' I said.

He rolled over.

I rolled a condom onto his cock and sucked him. He stopped me.

'Stop, I don't want to come yet,' he said.

'Silly me. I don't want to spoil my own fun, do I?' I said.

'Why don't you fuck me in the arse then?' I said. I tugged at his body to indicate that he should stand up next to the bed.

I positioned myself so that I was leaning against the edge of the bed with my face resting on the mattress and my arse facing him. I fingered my arse-hole with one finger, applying lube generously. I inserted two fingers, working myself loose and spread my cheeks open, beckoning him to enter.

He pushed against the rubber rim of my unyielding hole. I pushed out with my muscles, gritting my teeth, ready for the pain.

He pressed into me slowly and then picked up momentum. I closed my eyes and screwed up my face, thankful that he couldn't see.

He rocked back and forth until warm semen flooded the condom. I registered it with enormous relief. I reached around and held the edges of the condom as he withdrew.

His face was red and moist.

He lay down on his back and put one arm out for me to lay down beside him. I put my head on his chest and lay silently for a few minutes. I raised my head and let my hair fall in a curtain, moving it down his chest.

'Would you like another massage?' I asked.

'I never say no,' he said.

'Me neither, it's not in my vocabulary,' I said.

He relaxed under my hands as I karate-chopped him from head to toe up and down his legs and body, vigorously.

I counted how much money I would make today. I had one booking later in the afternoon—six hundred dollars. It was a good day. I could buy a new pair of 'fuck me' boots.

'Don't be a stranger,' I said, as he left.

He was to become one of my favourite regular clients, purely because he made me laugh. He was also a generous tipper. We became friends. I often bumped into him at local bars and restaurants with a woman who I suspect was his wife. She was a petite, young, pretty Indian woman.

I never acknowledged him in public; it was in the unwritten rulebook that we would never recognise each other outside the bedroom.

I was used to feeling my arse sticky with a sugary film of lube. I wiped myself with a hot, wet face washer and got dressed.

I was accustomed to getting semen in my hair, on my skin, on my clothes, in my bed, on the floor. It didn't bother me; it was just a fact of my life. The familiar smell of rubber and semen wafted up to my nostrils every time I used the flip-top rubbish bin. The smell had permeated the plastic from many tissue-wrapped condoms.

It smelt like bleach or old potatoes.

My immune system was strengthened by continuous contact with germs. I could see men who had colds or flus without catching the virus. I certainly never caught a sexually transmitted disease.

Every month I had swabs for venereal diseases and every three months I had blood tests for AIDS and hepatitis. I was careful not to allow semen to enter my body. I could never have had unprotected sex with a client. Perversely, I couldn't enjoy casual sex with a condom. It was a point of differentiation. Luckily, or unluckily, I didn't usually have casual sexual encounters.

My heart lurched at the sound of the home phone ringing. I dashed at to it but missed the last ring.

'Damn!' I waited anxiously to see if the caller would leave a message. I didn't dare hope that it might be the guy I'd met. I wanted it to be him so badly I ached. I thought of the delicious ease I'd felt fucking him. I was attracted to him. It was a feeling that seldom came along.

I waited but there was just a hang up. My heart sank.

I dialled star, ten, hash on the phone to get the last unanswered call. I didn't know the number. Only my closest friends had my home number.

I dialled the number quickly and held my breath.

The sound of his voice on the message bank was smooth and vibrant. I felt the way you do when you eat chocolate.

'Hi, I missed your call, it's Lisa. Speak to you soon,' I said. I hung up and wondered if I should have left a message. Would I seem too eager?

6
Medication:
the gangster

It was winter in Melbourne, all silver on black. Olives and greens ripened in the wet. Dewy diamonds hung from the branches of trees that formed a canopy between heaven and earth.

Drops of rain fell from misty skies, making a musical sound as they fell on mouldy autumn beds. A strong sculpted landscape of entangled lacy patterns reached skywards.

Yellow stamens trumpeted out of pink hibiscus flowers, misplaced miracles of colour. Soft drum-rolls of thunder shook the ground. Waves of rain washed through my thoughts and cars splashed on tarmac: silver streaks through my brain.

The private streets were sanctified by endless rain and the death-like woody smell of lichen on tree bark.

Life lay sleeping. People shuffled in grey lonely bundles, hurrying from home to work and back again, pressed as close to their heaters as possible in gloomy apartments, shadowy and reflective of the day. Melbourne was a breeding ground for escapism: wine, art, love.

My first client that day made a booking for twelve-thirty in the name of Charlie. I don't know if that was his real name, they often used false names.

He arrived wearing a big, black wool coat. He was a heavy-set man with wavy grey hair that looked as though it needed a cut.

He looked as though he'd slept in his clothes.

He had.

'Hello, sexy.' I greeted him at the door. I kissed his lips gently and pressed my breasts against his chest. He smelt strongly of stale cigarettes and whisky.

I was dressed in a low-cut, slinky red dress that clung to the curves of my body with white lace lingerie underneath and matching lace-top stockings.

'Can I get you a drink?' I asked.

'What have you got?' he asked.

'White wine, tea, coffee,' I said.

'I'll have a glass of wine. Thanks. I've been on a bit of a bender for a couple of days.' His voice was husky and rough.

'You poor baby, you need a rest,' I said

'I need a fuck, and some company. My wife's in hospital having a hysterectomy,' he said.

'Oh, the poor thing. That's a big operation. I hope you're going to look after her when she comes home,' I said.

'She hates my guts,' he said.

'I'm sure she loves you. Look at you, you're so cute,' I said in my talking-to-a-baby voice.

I rubbed his chin and the jowly cheeks of his face with my hand.

'I think she wants a divorce. She found out I was screwing around.'

'I'm sure you didn't mean it. It was an accident, wasn't it?' I said sympathetically. 'You probably just tripped up and fell into some woman.'

'Yeah right, I'm a prick,' he said.

'You mean you've got a prick, a nice big one and he has needs, and a mind of his own, just like the rest of us,' I said, pouring a glass of white wine into a glass for him and a small one for myself.

I gave him the glass and caressed his groin with one hand.

'Poor darling, he's neglected,' I said.

Gangsters usually look and behave like gangsters. Killers have a dead look in their eyes as though some part of them has been extinguished. He was probably both. I was always especially nice to shady characters. It's good to have friends in low places.

'You don't work nine to five then?' I said.

'Na. I do a bit of this, a bit of that,' he said.

'Me too,' I said, 'especially a bit of this,' I pressed my breasts against his chest again and ran a hand over the back of his neck.

'Come and get comfortable. Let me relax you,' I said, helping him to loosen himself out of his coat.

I knelt down to untie his shoelaces. He staggered slightly as he lifted a foot for me to ease off a sock.

'You'd better come and sit down on the bed, or you'll fall over,' I said.

He followed me to the bed and let me undress him.

He was big and hairy—a silverback, from the urban jungle.

'Can we watch a porno?' he asked.

'Of course, we can do anything you want,' I said, 'well, almost anything.'

I put a tape into the machine and turned on the television.

He sat propped up by pillows watching the credits roll.

'I might have a bit of trouble with me old fella,' he said, looking down forlornly at the small, limp, piece of flesh rolled against his thigh. 'Look, if it's not happening, don't worry,' he said.

'I'm sure it'll be fine. I have special tricks,' I said, smiling cheekily.

'Here, pass me my pants,' he said.

I handed him his trousers.

He pulled out a plastic bag full of small beige pills, maybe five hundred, and another bag with a large, powdery white lump of cocaine.

My eyes widened.

He handed me the cocaine.

'Here, chop some lines.'

'Sure, I'd love to,' I said.

I took the cocaine to the kitchen bench and shaved a chunk off the 'rock' with a sharp kitchen knife. I chopped it into a fine powder and formed two fat lines.

'You have some,' he said.

'Thank you, you're so kind,' I said.

Clients who take drugs like you to do them too so that you're on the same wavelength. I liked being full of energy and off my face, it made the time go faster. Almost fun.

I took a drinking straw from the cutlery draw and snorted one of the lines and took a sip of wine.

He laboured across the floor to where I stood and took the straw from me. He snorted the other line and returned to the bed and lay down. I pulled my dress over my head and lay next to him with my arm across his chest.

'Do you want a massage?' I asked.

'No, not yet. Let's just watch the porno for a while,' he said.

He seemed happy just to be there with me.

'How long have I got you for?' I asked.

'How much am I paying again?'

'One hundred and fifty an hour,' I said, 'but if you want to stay all afternoon, I can give you a discount.'

'How much?' he said.

'Say four hours, five hundred,' I said.

'Alright,' he said.

'Aren't I lucky?' I said, squeezing him tightly.

After an hour of lying together watching the porno and snorting lines of cocaine I had excessive amounts of energy and an impulse to tell him my life story, but I resisted the urge.

I felt like jumping up and down on the bed.

'Isn't this fun? It beats working, doesn't it?' I said. I sat upright, cross-legged, as I chattered excitedly, jiggling from side to side on the bed. 'What are you doing later?' I asked.

'Going back to my place. Do you want to come? I don't want to be alone,' he said.

'Sure, but I'll have to charge you,' I said. My jaw felt tight as I spoke through my teeth.

'I'll give you one twenty,' he said.

'OK. I've got a hairdressing appointment at five and then I'll come straight to your place. Is that OK?' I said quickly.

I was having fun.

My mind was on the bag of pills. I thought he might throw some in later to keep the party going.

I spent three hours teasing his cock and performing gymnastics around the bed for his entertainment. I threw in some erotic dancing.

We finished the wine. I snorted an obscene amount of cocaine and felt, as they say, ten foot tall and bulletproof.

At five I ushered him out and dressed in a frantic hurry. I raced to the hairdresser in my car.

I arrived for my appointment five minutes late.

My hairdresser was a young gay man who I knew well.

'John, I'm so high you'll have to strap me to the chair. I've been doing cocaine with a friend all afternoon,' I said.

'Lucky you,' he said.

'You can do anything you want with my hair. Go wild,' I said excitedly. 'I want a change.'

'OK. Well, let's get rid of these dead bits and let me see. What about Madonna, early days?' he said.

'Anything, it's up to you. I don't care,' I said.

He laboriously untied my hair extensions and shampooed what was left of my barely shoulder-length hair.

An hour later I walked out with soft silver waves, feeling supernaturally amazing. *Astro Girl on acid.*

I had Charlie's address and phone number scrawled on a piece of paper in my pocket.

My Morris Minor was parked across the road. I consulted the street directory in the glove box. It was only a suburb away, not too far.

'Come on, Gertrude,' I crooned seductively. The car coughed and spluttered and finally started. It sounded like an old man coughing up phlegm. I was relieved; I didn't feel like cranking the oily guts with a spanner.

His house was in a residential area that I wasn't familiar with. It was a one-storey, brick, Californian bungalow with a small front lawn. The front door was at the side of the house. I knocked with the brass knocker.

'Hello,' I said.

'Come in. The door's open,' he called.

I pushed the door and walked in.

'What's your name again?' he asked.

'Ruby,' I said.

'Oh yeah,' he said.

He was sitting at a long, wooden dining table with a glass of white wine in his hand and cocaine laid out in five or six lines on the timber top.

The bulging bag of pills was on the table in front of him.

He looked tired or just a lot drunker. The house was small, dark and untidy.

A low, gold velvet couch had the permanent imprint of a large backside in its seat and took up most of the floor space.

'Do I look gorgeous?' I asked. I did a twirl and laughed to myself.

He didn't answer. He just looked up with hound-dog, bloodshot eyes that drooped over the tabletop and nodded.

'Here,' he said holding a fifty dollar note rolled tightly into a straw in my direction.

I moved around the table behind him and leant over his shoulder to snort the line.

'Shall we go into the bedroom?' I asked.

'In a minute,' he said, slowly.

'I'd better get some money from you before I forget. Do you want me to pass you your wallet?' I said, looking around.

'Na, it's here.' He reached into his trouser pocket and fumbled around until his fingers made contact with leather.

'How much?' he said, opening the battered brown wallet to reveal a wad of cash. His bottom lip drooled a little.

'One twenty,' I said.

He handed me the money. I tucked it into my bag.

He snorted two more lines and slugged back the wine in his glass. As he poured some more he missed the glass and christened the table.

'Do you want me to help you?' I asked, feeling a little concerned.

I rubbed his shoulders with my hands.

'Come to bed,' I cajoled.

'Alright,' he said. I helped him to stand up and supported the weight of his bulky frame into the bedroom.

He lay on the bed while I wrestled with his shoes and tugged off his pants. I undid his shirt buttons and pulled off his trousers.

His body had slumped into a leaden mound. He looked like a dead walrus.

There was no visible sign of life.

I tried to check his pulse but I've never done first aid and I had no idea where to find it.

His breathing was shallow.

I tried to revive him by slapping his face and shaking him. There was no response.

'Come on, big boy, don't die on me,' I pleaded.

I'm not good in emergencies. I did what I usually do. I panicked.

I hid his pills under the low-slung couch, confiscating three for my trouble. I left the door slightly ajar as it had been when I'd arrived. I left quickly. Once in my car I called an ambulance and gave them the address. I told them he'd been using cocaine for three days.

I thought, *well, that's all I can do.*

I was too high to go home. I swallowed a pill and headed to a nightclub.

I don't think Marilyn , Madonna and Anna Nicole Smith put together have partied like I partied that night with my blonde hair.

Perhaps blondes do have more fun.

The next morning at eight-thirty I went to a doctor I knew well. He was a recreational drug-user who I bumped into at nightclubs occasionally.

I was still wearing the cream, fake-fur jacket and black leather mini-skirt I'd had on all night. I was the first one in the small surgery.

'You have to give me something to come back down to earth. I've never been so high in my life. I can't function. I might never sleep again,' I said, pacing around his surgery.

'Was it good?' he asked, dribbling.

'Amazing. I had the best night. I danced for eight hours,' I said.

'I'll give you these slow-release capsules, take one this morning and one tonight,' he said.

'You're an angel,' I said, kissing his cheek and wondering if he'd like to marry me.

I was in a good mood.

I went home and took one of the capsules. I was far too wired to sleep, and far too horny. I called the guy I'd picked up at the night club. He'd told me his name was Rosso but he wasn't answering so I hung up. He hadn't called me. I was trying so hard not to obsess about him that I was doing just that.

Weeks earlier I had seen an ad in a free gay magazine I picked up in a trendy bar. It said 'Girls for girls. Lesbian escorts.' I had fantasised about calling them and had stored the phone number in my address book.

I looked it up and dialled the number.

'I'm calling about your ad. How much do you charge?' I asked.

'One hundred and fifty dollars an hour as long as you're within thirty minutes of the CBD,' said the woman's voice. She spoke with a warm smile in a mature, intelligent voice. I was impressed that she wasn't sleazy or seductive. Her well-groomed voice stroked me.

'I'd like to see a pretty, slim girl, up to thirty but not older,' I said.

'I have someone for you. Her name's Julie. She's got dark hair, brown eyes. She's slim and attractive. I think you'll like her,' she said.

'Can she come straight away?' I asked.

'Where are you?' she asked.

'St Kilda,' I said.

'She's about thirty minutes away,' she said.

I gave my name, address and phone number so that she could crosscheck my address with the listing in the phone book. She called me back to confirm the booking.

I ran a bath and lay in the blissfully enveloping water. My skin dissolved in the comforting, maternal warmth.

The white-tiled room shone with icicles of light. A white rubber duck with a yellow beak that I'd taken from a booking in a hotel eyed me from sthe ide of the bath.

The water gurgled down the plughole hypnotically.

I dried myself and rubbed chocolate-scented body cream over my skin. I put on my white lace lingerie and sat on the bed in my dressing gown.

The knock at the door made a soft musical note that echoed through the room. As I let her in the sunlight from the window shone across the top of her chocolate brown hair in a golden halo. Her smile was warm as summer. Her brown eyes flashed animal gold. *The eyes of a leopard. A Japanese Geisha.*

'Hello, gorgeous,' she said in a melodious voice. I softened inside as though my kidneys were melting.

'I've never done this before. I see men for money,' I said. I felt sad for a moment, tragic and worn. *My life as Betty Blue.*

She looked at me sincerely but didn't say anything. *Sometimes there isn't anything to say.*

I took the money from my purse and handed it to her. She tucked it into her bag and took off her wrap. She was wearing black pants and a roll-neck jumper.

She stood two inches taller than I. Her hair and skin were as gold as the sheen on a calm sea at sunset, or the late afternoon sun reflected in a mirror.

She had the strong presence of a wild cat of jungle shadow. I caught her peculiar fragrance: scented ambergris, sand, sea, alpine mint. A smell that I would be able to carry with me on the winds of my memory to any place in time.

She undressed.

'Take off your underwear,' she said. I dropped my bra and panties on the floor and lay on the bed, newborn naked, soft, vulnerable.

My membranes vibrated like the strings of an orchestra playing in harmony.

She lay on top of me and kissed me softly, her hair was in my face; a soft storm that blinded me. I held the fine strands in my hands.

I sucked in her juices.

She held me tightly, unlocking strange feelings. Mind images exploded inside me, of sunflowers, a mother.

Her hair was in my mouth and over me, on my stomach and then my legs. Her skin on mine felt as satin as cream pouring over strawberries.

'Olive flesh, cherry sweet,' I said, stroking her skin.

'Think of me as a priestess saying high mass on your body,' she said, as her hands moved over my breasts. She kissed my stomach.

We rolled over together with the entwined, melting limbs of lion cubs playing together.

She fingered my vagina with tiny fingers. I felt the fizz of pleasure as her head moved between my legs and her warm tongue found my clit. A dam of water inside me released as I moved against her tongue to accentuate the pleasure.

I was aflame, hungry and insatiable. I gripped the flesh on her back with my hands. A white dove inside me was fluttering.

'Sex is liberty,' I breathed.

I put my head between her legs. I tasted her salt.

I was at the seaside—the sensual seaside. The sweet warm smell of seashells glittering in tiny particles of warm sand assailed my senses—the fragrance of mermaids.

Diamonds sparkled from soft gold, grey and vanilla sea-walls that had crumbled so that faces smiled out of the patterns. I heard the shimmering sand dancing in the waves as water crashed and slipped away. The blissful sun kissed my back, seagulls cooed, motors hummed. I was transported by the symphony of sound and movement, the somnolent sound of a sleeping person breathing.

My eyes opened wide with lust, glistening and moist. I licked her clit, running my hands over her large milk breasts, her soft dough belly. I pushed two fingers into the warm sap of her vagina.

My hair dripped over her stomach like a shroud.

'You are a veil over me,' she said.

I felt the white wool of her thighs. Her breasts were dark-tipped domes.

I slapped her ripe peach arse, the sound resonated. Her cheeks rolled upward in slow waves, pink-stippled from my fingers.

I thrust my breasts out and threw my head back, taut like the prow of a ship. We tumbled through the sheets together, striking out at the cold places with our legs.

She sat on my face, grinding her strawberry coloured clit onto my chin, rotating the stiff, wheaten hairs over my mouth with feverish urgency. It was hard to breathe.

She ejaculated a spurt of clear liquid.

We lay together for a moment.

'Thank you,' I said. 'I hope your experience of working isn't as tiresome as it is for me,' I said in a timid voice.

'No, I love it. Giving pleasure is highly spiritual,' she said.

She dressed and kissed me goodbye. I closed the door and sighed.

Two weeks later I took a phone enquiry from a woman.

'Hello, I'm interested in booking you for a threesome with my husband. Can you tell me how much you charge? I got your number from Charlie.'

It wasn't an unusual request.

'How nice, he's very sweet. I charge three hundred dollars for two people,' I said.

'You slut. You fucked my husband,' she said and hung up.

Oops, I thought, *I didn't see that one coming. Oh well, at least he's alive, well, for the moment anyway.*

Two days later Charlie called me,

'Why did you dob me in?' he said.

'I didn't. She said she wanted to book me for a threesome and that you recommended me. I would never have admitted anything. I'm really sorry,' I said.

'Where are my pills?' he asked. My heart lurched in disbelief.

'I pushed them under the sofa because I didn't want the ambulance officers to find them. I thought you would have found them. I thought you were dying,' I said.

'I've fucking looked under the sofa. I've looked everywhere,' he said.

'I promise you I'd never take anything that didn't belong to me, honestly. Go and look again. They must be there,' I said.

I was worried. I wondered whether the ambulance guys had taken the drugs or whether he was lying to scare me.

Good deeds don't always pay.

I hoped I hadn't ruined his life. Years later I heard a rumour that he was killed in Melbourne's gang land war.

I played the tape on my answering machine to see if there were any hang-ups or messages that might be from my one-night stand. He hadn't called. *What*

the hell. I haven't got anything to lose.

'Oh hi. I had an hour to kill and I thought I'd give you a call. We met at Saratoga last week, I hope you remember me.' I said the last words with a teasing tone.

'Sure I do, how are you, gorgeous?' he said in a pleasantly relaxed voice. I felt warm chocolate pouring over me.

'I'm extra gorgeous, of course. I thought we should have dinner one night, would you like that?' I said in my most seductive, happy voice.

He paused.

'OK, why not? Friday night?' he said.

'I'd love to. Why don't I meet you at the Dog's bar at seven? We can go out from there,' I said.

'Cool. See you,' he said.

I hugged myself and laughed joyously.

'There is no drug as good as this feeling,' I said out loud.

Maybe my date would be the beginning of a new relationship. I hugged the thought happily and wondered what to wear.

7
Subordination:
submissive fantasy

I called the local newspaper and placed my usual ad. It came out every Wednesday. It read:

> 'Ruby. Extremely attractive, discreet, petite, size eight, bubbly, intelligent, sophisticated, warm, affectionate, fit, fun, playful, adventurous, sensual, sweet, stylish, well-groomed, green-eyed, blonde/ brunette/ red-head.'

Depending on what John, my hair-dresser, and I had decided that month. My eyes also changed with coloured contact lenses. My hair was either long or short depending on whether my hair extensions were in or out. One month I had three colours in my hair and that was difficult to describe, tri-colour sounded strange. I looked like a very attractive bandicoot.

The message bank on the mobile phone was full. Some of my regulars had called. I didn't call them back. They'd get in touch with me when they felt like seeing me. There was no point me calling them at any other time. Men would call me up to two years after they'd seen one of my ads in the paper.

There was more demand than supply, even though there were probably more than a thousand girls working in Victoria at any time.

I had met fat women, ugly women, gorgeous women, black, white, Asian, short, tall, rough, old, young, anorexic, alcoholic and drug-addicted women and all of them had a following of regular clients. I even met a young woman who had lost some of her front teeth.

There were someones for every-one.

I made a booking for lunchtime with a client I had seen several times. I could usually guarantee a booking in the lunch period and one at around five-thirty, the end of the working day.

I vacuumed and tidied and changed the sheets. I washed and blow-dried my hair and applied plenty of make-up.

I decided to wear a very short black dress that barely skimmed the bottom of my arse, cut low at the front to show off my cleavage. I put on black lace lingerie and stockings and black stilettos. I lit the candles and oil burner and put on a Vince Jones CD.

I opened two condoms, wrapped them in tissue and hid them under the pillow with the lube and changed the vibrator batteries. I had left it on by mistake and it had buzzed itself to death.

I sat on the bed waiting for a knock at the door.

'Hi, come in, Marvin, how are you?' I assumed my usual chirpy voice.

'I'm good. I've been trying to ring you,' he said. He sounded offended.

'I know. I had the flu, sorry,' I said. I hadn't, but it was an easy answer.

'I had that flu, it was a bad one,' he said.

'Have you got any hot racing tips for me? Have you had any big wins?' I asked. Marvin was a racehorse owner who was married to a well-known artist.

'We had a place on Saturday at a country meet,' he said.

'How's your family?' I asked taking his tweed jacket.

'They're good. My girlfriend is driving me mad. She's my wife's best friend and she's becoming very demanding,' he said.

'Don't you hate that? How many wives have you had?' I said.

'This is my third,' he said.

'You didn't learn the second time, that's the problem,' I said.

'I was wondering if you'd like to go out for lunch or dinner this week?' he asked, undressing himself and heading towards the shower.

'I'd love to, but I've got to make some money because I took a couple of days off,' I said. 'Maybe next week.'

I had been putting him off for a while. Clients were tedious enough, without having to socialise with them *without* being paid.

While he showered I shook my head at how ridiculous he was. He'd offered to put me on a retainer to be his girlfriend. *As if I wanted to be one of his harem!* It wasn't just that he cheated on all of his women that made him unbearable. He had ginger hairs growing out of his ears and nostrils and dressed and behaved like an old man even though he was only in his late thirties. *Don't men look in the mirror?*

'Hello sexy, come to mummy,' I said, 'I've missed you.' I held my arms open to receive his pale, freckled body in an embrace.

'Now roll over on your stomach and let me spoil you,' I said. He lay on his stomach with his head to one side and his eyes closed waiting for me to begin my routine. *It's just like riding a bike; you get off, you get back on, you don't even have to think, it becomes second nature.*

I saw my usual quota of around eighteen clients that week. On Friday at two in the afternoon I took a phone enquiry.

'Hello, I'm ringing about your ad in the paper,' he said in a Canadian accent.

'Are you here on business?' I asked. You could charge tourists more.

'Yes, a conference,' he said.

'How lovely. OK. I'm five-foot-three, slim, with curves. I'm very attractive with blonde hair and green eyes. I charge two hundred dollars an hour. That's cash only because I'm not a big business. I only see a couple of people a week privately. I'll need your phone number to take a booking so that I can call you back and confirm the address. I'll be available all day until nine pm. If you want to see me later you need to let me know before six because I sometimes go out socially in the evenings. Is there anything I've forgotten to tell you?' I asked.

'Can I bring another girl?' he asked, 'I want a special service.'

'How exciting,' I said. 'I can't wait. What will we do to you?' I said huskily.

'It's more what I want to do to you. I want a submissive fantasy,' he said

'That's fine, but you won't be able to restrain me, or cut or scar me.' I laughed as though I was making a joke.

'That's fine. I just want to spank you,' he said.

'I'll have to charge you four hundred dollars,' I said. I didn't mind if I didn't get the booking—it sounded like hard work. I hadn't done a submissive booking before. I was a little apprehensive.

'That's fine. Do you have a French maid's outfit?' he asked.

'Yes, of course,' I said. I took his number and called him back to give him my address. He was to arrive with the other woman at four.

I prepared the room and dressed in my short, fitted, black vinyl dress with a white apron, a low scoop-neck, a lace-up choker and a matching cap with a white frill. I had a pink feather duster to go with the outfit. I put out my riding crop and black leather, fur-lined handcuffs that slipped off my wrists easily so that I could escape from them if I needed to.

I laid out on the bed a leather bondage outfit with chains across the front that resembled a backless swimming costume. I thought it might come in handy.

I took stock of the girl as I showed them in. She was tall with very curly, long, dark-blonde hair. She was big-boned but not fat. Reasonably attractive, I thought, a bit horsy.

'Hello,' she said, 'I'm Blush.' She was Australian. I could tell from her artificial manner that she was working. I was relieved. She would know the rules and I wouldn't have to worry about pleasing her. We would both work together to satisfy him. It made my job easier.

'Hello, I'm Ruby,' I said. 'Would you like a drink, a glass of chardonnay?'

'Yes please,' said Blush. He didn't reply. I poured him a glass anyway. I usually kept a cask of white wine in the fridge for clients.

I handed them their glasses.

'Now, let's take our clothes off and get nice and friendly,' I said.

'You can leave your clothes here,' I said to him pointing to the chair. 'I'll go and turn on the shower,' I said.

I went into the bathroom and turned on the taps and returned.

I handed him a towel to take with him to the bathroom.

I had the condoms and lube positioned under the pillow ready to use and the massage oil and lotion on the floor next to the bed.

'Have you seen him before?' I asked Blush.

'No, this is the first time,' she whispered. She took a sip of her wine and put her glass on the floor next to the bed. She took off her coat, skirt and shirt and placed them on the floor in the corner of the room over her handbag. I sat on the edge of the bed.

Blush came and stood next to me, she was wearing matching red lace lingerie and flesh-coloured stay-up stockings. She wore shiny, black, patent-leather stilettos.

We watched him walk back into the room. He was fit and suntanned with blond hair and an attractive face and manner. *What a shame he's a freak.*

He paid me four hundred-dollar notes and I pushed them into the bottom of the wardrobe.

'This is my queen,' he said, indicating Blush with a wave of his hand, 'and you are our slave.'

'You have to do everything we tell you and Blush will punish you for being bad,' he said.

'You must address us as master and mistress, do you understand?' he said sternly.

'Yes, master,' I said meekly.

'Kiss your mistress's feet and her legs,' he said.

I knelt down in front of her and kissed her shoes. Lifting my body to kneel, I slowly kissed her ankles, her calves, knees and thighs.

He walked behind me and bent down to spank the cheeks of my arse. I tensed as the first few slaps stung. The slaps continued as I kissed the inside of Blush's thighs. She looked down at me, smirking. She was obviously in character.

He sat back on the bed.

'Queen, come and sit beside me,' he said.

'Slave, clean the room on your knees,' he commanded.

I dusted the skirting boards and tabletops, bending over to expose my branded red arse.

'Hold the duster with your teeth,' he said. I held the duster to my mouth and gripped it with my teeth and continued on all fours dusting the skirting board that ran around the edge of the room. *It needed a clean.*

'Come over here and bend over,' he commanded.

I moved close to him, stood up and bent over, facing away from him so that he could reach me.

He slapped me harder than before. I flinched. The queen decided to join in. I cursed her. *Thanks bitch.*

My arse was beginning to smart, it was making my mind numb and dizzy.

'Even my queen is spanked sometimes,' he said. He proceeded to spank her bottom. She smiled at him cheekily as though she enjoyed it.

I caught a glimpse of his face, it seemed grey, ghoulish. His eyes had a hollow look in them. He looked different, older.

'Get on the bed with us,' he said. I walked to the other side of the bed and sat next to her.

'Kiss each other,' he said. She kissed me hard, opening her mouth wide over mine, pushing her small tongue into my mouth.

I groped her breasts.

'Mummmmmmm,' I moaned, still full of hatred. He slapped my arse hard, six or seven times.

'Crawl around the room on your hands and knees again,' he said. I got onto the floor and began to crawl.

'Faster,' he shouted. I crawled in a circle around the bed and turned as fast as I could and crawled the other way. My knees were sore.

He took the vibrator from the middle of the bed and gave it to her.

'Fuck her with this,' he said.

She took the vibrator and knelt on the floor next to me. I bent down with my face on the floor and allowed her to pull my dress over my shoulders. She eased my G-string down to my knees and pushed the vibrator into me, gathering momentum, pushing it in and out forcefully. She slapped my arse with her free hand. The burning sensation on my cheeks felt icy. Hard goose bumps had formed from the shock.

My mind was shocked into stupor by the pain. I gritted my teeth. I began to feel angry. I looked at her. Her face was stern. I thought of Joan of Arc, iron maiden.

I hate you both, eat shit and die, I thought, feeling fierce. *This is how they make people soldiers.*

I wondered how much she had been paid. I hoped it was a lot less than me.

'Please master, can I spank your queen?' I asked. I had been inhabited by his demons.

He thought for a moment, he looked at her.

'OK, then you can lick her pussy,' he said. I got up and took a condom from under the pillow, returning to the floor where she knelt. She leant forward on all fours.

I slapped her as hard as I could on both cheeks using both of my hands until she shifted positions to escape from the spanking. She lay down on her back on the rug. I put the condom over the tip of my tongue and began to lick her, around the edge of her vagina and on the clitoris. I pushed my tongue into her as far as it would go, holding her thighs apart roughly with my hands. He got off the bed and came closer to watch.

He leant down and spanked me while I licked her. My tongue was beginning to ache but at least it took my attention away from my raw buttocks.

I really hate this. I lifted my head and removed the condom.

'Please master, can I suck your cock?' I asked.

'Yes, while the queen punishes you,' he said, lifting his chin in a regal manner.

I fetched a condom from the bed and put it in my mouth. I took his cock deep in my throat and began to suck hard. Adrenaline gave me strength.

I was sure the queen was taking all of her psychological problems out on my arse as she smacked me as hard as she could. I remembered then that women can be just as cruel as men. Queen Boadicea of the Britons had the innocent women and children in the Roman camps killed by her men.

I contemplated turning around and slapping her across the face.

'Bend down,' he said, pushing my head down roughly. He got behind me on all fours and thrust into me. He fucked me hard for six or seven thrusts and throwing his head back, came silently.

I held the condom with the fingers of one hand as he pulled out of me, getting up to dispose of it.

He sat on the bed with Blush cuddled into his side. The mood had mellowed.

'Have you always been into discipline?' I asked. His voice was soft and relaxed, the contrast was remarkable.

'Yes,' he said, 'but I need more and more as I get older.'

He was thoughtful for a moment. His brow creased into furrows.

'I'm frightened that I'll meet a woman who's into it as well and we'll do it together. I don't know where it'll stop,' he said. He seemed genuinely afraid of his dark side.

They left. I was exhausted and sore.

I finished the wine in my glass and then finished Blush's wine. I turned on the television to bring some normality back into the room and ran a bath.

I shivered. *I wonder if men like him end up becoming serial killers?*

Interlude: Fascination

Falling in love

I spent ages getting ready. Finally I was happy with my appearance. I drove to Acland Street. Rosso was already sitting at a table in the bar.

As I walked towards him my body moved seductively. I wore high-heeled black slip-ons that threw my body so that my hips swung. My legs looked long and shapely in a short red skirt.

A jazz band was playing in the corner and the sound of the bass stirred my stomach.

He rose to meet me. My face burned. He kissed my lips gently. Delicate cushions of flesh touched mine. My breath came faster.

'Let's pick one drink for the evening; Frangelico, Grand Marnier, Pimms or neat vodka with oysters? What do you feel like?' he said.

'An alcohol theme to colour our mood. Let's be sweet with fermented sugar and hazelnuts. Frangelico would be nice,' I said.

I smiled as I watched him buy the drinks and return to the table. He sat down and smiled at me.

'What do you do?' I asked.

'I'm a musician,' he said.

'That's right I think you told me,' I said. 'Are you famous?'

'We were. We made four albums in the eighties. One of our singles was in the top ten all over the world. Our management ripped us off, so I'm not rich,' he said humbly. I was impressed.

'How long have you been single?' I asked.

'Years. I was in one long-term relationship for seven years. I haven't met anyone special since,' he said.

'Let's get sentimental and morose,' I said.

He leaned deeply towards me. I inhaled his faint soap and citrus smell. 'Let's get messy,' he said. He looked impish.

I laughed, throwing my throat back.

'What do you do?' he asked. My heart sank. I hated lying.

'I'm an interior decorator,' I said. My smile felt crooked.

He ordered a cheese plate with waffle biscuits, dried figs and large flat sultanas. We sat side by side and fed each other, taking it in turns to place food on each other's tongue.

My fine chestnut hair fell over my face and brushed his shoulder. Our hands skimmed each other's arms, backs, thighs like elegant birds skipping along a branch.

Our words laughed and ran together in a song. A love song; poetry— Ovid.

Alcoholic vapour in my knees, lungs and brain slowed me pleasantly. We walked out arm in arm into the golden glow thrown up the tree-lined, night street by the street lamps. I nestled against the fine wool cloth of his jacket. It was chilly but not cold.

'Melbourne weather, heh?' I said. 'It's so non-committal.' I paused.

'Do you want to come back to my place?' I asked.

'Sure, have you got any etchings to show me?' he said.

He hailed a taxi with an imperious arm that made me think of a Roman conqueror.

'Hail Caesar!' I said.

I laughed and bent forward holding my stomach.

'I crack myself up!' I said.

He laughed.

He held my arm to steady me.

'My husband and I,' I said in my Queen-of-England voice.

Amusement spilled onto the pavement like lamplight.

'You're fun, Lisa. Unique is the word I would use to describe you,' he said. I liked the way he said my name.

He followed me upstairs. I let us in and turned on the light.

'People's things hold molecules that magnify them,' he said.

'I love being spontaneous. I never plan, do you? My life has been a series of sudden decisions for money or pleasure,' I said.

'Sounds like a dangerous ride,' he said.

'I've had a chaotic life. I'm a bit of a rebel. Being angry is like a furball you can't cough up,' I said. 'Sorry, that's a bit heavy.'

I drifted around the room brushing things with my hand.

'I feel like Greta Garbo,' I said.

I finished lighting candles around the room. The moving yellow lights deceived and flattered.

'The smell of wax triggers strong emotions. It's from church or vampires or long-ago lives in castles,' I said.

I draped myself across the sofa with one arm dragging on the floor.

His fine straight hair fell over one side of his face. 'I'll be a Man Ray muse—a 1930s screen goddess. You can be Cary Grant,' I said.

I fetched two wine glasses and a bottle of red wine. We sipped together in silence.

'The spiced blood of the French vine—it warms your veins, doesn't it?' I said.

I lay on the couch for a while with my head on his chest. I was walking a tightrope of semi-consciousness and then I fell softly. I felt him valiantly carry the sleeping princess to bed. I loved the feeling of my slight body in his arms.

I woke feeling euphoric, or just drunk.

I had been dreaming that he made love to me. I wondered at the suede of his new skin thighs, at the warm marble skin, his scent.

Fever crept through me. I inhaled his smell and savoured it as though he was inside me, in the way the Holy Trinity was when I was a child—a pure white glow.

His naked body was moulded against mine. I felt every contour of armoured bone, rolling muscle and skin in my mind. His strong male thumbs, hands, collarbones, abs and firm trunk thighs. I was part of him. The warmth from our bodies crept into one another.

I was beauty: Venus. He was a connoisseur.

My body was warm wax that moulded perfectly into him. My bones turned to rubber as we writhed together in a trance.

His large male hands pushed between my thighs. I sighed with relief.

I trusted him, I loved him. I didn't think. I felt as I had never felt, with my anima, animus, my primal senses.

I moved across the cold sheet with my shoulder blades, positioning my pelvis closer to him.

I made guttural low noises in the base of my throat, low frequency growls and feral sounds. My teeth were bared.

I braced. As he thrust into me his strength surprised me. The strength of lust.

I was in the grip of moon fever. We waxed and waned together.

I felt like a river bursting its banks in a storm, with water sloshing around inside me.

We came together—two semi-trailers crashing head on to the accompaniment of symbols.

He cradled me against his furry warm body. A tear of joy ran down my cheek onto the pillow.

We woke late.

'Fuck, I'm late. I have to meet a friend,' he said. He jumped up and got dressed.

'My head is pounding like a brass band,' I moaned.

'You sleep, I have to go,' he said.

I rolled into the warm spot that he'd left and drank his smell deeply. I was glad. Love was risk. I felt alive, even the pain was worth it. I slept for an hour or so and then showered.

I wondered fearfully if he was glad to sneak off like a coward.

Stupid woman! Will I ever learn?

The problem is I really like him.

Shit!

My head.

8
Abomination:
bestiality

Saturday and Sunday were quiet days. Most of my clients were with their partners. I would be lucky to do a booking.

I'm so bored. Intelligence is the enemy. If I was were dumb I'd be happy. Maybe I just need to take more drugs so I don't have to feel or think or get that stab of pain every time I think about my children.

I took a couple of calls.

'I've got a big cock. I want you to swallow my come. I'm gonna fuck your arse, you filthy slut,' said the voice.

'Oh, stop it you're turning me on,' I said and hung up and continued filing my nails.

The next caller confirmed an appointment for two-thirty.

I sprang into action with a cloth, dusting and putting clothes and underwear back in cupboards. I put on black velvet lingerie, black stockings and a skin-tight black vinyl skirt and matching zip-up vest.

I applied deep red lipstick, smoky eyeshadow and blusher. I put my improbably high stilettos that I'd bought in a Gucci sale next to the front door.

I decided to listen to old jazz. It brought out the romantic in me.

'So deep in my heart,' I sang in full voice to the Cole Porter arrangement, with a hand placed melodramatically over my heart.

Great romantic, two-timing, cynical, deceptive, dysfunctional man that he was. Cole Porter was the kind of man I'd be attracted to, the type who I'd always fallen for—gay, emotionally unavailable.

I gazed into the rose-tinted past and revelled for a moment in melancholy.

The knock at the door made my heart leap. I always had a nervous moment when someone I didn't know arrived.

I'd been caught out once before. A man had arrived at the door at the appointed time. I'd showed him in and said, 'Come in, sexy.' I'd pushed my arse into his groin as I pulled him by the hand towards the bed. He'd looked flushed and confused.

'I'm collecting for Red Cross,' he said nervously.

'Oh, I'm sorry, I thought you were a friend,' I said blushing. I gave him five dollars.

My client had arrived as I was showing him out.

I took a deep breath to calm my nerves and smiled warmly at the fair-haired young man who stood on the landing looking slightly nervous.

'Hi,' I said enthusiastically, as though I was delighted to see him, as though he was a dear old friend who I hadn't seen in ages.

I put both my arms around him and lay my head on his chest.

'I need someone to entertain me. I've been so very bored,' I said, pulling him into the room by his tie.

God. Here I go again.

I wish I had a fast forward button so I could cut to the part where I'm kissing him goodbye and savouring the warm, woody smell of his money, feeling the silky caress of notes in my hand—calculating the pleasure of spending it.

'Come and take your clothes off and get comfortable. Here sit down,' I said. I took his hand and pulled him towards the bed. I was aware that I sounded slightly bossy and flippant and made a note to myself to try to be more sincere.

'I didn't realise you were going to be so good-looking,' I crooned.

He smiled and relaxed. I eased his suit jacket off.

'Are you working today?' I asked.

'Yes, I'm a real estate agent,' he said.

'I love talking about houses. We're going to get along very well,' I said, as I undid his shirt buttons, kneeling in front of him. I stood up to loosen his tie and slid it over his head with the knot intact.

'I'll let you do the rest while I adjust the water for your shower,' I said. I felt like saying 'good boy' and patting him on the head.

He went to take his shower in his socks. I observed that a lot of men like to keep their socks on, even when they're having sex. *Strange creatures.*

I applied lube to my arse and vagina and made sure everything was in place. After ten minutes or so he emerged from the steaming bathroom with his socks neatly pulled up again.

'I missed you,' I pouted at him and picked up the vibrator, playfully running it up the inside of my thighs. I put it in my mouth and sucked it slowly. I lay on my back and pulled aside my G-string to push the cold plastic phallus into my pussy. I threw my head back and closed my eyes, relaxing my face as though I was abandoning myself to the feeling of pre-orgasmic ecstasy.

He stood still and watched me. I patted the bed beside me.

'Come and play with me,' I said.

He lay down on his back next to me. I stroked the sparse hairs on his chest with one hand and took his cock with my other hand. I sat on top of him, facing the other way. Taking the lube from under the pillow, I squeezed some into the palms of my hands. I pulled his cock slowly with one hand at a time and then held his shaft against the crack of my arse.

'Doesn't that feel wonderful?' I asked. He made an indescribable noise in his belly. He's hungry I thought. It was lunchtime, after all.

I felt him tense as he ejaculated over his stomach.

'One down, several to go,' I said, moving off him to take a handful of tissues from the box next to the bed. I wiped his stomach.

'Roll over and let me massage you while you recover for a few minutes,' I said.

I squirted Nivea cream onto his back liberally. I began at his shoulders and neck and squeezed each muscle one by one.

'Tell me, where should I buy a house?' I asked.

'Balaclava is good value at the moment, but anywhere around here is good,' he said.

'I thought it would be,' I said, pulling large chunks of flesh from his back towards me with both hands. I rubbed his arse cheeks and then parted them and squeezed some lube onto his arse-hole. I reached up and slid a condom from under the pillow with one hand. I broke the wrapper with my teeth and put it over my tongue. I held his cheeks wide apart with both hands as I leant down and pushed the tip of my tongue into his arse, licking the edges. I removed the condom from my tongue and discarded it on the floor.

'Was that your tongue,' he asked incredulously.

'Yes, of course,' I said.

I knew I was going to have to employ all of my special gifts to get him aroused again. It was hard work to make them come twice in an hour but if he didn't he'd feel cheated.

'Next time I see you I'll have to get my girlfriend to come over and have sex with us both,' I said.

'She loves it, so do I. We can lick each other and then you can fuck us both. Roll over and let me play with your cock,' I said, pushing him to help him roll. I didn't want him to get too comfortable.

I applied more lube to his semi-erect shaft and began pulling him as though I was seducing the reluctant udder of a cow.

'My girlfriend likes to be fucked in the arse while I lick her clit,' I said. 'Do you have a fantasy?' I asked innocently.

'Yes, I'd like to watch you fuck animals,' he said. I was stunned. He was the first client I'd ever seen who'd said that.

'A nice big horse cock?' I said.

'Yes,' he said, breathing heavily. His cock was hardening.

'Perhaps you could bring a big Alsatian with you and I could suck it off until it got hard and then you could watch it fuck me,' I said.

'Oooh, yes. Would you like that?' he asked, barely able to contain his excitement.

'Oh, yes, I'd love it. Especially a giant horse dick.' I pulled his cock faster, changing hands. His face went red and contorted as he came again.

'Would you really like it?' he asked.

'Of course,' I lied.

'We'd better get you back in the shower so that you can sell some more houses,' I said. I handed him the towel that we'd been lying on.

'Take this one, it's nice and warm,' I said. I went with him into the bathroom to help him adjust the water.

He dressed himself and left. I doubled over naked, laughing,

'Come here, Lassie. Mr Ed, give it to me, baby. Oh, what the hell, Three Little Pigs, Big Bad Wolf, what about an orgy? Why not?'

I couldn't wait to ring Apple and tell her about it. She told me this story.

It was dark. He parked his car in the same place as usual, at the end of a deserted farm track behind a metal gate. He could see the tall metal shed as he hopped over the gate deftly, using one hand to fling his slim body over.

He was fit from diving. He made his money selling illegally caught abalone to restaurants in Chinatown. He walked quickly, looking around for the night watchman. He was pretty sure he'd be right. The lazy fat bastard would be sleeping. It was around midnight.

A strong, sour odour filled his lungs. Hay, faeces and rotting vegetables, laced with some sort of disinfectant that they hose the pens down with. He knew the smell well, he wasn't deterred by it.

His compulsion, his purpose, caused him to clench his jaw, working the muscles of his cheeks.

He stopped to listen for approaching footfalls but all he could hear were the animals shifting and grunting.

He clicked on a short black torch to light the path in front of him.

He knew his way.

He approached the metal-fenced pen quietly, lifting himself onto it and then eased himself slowly down.

Standing in between two large sows, he bent down and removed his shoes and socks, leaving them at the side of the pen.

He pushed the solid body of a sow away from him so that he could pull his jeans off. He let them fall on top of his shoes. He unbuttoned his flannel shirt and left it on top of his trousers. He crouched amongst the pigs. His smooth body was pale and naked next to the ruddy, bristled hides.

A short green plastic hose was hung over the tap near a small gate. He shone the torch around the fence until he found the tap. He reached across and pulled the hose down, inspecting the pigs in the small circular beam of torchlight. He could tell them apart by their size and markings.

His favourites were the sow with a big black spot on her left ear and the largest of the six sows in the pen.

He felt that they knew him, that they enjoyed him. Perhaps they loved him.

The concrete flooring was jagged and cold under the soles of his feet, but he was distracted enough not to care. His hard-on knocked against his thigh.

He turned the tap on, almost losing his balance as he leaned over. He directed the stream of icy water under the tail of the largest sow, brushing her arse free of sticky black meconium with his free hand. He turned off the tap and pushed the rear-end of the big sow down hard, until she lay on her side with a deep exhalation and a grunt.

'Come on, baby, it's me, you know you want it.' He spoke into her ear lovingly. He caressed her cumbersome body with a tender, circular stroke of one hand, steadying himself against her with his other arm.

He lay down, crouched around her rear-end in the shape of an embryo.

He was sure she responded. She seemed to grunt with pleasure as he contracted his arse cheeks and thrust his pelvis towards her. He felt for the tight hole with his fingers, not her arse, but the smaller hole under it. He loosened it slightly, by inserting one finger. He thrust his cock into the elastic hole, it tightened on him almost painfully but he persisted, easing himself in a little further with each stroke. He came inside her after six deep thrusts.

He was panting with excitement more than exertion. He waited for the joyous spasming to subside before pulling out of her.

He patted the head of his other favourite.

'Your turn next time,' he said fondly.

He hurriedly pulled his clothes into his arms.

'Ooi! What the fuck are you doing in there,' an irate voice shouted from inside the entrance of the large shed opposite.

Torchlight caught him in the eyes as he bounded over the fence. He hit his knee with a loud clang on the metal fence and dropped one shoe in the pen.

He fled, leaping the fence in a single bound. He threw the car door open, threw his clothes in. He'd left the keys in the ignition, just in case.

He was breathing heavy chain-saw breaths as his shaking hand turned the ignition key.

The fairly new Holden started first time.

He backed up the lane with the door still open. He slammed the door shut as his wheels reversed onto the tarmac road. The car screeched and lurched forward as he sped off. He could hear the man's shouts dying off in the distance.

He was thankful the old fat guy would have got stuck on the fence.

As his heartbeat slowed, he thought sadly that he'd have to find a new place. He'd look in the Yellow Pages.

His girls would miss him.

He drove home naked. He dressed himself in his driveway before he went indoors.

'Where's your shoe, luv?' his wife asked. She'd been waiting up for him.

That night he had a dream that he saw a litter of piglets who all had his face.

He never could eat pork.

He was a regular client of Apple's. She said he looked normal; he was nice to talk to. She'd seen a picture of his wife and kids, they were an attractive family. You just couldn't tell.

We called him the pig-fucker.

A year later he went missing. Apple believed he'd been taken by a shark while out abalone poaching, either that or some drug dealers he was involved with had him killed. Perhaps the pigs ate him. *Sausage anyone?*

Sunday morning.

I dragged myself around the apartment in a pair of overly-large flannel pyjamas with tiny sprigs of pink flowers on them. I'd rolled the trousers over at the waistband. My silver belly-button ring peeped from the downy skin around my navel.

My fine hair was tangled into clumps at the back of my head. Black circles under my eyes made them look deeper green—two onyx stones.

I often slept all day when I was depressed.

I reasoned with myself, I wasn't dead, therefore I'd have to keep living, for the moment anyway.

I wasn't in an up mood, which meant I was down. I was seldom in the middle. I was either too high or too low. The lows were unbearable. I could hardly walk let alone function. The highs were also unbearable in their own way, a feeling of anxiety and restlessness meant I couldn't stay still. I had to keep moving. I had to party—hard.

The phone rang, probably some telemarketer wanting money for charity.

'Hello,' I said, impatiently.

'Lisa, Rosso. Do you want to catch up?' he said.

A surge of adrenaline rushed through me.

My voice changed.

'I'd love to, I'm really bored,' I said.

'We can't have that. I'll pick you up at seven.'

I waited anxiously for Rosso to pick me up, he was ten minutes late. I answered the door in a short, tight black dress.

He had dressed-up in a funky printed t-shirt under a black velvet jacket and casual pants.

'You look great,' he said.

Of course I do, I just spent two hours getting ready.

'Thank you, I got ready in a hurry,' I said, flicking my hair back with a shrug of my head. 'I thought we'd go to the Espy, Midnight Oil are playing, they're friends of mine,' he said. The run-down Esplanade Hotel on the waterfront in St Kilda is well known for launching the careers of Australian bands.

'Great, I've always wanted to be a groupie, especially since I'm now doing Australian bands,' I said.

The rambling hotel was packed. We squeezed through the crowd to the stage. Rosso put his arm around me. Peter Garrett strutted and sang familiar words into the mike, 'US forces give the nod'.

After the show Rosso led me by the hand to the band room at the back of the stage. The crew were smoking joints and drinking beer.

'Brother, how's it going?' said Peter. Rosso clasped Peter's hand in greeting.

'Great yeah, working on a few things, you know,' Rosso said. I noticed Rosso said virtually the same thing to everyone he met.

'I suppose everyone expects you to release another album or killer song. It must be hard having been famous and having the weight of expectation wherever you go,' I said to Rosso.

'It's all cool,' he said smiling. He had an infectious smile.

A roady handed me a joint with a nod. I didn't usually smoke but I took a puff to be polite and handed it to Rosso.

I held the smoke in my lungs for as long as possible and leaned back. The oil-painted brick walls were covered in writing. Every band for decades had added a message and signed their name. I'd never heard of most of them. I smiled at everyone vaguely and took the joint again from one of the guys and inhaled. Rosso was busy talking to people he knew. I felt reality draining from me.

Rosso's lips were moving, he was talking to me but I didn't have a clue what he was saying. I smiled back, feeling self-conscious. A few minutes later the words reached me, they must have circled the room before reaching my ears. 'I feel as though I'm cross-eyed and standing on my head,' I said to Rosso. 'I really should go and get some sleep.'

'Don't you want to have dinner?' he said.

'No thanks, I couldn't eat a thing. The room's on holiday with Alice in Wonderland and the conversation's backwards. It's really confusing,' I said.

'Wicked weed, huh?' he said smiling.

I didn't like the feeling.

'I'll take you home,' he said. He led me outside where his car was parked illegally.

I noticed we were driving very slowly.

'Do you think you should drive faster? The police will stop us,' I said.

He giggled to himself.

Outside the apartment we stopped to watch two snails on the garden wall. 'Amazing, they're fucking,' I said. I started to laugh at how ridiculous it was. 'Two snails fucking,' I said screaming with laughter. Rosso laughed at me.

'I can't stop laughing, it hurts,' I said.

'Shut up,' said Rosso laughing and holding his side.

We held onto the banister as we slowly climbed the stairs, laughing all the way to the top.

Rosso was dressed and gone before I got out of bed. He'd told me he was working in his friend's studio, recording a track for a new album.

Interlude: Infatuation

Romantic weekend

During the week I spoke to Rosso on the phone. I talked him in to going to Daylesford for a romantic weekend. Because it was my idea, I offered to pay. I would have paid anything to go away with him. I didn't mind.

We drove there in his old cream Mercedes.

Daylesford was only an hour and a half from the city. The small town was originally a Victorian mineral spa, the source of briny, metallic, magical springs.

Usually I stayed at a cheap, rambling, rainbow-painted house with uncomfortable iron bunks. This was special, so I splashed out on a room in a romantic Italianate villa.

On the large block of land sloping away from the house the owner had planted a sculptural terrace of topiary and rose gardens with vine and wisteria trailing over cedar arches. Narrow, white, loose-stoned pathways led to the heart of the garden with surprising twists that revealed statues and a mosaic pond. By the back door was an urn inscribed with messages dedicated to the owner's gay lover who'd died of AIDS.

The house was near a lavender farm—the fragrance filled the air.

Nottingham lace curtains murmured against quaint, small square windowpanes. A collection of Victoriana was carefully placed around the house. The old floorboards creaked softly underfoot, a song of hundreds of comings and goings. Hand-finished lime-washed walls in sky blue and terracotta were painted with vines that ushered the garden and sunlight indoors.

I bathed in the old claw-footed tub. From the small window I could see Rosso in the parterre garden below talking with the owner. Small birds hopped onto the windowsill and chattered.

I'm in heaven.

I got dressed and clattered down the wooden stairs to collect Rosso.

We drove to the lake nearby and parked the car.

Rosso stood next to a twisted, budding tree, that leant at the water's edge, gently dipping a wrinkled branch into an oblong of pure silver light on the surface of the water. He turned, feeling my presence, my heart expanded and bounced against my ribs so that I couldn't breathe. It felt like a giant bird trying to escape from its cage.

His eyes melted into mine, reflecting the still, silver water.

He looked as defenceless as a rabbit with his hair almost touching his shoulder. It was that distinctive picture that I always saw in my mind's eye, his curls kicking up slightly off the collar of his leather jacket.

I felt him strongly, familiarly—his warmth and smell, his gestures, the way he spoke, the light in his eyes.

His eyes were the colour of a summer evening. His cheekbones made his face look strong. He had a small dimple in his chin, one that I had traced with the tip of my finger many times.

I closed my eyes and saw the line of hair that ran from the soft thatch of chest hair down to his navel, forming a valley of shadow between gently curving ivory hillocks of abdominal muscle.

The fine line of fur disappeared into the tuft above his cock.

His cock, with its distinctive helmet as soft as cashmere.

I was addicted to his smell, the scent of aftershave, semen and perspiration that faintly lingered around his balls that on another man might have repulsed me.

I began to pant with an overwhelming desire to have him inside me.

My arms gripped him until blood no longer pumped through them. I barely remembered to breathe. As he bent and kissed me slowly, my mouth devoured his, my eyelids fluttered in a swoon.

Nothing in life seemed to matter at that moment than that I stood before my mate. I felt animal instinct overwhelm me. Lust is more powerful than hunger or any other physical need.

The need to be loved—that is all.

As he looked down on me, he had a way of raising his eyes from mine and tilting his head backwards, quizzing me comically.

I laughed giddily. My heart jumped, tears welled in my eyes. Words seemed superficial as I moved my body against his.

He rested his chin on the top of my head and held me against him.

I looked down at his wide feet. His toes were pushing against mine, connecting us through the entire length of our bodies and on some meta-physical level that I felt more strongly than with my physical being.

We lay on the soft, freshly mowed grass at the edge of the water. There was a strong smell of mulch and duck droppings. I laughed at two snowy-haired, stooped ladies berating each other in a sharp indeci-pherable tongue—'nei' and 'neish' and 'eschka'.'

'Russian makes me tongue-tied,' I said, sucking honey from the spiny segments of clover flowers to the chagrin of a bee.

'Nothing would stop you talking. If you could only speak in Russian you'd find a way,' he said.

Tousle-headed brown ducklings followed their mother in small groups, looking confused. Dainty yellow fronds of willow brushed the surface of water.

As we kissed, a child splashed into the slightly stagnant murky shal-lows from a suspended rubber tyre. My skin shrank at the thought of the bracing cold water.

The next morning Rosso and I made love quietly so the owner would-n't hear us.

After breakfast we walked to the large modern spa complex. We lay in a bathtub full of rusty mineral water perfumed with aromatherapy oils. Our bath looked out over native gardens.

'The purity of nature fills you with wholesome thoughts, doesn't it?' I said, aware of my impurity. 'Memories like this are precious jewels.'

Our relationship will probably be over soon. I wish I could hold onto this moment.

The weather was unseasonably warm. As we ambled along a narrow path next to a fir forest my feelings fermented in the humidity.

The air was still. A storm was coming. The sky was a duck egg blue stage drawn over with a heavy grey curtain. Soft track yielded underfoot. A film of pale sand covered the soil. Damp, snapping twigs and grass smelt of truffles. Insects buzzed seductively.

'The weather is a woman, all change and hormones. The sex of spring is opening her fleshy petals, can you feel it? Pollen is just powder semen. The land is a body waiting for orgasm,' I said.

'I can feel you,' Rosso said, squeezing my waist. I laughed.

Small strips of sun escaped through the cloud in cones of light, picking out the colours of Monet's palette in the grasses: lilac, tangerine and pinks. Light sparkled over the top of the grasses. Yellow tips of tender new leaves poked out. The happiness was too much to bear.

Lightning cracked above us and rain began to fall.

I broke with the storm. Bursting into tears I ran back to the house leaving Rosso to follow. I was red-faced and ashamed as I packed my things ready to leave.

I feverishly tried to manufacture a plausible excuse for my behaviour but couldn't think of anything to say. I sat self-consciously in the car as we drove home.

'Sorry, I'm insane,' I said. Rosso looked at me with a raised eyebrow.

Rosso was still asleep. I woke feeling restless. I often felt anxious in the mornings, as though I had to hurry. I dressed quickly, grabbed my handbag and tiptoed out. I returned shortly afterwards with two crisp, rustling paper bags full of groceries under my arms.

Rosso stirred as the saucepan jiggled on the graphite coil on the stove-top. A plate connected with the plastic covered bench top. Cutlery rattled; the sulphur smell of eggs cooking wafted across the room. Water sighed into the teapot.

As Rosso sat up rubbing his half open eyes and yawning he saw my figure approach the bed through the semi-darkness. (I had covered the window with a sheet to protect us against morning.) Then the unexpected thing happened. I tipped a plate of hot, buttery yellow scrambled eggs and toast onto his lap, then turned quickly and walked back to the kitchen. I began to wash dishes.

Violently.

9
Amputation:
Salon Kitty

'Why did you do that?' Rosso shouted.

I steamed back, hands on hips, red cheeks, hot breathed.

'Why should I cook breakfast?' My eyes sparked red darts that hit Rosso with hot pokers.

'What do you mean? I don't care. I didn't ask you to,' Rosso said.

I threw myself on the bed and sobbed.

'I know women reserve the right to be completely illogical, but even using the female yardstick this is a little extreme,' Rosso said, as I collected the lumps of egg and pieces of toast that resembled little pieces of tree bark onto the plate, and returned to the kitchen.

Rosso placed an arm gingerly across my butter-flyingbutterflying shoulders. He waited for the hurricane to subside.

'Are you feeling better?' he asked.

'I'm sorry, I can't help it. I feel so stressed,' I said.

He looked thoughtful.

'I'll make some toast. You know, next time it might be easier to just ask. I know they call it breakfast in bed but you're supposed to leave it on the plate,' he said.

I laughed wetly.

'A doctor told me I have bipolar disorder. But what does it matter what label you give yourself? It doesn't make it any easier, does it?'

'You're just like the weather. It might storm out of a clear blue sky, be sunny for days or experience several changes in one day. The bureau of meteorology can't give me a three day forecast, so I'll have to guess what's coming next,' Rosso said. 'I suppose if it was summer all the time it would get boring,' he added.

'Don't make excuses for me. You don't know how guilty I feel. Once I smashed all my framed pictures with a brick. I sat on the floor with them lined up like prisoners for execution. Usually I have the sense to save the necessities from destruction. After I lose it I'm usually calm for weeks. I only lose control every six months,' I said sadly.

'That's good, I've got six months of good weather to look forward to,' Rosso said.

I looked at him gratefully.

We spent the rest of the day sitting in bed watching videos. I'd hired *La Belle et La Bette* and *Cyrano De Bergerac* to impress him.

As he left I felt sick in the stomach.

I wonder if I've ruined everything.

The next day I looked outside. The weather mimicked my mood.

Pale, bird-feather brown smoke lay over the city, nesting down from the mountains from some 'burning off' of brush to protect against bush fires, whose orange flames destroyed indiscriminately each summer.

The pall hanging in the sky looked like rain clouds.

It was hard to breathe in the cigarette-smoke atmosphere.

I felt like an acrobat tumbling through the air with a silent whoosh, with my hands stretched out, hoping a stranger would grab me by the wrists and pull me up to safety.

Sometimes I just fell with melancholy abandon into the burning net, at rock bottom. Up high, I swung to and fro in elation on my emotional swing, eyes bright with the shine of sequins, feathers nodding joyously.

Each performance might be my last. It was the thrill of life in the circus.

My life was a circus.

My infatuation with Rosso was impractical—how could I think our fling was permanent? I had three children; he would probably want at least one of his own sooner or later. I had no way of supporting my children if I gave up working. He was broke. His income came from a weekly gig at a local pub and the dole. Musicians in Melbourne didn't make much money. It was unlikely he would accept me if he knew the truth about my working life.

Dread and guilt fermented inside me.

Can I lie to him forever?

I was itching for some excitement to distract me from the stress I was feeling—something new would be a challenge.

I'd often wondered about becoming a mistress.

It was aesthetically stimulating and carried less shame.

It was an occupation that could almost be considered an art form, mysterious, with a tantalising undercurrent of subversion.

There would be costumes and drama.

I found the largest ad in the Yellow Pages directory that said 'House of Domination' amongst the usual assortment of advertisements for brothels and escorts.

I called quickly, embracing the fear that laced my body with adrenaline. It was good to be distracted by some form of action.

A pleasant voice at the other end of the receiver told me to come for an interview in an hour or so.

I cited my experience in a brothel but the woman didn't seem interested.

I expected there to be a sign or a red light at the door or a plush frontage advertising a business, but it was an anonymous, slightly run-down terrace house with a plain black door and heavily draped windows, all closed to the light.

I pressed the buzzer and spoke my name into the intercom. The heavy Victorian door swung open. I was greeted by a pleasant middle-aged woman.

She asked me to wait in a small reception area, handed me a basic form to fill in and vanished.

I sat on the well-worn couch, a black leather two-seater that had been popular in the eighties.

I was told to wait, the head 'mistress' was to show me around.

She arrived shortly, entering the badly lit room with a stern face.

She didn't respond to my smile. I immediately felt I had done something wrong. She led me up a narrow, ill-lit flight of stairs that creaked beneath carpet that had once been cream.

I followed quietly.

The 'mistress' wore black leather pants and a bra top. A chain ran from her nose to her ear. Her hair was cropped and black against her white skin. Faint muffled steps and movements around us were hard to identify or locate.

She turned to look at me.

'Why are you smiling?' she asked me.

'I do that when I'm nervous,' I said.

'This isn't funny,' she said.

'Sorry,' I said in a meek voice.

She opened the door to a small room at the top of the stairs that would originally have been a bathroom.

In the centre of the room was a cream-painted metal chair, a modified dentist's chair or surgical apparatus for gynaecological examinations.

'We strap the legs and arms here,' she said, indicating leather straps at the sides of the chair.

'It's not unusual to cut the client open and suture them, sometimes sewing his penis to his leg.'

'Of course,' I said, knowledgeably.

'Occasionally we perform a small amputation. Once we cut off a guy's hand but that's rare, usually it's just a toe or a finger,' she said.

'You won't be allowed to participate for the first few months. You won't be paid anything until you're trained. If the head mistress allows it you can watch, but you must have respect and do everything you're told. This is a very serious business,' she continued.

'I see,' I said.

I looked at her with a dead stare. I could taste blood in the back of my throat.

'Do you get law suits if something goes wrong?' I asked.

'No, never,' she said, as though I'd said something incredibly stupid.

The walls were lined with locked, slim glass cabinets full of silver cutting implements of every size and style, tweezers, pliers and the like.

A single window looked out at the back of the building onto a laneway.

A small sink in the corner for washing up and light rubber floors made the room easy to clean.

I looked at the rubber floor covering that was curved up at the edges to form a skirting and imagined there would be a lot of blood to clean up.

She showed me into the next room.

At the far end of the long narrow room was a large mirror on the wall and down the side walls were racks of clothes, wigs, accessories and rows of shoes. Halfway down, forming a partition, was a dressing table full of make-up.

Long gloves, costume jewellery, feather boas and hats were buried within the deep, dusty smell of the theatre. There were uniforms: French maid, nurse, schoolgirl and boy, fireman, policeman and woman, army officer, vinyl and rubber.

As we left this room I looked down from the top of the stairs and saw a man crawl away on all fours. A leash was attached to a black studded collar around his neck. He was wearing only leather straps and was closely followed by his 'mistress'. She wore a black cap, a laced satin bodice, stockings and stiletto boots. She held a whip in one hand and the end of the leash in the other.

We passed into another room. I wondered more about the shuffling noises from padded, far-off corners.

The third and largest room was the most equipped, extending into one long area that would have been converted from two bedrooms.

It was the torture chamber or traditional dungeon. I drew breath, which was the desired effect, at the impressive fittings.

I inhaled the smell of fear and sweat tinged with leather and something else, perhaps old blood?

The equipment would have been rare and expensive but this *was* one of the most established salons of its kind in Australia.

'We have screws for fingers and genitals, a selection of large whips and hooks for the gimp. Sometimes they hang here for days,' the mistress explained.

There were coffins. Leather wrist and ankle cuffs attached to the walls, chains, and a rack of ropes and a large wooden bench like a conveyor belt with restraints for stretching.

There was a freestanding wooden upright rack to hang people upside down on and large metal hooks on the ceiling to attach ropes for hanging.

The drapes were black velvet, there being absolutely no light, no hope.

I felt sick in the stomach.

The screams of the night still haunted the room. I could feel them.

The Marquise de Sade would be proud.

I understood fun and pleasure but *this* I could not comprehend.

'I can't show you the other rooms, they're busy,' she said.

'No, really, that's fine. It's lovely. I'll have to go away and think about it,' I said in my jolly British voice.

It was all I could do to walk away from the house with a measured step and not run from the unearthly cold in my throat and stomach.

I returned to the apartment whose cool spaces had grown larger. My footfalls startled the dust.

There was a silence full of dread and a sense of something missing.

There were several hang-ups on the message bank and a message from a client I had seen several times. He had left a number.

'Hello, Rojo. Are you coming to see me today?' I said.

'I'm going to Tasmania tomorrow. If I book you a flight would you like to have dinner at the casino and fly back the next day?' he said.

'I'd love to, but I'll have to charge you two thousand dollars to compensate me for missing work,' I said, knowing he was a big spender.

'I thought you'd come for French champagne and a nice dinner,' he said.

'Sure you did, you thought I'd come for the free sex,' I said.

'I'll get my secretary to call you with the flight details,' he said.

'Woohooo, two thousand dollars and a trip to Tasmania,' I sang as I danced around the room.

I selected a pale-pink linen pantsuit and pale-pink and white lace lingerie. A woman rang me with flight details there and back. The next morning I took a taxi to the airport. It was only an hour away but I enjoyed the feeling of being the mistress of a wealthy entrepreneur. Rojo's wife owned a modelling agency and he was reasonably attractive with an interesting personality. I wondered why he needed to pay me. It was probably the thrill of being naughty and because he could afford it.

I arrived at the Hobart casino by taxi and asked for Rojo at the hotel desk. I was sent up to the room on the ninth floor.

He answered the door in his robe. He had a typically Spanish complexion, black hair and dark eyes. I like Spanish men, there's warmth and passion in cultures that come from sunshine—they call it hot-blooded.

'Hi, sexy,' I said. I sparkled at him and kissed him passionately.

He lay on the bed and watched me undress slowly. I looked at him shyly with my chin on my neck, looking up from under my eyelashes. I smiled innocently. We locked eyes but didn't speak. He held open his robe so that I could press my lingerie-clad body into his chest. I closed my eyes and absorbed his warmth the way you feel the sunshine warm you. His skin was naturally hairless.

'You feel like butter,' I mumbled.

I slid over his smooth skin as easily as though we were lathered with soap.

The sun shone onto my skin though the window.

'Mmmm, spring,' I said.

'Why do you do this?' he asked.

'Because I love sex, silly. Wouldn't you rather have sex all day than run your business?' I said.

His brow furrowed. I was convincing, but he was too intelligent to believe me.

I had perfected a series of coy looks, postures and tilts of the head that were designed to be cute and sexy, they were my stock. I plied him with a half-smile, a left tilt of the head and flutter of the eyelids. I grabbed his cock with one hand and began to pull it with languorous strokes.

'I want you to fuck me,' I said aggressively.

His face looked hot. He grabbed my arse with both hands.

'Nice arse,' he said.

'Think of it as a big hot-dog bun waiting to be filled,' I said.

I hopped off the bed quickly to fetch condoms and lube from my handbag that I'd dropped on the floor nearby.

I held up the lube.

'I brought the ketchup, let's heat up that sausage,' I said. I leant over him letting my hair fall over his thighs as I ripped open a foil packet.

'Mmmmm,' I made a sound in my throat as I sucked his cock slowly.

He pushed me down on the bed and slipped into me. It felt pleasant, not just because I like the feeling of his incredibly soft skin but because I felt relaxed in his company. After he came and I'd finished my fabulously vocal imperson-ation of an orgasm, we lay together and watched the sky darken.

'Look, it's a full moon,' I said. 'Close your eyes, can you feel it? If the moon pulls the tides and we're made of water, imagine what it does to us. I can feel the energy pulling me,' I said.

'Let's go and have dinner,' he said.

We tidied ourselves and took the lift to the top floor.

The restaurant was round with long glass windows that looked out over the city and surrounds. We were seated at a white-clothed table in the centre.

'Do you drink Bollinger?' he asked.

'All the time,' I lied.

'A nice cold Bollinger please and a dozen oysters, thank you,' he said to the waiter.

'You can't drink champagne without oysters,' he said.

'No, I never do,' I said. I had never eaten oysters before. They looked weird. I thought I'd heard that you have to swallow them whole.

I opened my eyes wide to show them off, tilted my head to the right and rested my chin on the back of my hands.

'Tell me about you,' I said.

'I love my wife you know, but she's preoccupied with her business and the kids; she doesn't have time for me,' he said.

'It's hard when you have small children, it puts a strain on the relationship,' I said.

'Every year at Christmas we invite fifty homeless people to lunch at our house. I have it catered for, it's a wonderful thing to do,' he said.

'That's wonderful, you have a big heart,' I said. I felt as though he told me because he needed to let me know he was a good person.

The Bollinger had been poured. As I sipped I felt my petals open. I unfolded, I smiled, I laughed.

'Excuse me, I must go to the ladies and powder my pussy, I mean nose,' I said. The waiter overheard me. He looked embarrassed as he pointed to a door up a short step in the centre of the room.

I used the toilet, washed my hands and applied more lipstick, feeling slightly light-headed from drinking on an empty stomach.

I emerged from the toilet and looked for my table in the centre of the room. There were several empty tables. There was absolutely no sign of Rojo, not even the bottle, glasses or plates we had used.

Shit, I can't be that drunk. He wouldn't be playing some kind of weird practical joke on me, would he? I felt panicky. *I don't know the room number. Maybe I've gone insane. I can't believe he's left me here alone.* I stood staring with my mouth hanging open for a while.

'Excuse me. My table has gone,' I said to the waiter, trying not to sound hysterical. He looked at me strangely.

'Madam, it's over there,' he said, pointing around the corner to the other side of the room.

'Oh, yes, of course, thank you,' I said. I staggered across the carpeted floor and sat down.

'Are you OK?' Rojo asked.

'Yes, sure, fine. I couldn't find the table.' I felt a little dizzy.

He laughed at me.

'I'll give you a tip,' he said. 'When you're eating in a round room with a platform in the centre, at the top of a building, always consider that it might be a revolving restaurant,' he said, still laughing.

'I had no idea,' I said, feeling foolish. All my efforts to appear sophisticated had just flown out of the window. I gave them a wave as they plummeted to earth. I ate my meal with a second bottle of Bollinger. I smiled and nodded and said, 'How interesting' at polite intervals. I was drunk and confused.

'You're such a good conversationalist,' he said.

That's funny. I don't think I've said anything.

I don't remember passing out. I woke up the next morning alone in the room. Two thousand dollars was sitting on the side table with a note: 'Didn't want to wake you, have a nice day. Order breakfast before you go.'

'How sweet,' I said. I kissed the note. I ordered tea and fruit from room service and showered.

My flight home wasn't until two. I took a taxi to Hobart harbour, admiring the attractive buildings. The stones used to build the houses were hewn out of sandstone, quarried by convicts a hundred years before.

I walked around brightly painted fishing boats nestled in the small harbour. The sparkling water winked and twinkled. Seagulls squawked at fishermen selling their catch from their boats.

I felt lucky and pretty and free. *Forget blondes—scarlet women have more fun.*

Rojo called me a week later.

'My wife has just received a package from the Hobart casino. You left your underwear in a drawer,' he said.

10
Covert Operation:
busted

'Oh no, I'm so sorry,' I said. 'Oops.'

I felt terrible for him. It couldn't have happened to a nicer man.

I ran around the room, screaming to ward off the demons.

Years later I read that he went bankrupt in a very big, messy way.

Once again I resigned myself to the reality of making money. I turned on my phone and took a booking for one hour's time.

I'm not a bad person. No-one approves of me, they don't understand.

It's only a job. I'm not harming anyone. How much less morality does the average businessman or government have?

Someone wise once said to me, everyone has to bend over sometimes.

It has been speculated that some of the most inspirational people were prostitutes early in their career: Madonna, Roseanne Barr, Eva Peron, Billie Holiday. Perhaps it is true, perhaps it is not. Who will ever know?

How many Hollywood actors have slept their way to success? Or married their way to the top? Did Anna Nicole Smith love her husband for his gorgeous body or his scintillating wit or his millions?

Marriage can be prostitution.

I didn't feel bad about how I earned my money. It was honest. Sometimes I felt I was actually helping people.

The truth was, I couldn't go back to earning ten dollars an hour working in a department store.

I was spoilt. One day I would start some kind of business, maybe a café or a clothes shop.

Ginarelli lay back reluctantly into the yielding cushion.

He was uncomfortable, not only because his arm was crushed beneath his cumbersome body. His discomfort stretched itself into every aspect of his life. He had a deep-seated feeling, a gut feeling, if you like, that his life had been unfair in its twists and turns. His boss had barraged him for years with casual, derogatory words tossed carelessly his way—words that had wounded him deeply.

The little woman he had filled with his seed and railed at with his vitriol had become plump and numb. She had ceaselessly chipped away at his manhood with her nagging, her lack of passion, and her looks filled with contempt.

He felt the weight of expectation from his children, whose knowledge of him filled him with crippling guilt. The children, who were now cabbage-headed and grown, no longer heeded his words.

They knew his failings—the rushes of purple temper, often unprovoked; the animal lustings that drove him out of the house and into the angular streets late at night with spirits on his breath.

He knew that his stubborn assertiveness came not from rightness, but from his sense of failure and disillusionment.

Being a policeman had once been a profession that was respected; that gave you a position of dignity in the community.

People still looked at him fearfully in his department. He had a reputation as a corrupt bastard. He no longer wore a uniform; drug-squad had more perks. He felt he'd earned them after twenty years on the force.

One of the perks was looking at him now, trying to butter him up.

He'd spit on her kind for their lack of morals, he thought, as he unzipped his fly and removed his pants. He looked at her with disgust.

This one didn't seem to be a smacky, but you couldn't always tell.

It was routine to bust girls working privately. The CIB got a nice little Christmas bonus every year from the PCV (Prostitutes Collective of Victoria). Run by the owners of the big brothels to look after their interests.

He didn't usually do undercover work himself but he felt like a bit of sport.

All he had to do was fuck her; the boys would do the rest.

I felt uneasy with him. He didn't soften with my cajoling.

His face was hard and unsmiling as though he was made of cardboard.

'It's pretty dangerous working from home,' he said. It sounded more like an accusation than the voice of concern.

Bells went off in my head. That wasn't the sort of thing clients normally said. Usually they were more interested in being flippant and having a good time.

'No, I don't think so,' I said, surprised. He hadn't taken off his coat yet and sat stiffly on the edge of my bed.

'The crazies wouldn't call and give me their phone number. They'd probably just pick someone up off the street. Besides, I'm not here to threaten anyone,' I said.

I did a quick checklist in my head. I'd heard of girls being busted and I'd been careful when I spoke to him on the phone to get his number and call him back before I said anything incriminating. I'd taken the money from him as soon as he'd walked in.

I stripped slowly, dropping my gym skirt and blouse on the floor at my feet. I placed my hands on his head bringing my crotch in line with his face, enticing him with my eyes. I turned away from him and bent over so that my arse was pointing at his face. I pulled the red lace G-string aside to reveal my labia and pushed my index finger deep into my pussy and then into my arse-hole. I turned to face him and sucked my finger slowly, looking coy.

'Let's take those nasty stiff clothes off and pop you in a nice warm shower, shall we?' I reached for the shoulders of his coat and eased it down his arms. He relaxed very slightly.

I undid the buttons of his shirt one by one.

'You're in good shape,' I stroked his chest with one hand and knelt in front of him. I placed my head on his lap. His cock was bulging under my forehead, I stroked it lovingly.

'Ummm, nice big cock. I think he likes me,' I said, cheerily. I looked up adoringly at him and laughed softly.

'I'll turn the shower on for you, then I'll see if I can turn you on,' I said as I stood up and walked to the bathroom wiggling my naked bottom at him and slapping it with my hand.

'I'm very naughty, you'll have to punish me,' I sang out.

He followed me in his white singlet, tucked neatly into his white y-fronts. Of course he was still wearing his black socks, pulled up neatly. *Men and their socks!*

I sat on the edge of the bed waiting. I felt nervous. He returned with the towel wrapped around his waist. His scalp shone through his thin, damp, dark hair. Black hairs sprouted around his belly-button. He was swarthy and had the spread of fat around his middle typical of middle-aged men.

'Do you want a nice massage? It'll relax you,' I coaxed.

His face was stony.

He didn't answer me. *He obviously doesn't want a massage. OK.*

He lay on his back on the bed and waited. I leant across his body and sucked his stiff cock, emitting the sounds of enjoyment you make when you're enjoying food.

'Nice fat cock, yum,' I said. I pulled my body on top of his and eased his cock into my cunt, spreading my knees wide next to his legs for balance. I pushed myself up and down with my feet, riding him hard. I screamed loud.

'Uugh, oooh, wow, amazing, FUCK ME!' I cried out.

(If only I'd known how fucked I was going to be.)

He came quickly and left after a quick shower just before the hour was up.

Two days later as I walked to the shops, two plain-clothes policemen stopped me, flashing their badges.

I felt as though I was in a horror movie.

My face burnt hot chilli-red. My blood pulsated through my veins at such speed I thought I would die.

The sound of my heart beating in my ears sounded like thunder.

'It's all right; we're not going to take you to court. This is a warning. We know where you are,' the taller of the two policemen said.

'I didn't know I was doing anything wrong,' I lied.

'It is against the law to conduct a business from a residence without a permit. It's a contravention of the by-laws and carries a heavy fine. We're going to let you off this time with a warning, however,' the shorter one said.

I walked home quickly, feeling humiliated and powerless.

I locked myself in my flat crying.

I was sure unseen men were watching me.

I thought of the sinister man and shuddered.

I was aware of my mortality, of the humid breath brushing my cheeks as I breathed heavily in and out. I lay huddled on the floor motionless.

Darkness rolled over the room. I was too apathetic to turn on the light.

I dreamt: Blood wended its way down the rugged wall terrain and dripped purposefully onto the porous, grainy floorboards. Navigating a pre-ordained, designated route. Forming a lake: a natural phenomena ready to house shoals of dead fish and bullet wounded ducks.

Broken reeds rotted at the edge and, beneath, a bed of bodies decomposed.

An icy-cold waterfall flowed over slimy rocks.

I was part of a new ecology of death, squeezed from a painful abscess. I felt the uncaring slaughter that surrounded me.

I thought ... *careless.*

The next few days were featureless. I dragged myself around the room not daring to go out, not speaking to anyone, barely eating.

Would they have tapped my phone?

I cried frequently: for myself, for the past, for the ugliness in the world.

I didn't want to tell anyone what had happened.

My strapped senses reeled from the harsh tone of the words the police had used.

I could no longer muster the energy to be fierce, but rolled from side to side, buffeted and dull.

I pondered with confusion on the purposelessness of life and tried to sharpen my thoughts to some focus.

I thought I heard the wheels of the societal machine, as they turned over heavily, flattening me into obscurity—I, a misplaced cog rattling around, in danger of falling out the bottom.

I felt tired in the way that an elderly person must feel tired, in the bones. Tired and sad in my belly and chest.

Sadness pumped through me like jelly, making me bloated and heavy.

The flat was still the same, yet different—colder.

I slept badly, still dressed in my clothes, waking cold and then hot.

I was sweating.

I recited the Lord's Prayer over and over to ward off my fear. I had a feeling something bad was about to happen.

I had to see clients. I needed to make money. I decided I could only see men

I knew. If I was careful I might be able to survive for a while. I had to work out what to do but I couldn't think. None of my regular clients called. I was desperate.

I thought about the rent and bills that needed to be paid. I only had enough money to survive for less than a month. My mind was cloudy from stress. I was living in my own personal nightmare.

I drove to the supermarket to buy condoms and lube and some necessities.

I felt distracted and miserable. When I got back Rosso was standing outside my apartment with a stony face. My stomach turned.

'Hi, I didn't expect to see you. What's wrong?' I said tremulously. He was holding a paper in one hand.

'This!' He held up the paper. He had circled my ad in red.

My jaw dropped.

'Oh,' I said weakly.

I opened the door and let him in.

Interlude: Annihilation

Suicide attempt

He kicked the bed across the room, picked up the pillows and threw them on the floor. I put my arms over my head. I wondered if he would hit me. My heart was pounding. I began to cry.

'Why didn't you tell me?' He was screaming at me. His face was red. He was normally so placid. I was shocked by his anger.

'I was starting to like you. How could you do this to me?' he shouted.

'I'm sorry. I thought if I told you, you wouldn't see me,' I said.

'You're damn right I wouldn't. You're just a prostitute,' he spat.

'Please try to understand. I've got three children to support. I just do it for the money,' I said.

'Get a job like everyone else does,' he shouted. He stormed out and slammed the door. I sat on the edge of the bed and cried bitterly.

'Nooo, please no, please God, I'm sorry. Help me. What am I going to do?'

Morning.

I looked around my bedsitter.

My headache and dry throat had barged into my sleep like rude visitors that dragged me to the tap to appease my dry throat. People were living healthy, noisy lives in other flats, celebrating morning by chinking their crockery ferociously.

The water from the tap tasted dry and stale. The kitchenette walls had begun to turn stale, cooking-fat yellow. Cracks had begun to turn the paint away at the edges of the window in little crisp rolls.

The windows wore a film of brown mire.

The smell of something rotting in the fridge almost drove me out. I found a bag full of orange and black slush that must have been pumpkin and wrapped it in a shopping bag, sealing in the smell, though it continued to hang in the air in a swampy vapour.

If this was the sum total of my life it had putrefied.

Funereal dishes had piled themselves in the sink. Mainly dusty cups, brown and yellow-stained, and lipstick on all of them. Kissed sometime during the days or the nights or the dead afternoons long ago.

The slovenly kitchen mocked me. Linoleum slid under my feet, crunchy nuggets of dry bread wedged between my toes.

Domestic Beirut, or the National Centre for Penicillin Research and Development, I thought.

'Do you want scrambled egg?' I asked myself.

'Yes please, I'd love some. Thank you,' I said, in an unenthusiastic monotone.

'That's OK. Anytime,' I said aloud to myself in my polite English accent.

I poured the eggs into a pool of tomato sauce and threw triangles of toast around the edge of the plate. I wasn't hungry. I nibbled the corner of a piece of toast.

I drank the last of a stoppered bottle of woody red wine from a coffee glass.

I left the dirty dishes on the pile in the sink and sat on the bed and rolled a cigarette, dropping worms of tobacco on the sheets. I lay back in crumpled bed sheets that smelt of stale perfume.

I wanted to cry.

Irrational.

They say the bigger the city the lonelier you feel.

The bed was warm from the imprint of my body. I lay back and stretched out my arms. Cloudy sky reached into the room and soothed me slightly.

From my one tall window I could see the tin roof of another flat below and part of the overgrown garden, where an assortment of old sheds seemed to have rooted them-selves.

The clock ticked in the room but time seemed irrelevant here.

The dresser mirror had oily beige make-up smudges at the edge.

The paint on one glossy blood red wall behind the bed that I'd painted myself, didn't quite reach the white plaster cornice at the top.

My old teddy bears, knitted toys, and a one-eyed rag doll slumped over the bed like lifeless actors on a stage.

On the art-deco dresser, lay carefully placed collections of sea-shells. Amongst the dust, some dead pansies drooped from a shot glass.

Panic rose and fell inside me.

I was pre-menstrual. The beautifully gilded horse of the hormonal merry-go-round that lifted me up, had plunged me into emotional, sensory chaos. It had me in its heady grip.

What am I going to do? My life's a mess. I have no future! I can't stand it here. I can't stand being with myself. I have to get away! Help me somebody! I hate myself. I'm a failure. I've failed my children. I am completely worthless.

'Help me, God!' I shouted.

The television erased my thoughts with its banality.

I put on a navy blue, quilted, fake-fur-trimmed jacket and jeans and sat on the edge of the bed and let warm tears run into the white acrylic fur, wiping my wet nose with the back of my hand and tasting the salt.

It was Tuesday. *Bloody Tuesday.*

The sun did not rise. There was a dim half-light that surrounded me enough to tread a minimal path. Not to extend beyond the easily achieved: the basic needs of survival.

I walked through the streets, past mundane architecture. Ghost-people were silhouetted in the windows of the stores. Reflections of what they might have been. Their empty eyes stared out at me. The Pied Piper had summoned all the young people away and the old ones, bundled in colourless cloth, were all that remained.

Beside me strode anger and apathy, quiet companions.

A small festering abscess gathered on my gum, probably a penance for speaking untruthfully.

Nonentity is a lack of physical perfection. I wondered, *their lot?*

Mine? I hoped the sun would rise soon.

I like Sundays best.

I thought about innocence, pink fairy floss.

Pain peeled through my arteries, almost orgasmic.

A melancholy wrap warmed me. Sweet tears pricked.

I was overfull, yet so empty I thought I might implode.

I need to get away. My life has no meaning.

I keep paying my dues, doing my duty.

I'm not a machine. I'm an insect.

I don't want to remain a pupa.

If I weren't here tomorrow no-one would care. Why live? Why exist? It's all so meaningless and confusing.

The feeling of panic rose in my chest. *I have to see someone. I need help.* I wandered into a doctor's surgery on the way back. I tried not to let my loathing of him show. He represented the stupid establishment that I hated.

The receptionist took my details and ushered me into the doctor's room. She placed a thin manila file on the desk in front of him. He looked up from under half-glasses.

I sat in front of the old grey man, who seemed to know nothing, or very little. I felt as though I was there in the third person. He had a Uriah Heap hunch and demeanour and seemed eager for me to leave as if I might be contagious.

'I have a history of depression,' I said, in a clinical, matter-of-fact way that brooked no opposition and belied the turmoil in my mind.

I disliked his lack of caring and tried not to imagine his flaccid old penis. I couldn't even look at old men any more without thinking of them fucking me.

Zoloft made me tense and drunk with apathy. I liked Valium but no-one would prescribe it because of some stupid bureaucratic crap, so I'd have to settle for Aurorix, which was all right if you took plenty of it and used it regularly, which I did not.

'I'm having trouble sleeping as well, could you give me a repeat prescription? It'll save me coming back next time?' I said.

I thought he must be insane to believe me. I wondered if he was addicted to morphine or pethidine, whether he had perverse sexual fantasies.

Perhaps he just doesn't care any more.

I sat in front of him with absolutely no facial expression, while he wrote on his pad.

He wrote the prescription quickly with a suspicious yet resigned look on his dusty, nondescript face.

To stick it up the establishment I went to three chemists in a row with my health care card and collected all of the repeats for two dollars each.

How fucked up is this system? I laughed bitterly.

I couldn't stop thinking about my children, my life, all of the bad things that had happened to me. I reasoned that I was such a useless mother anyway, my children would be better off without me. I had called them the night before. I could hear the anger in my oldest son's voice. I was sure he hated me for leaving him. The other two didn't sound interested in talking to me.

Who can blame them? They'll get over me, after all, everyone has to die one day. Every child is likely to outlive their parents.

Mostly I thought that my life would never be anything other than it was. I didn't want to be a prostitute forever. I wanted to be loved, to love. To hold my head high. I was sick of lying to people.

Clients flashed into my mind unbidden.

I tried to block them out.

Not that I felt anything for them one way or another. The little plump comedian who fucked my arse with his skinny little dick; the racehorse owner who seemed to think we were in a relationship.

I couldn't help asking the same question over and over. What was it all for, the deathly life? Pain?

This was how mice felt on a treadmill in a research lab. You live, you die, so what?

The flat had become claustrophobic and yet I shunned people. I was frightened to turn the phone on.

I drank tea; it flowed through my veins and flooded my mind beige.

Sitting on the bed in old jeans, frayed at the ends and the edges of the pockets, and a soft velour top the colour of grape juice. I was aware of the soft pressure of dirt and untidiness around me.

I spread pills around me on the bed in small piles.

I crumpled up the paper bags and threw them on the ground. I poured a glass of red wine, its acid burnt my tongue and throat but I drank it quickly, attempting to drown the insistent pain, to block out thoughts that were getting bigger and more cumbersome.

I picked up little handfuls of shiny white pills from the doona and let them run through my hands. The sugar coating melted slightly and I licked it from my fingers, it was slightly bitter.

I felt hypnotised. What would it be like to sleep so deeply, blessedly? Never to wake up, never to worry or fear the future?

Old age would be no loss. I had done everything I wanted to: had travelled, loved. Why did people prolong their pain? How did they not see the truth? The ugliness?

I felt clear, relieved.

Death looked on, soft as rose petals, pure love: eternal.

I struggled with my will. I had to force my hands to hold the candy buttons to my mouth.

I gagged on their roundness. One, two, three handfuls, maybe one hundred and fifty pills.

A roaring wall of water carried me away, retching forward and then retreating, like a giant tongue, gurgling and mutating; a foaming, frothy, boiling sea. A shape-changing water cloud.

I smiled faintly.

It was about four hours later that Apple rang me, at eight pm. She hadn't heard from me for about five days.

She rang again at eight-thirty and again at ten. The mobile was switched off. She rang the home phone every half an hour or so until two in the morning.

She couldn't help feeling that something was wrong.

She was worried that I'd been seeing clients at home. Perhaps it wasn't safe after all.

She couldn't get the thought out of her mind, so she jumped in a taxi and was driven the short distance to my flat.

A radio was playing behind the heavy door. She walked away slowly, her knuckles smarted slightly from knocking, her brow was furrowed. What if I was out?

It was nearly three o' clock in the morning when Apple rang the police.

'Look, I'm probably being silly but my friend isn't answering the door and I think something's wrong.'

The woman police officer was pleasant. She didn't make her feel stupid. At four-thirty a flashing fire engine drew up outside the building to join the police car.

Apple stood on the grass verge outside the building; looking up at the first floor window. The lights were off.

A fireman knocked heavily before breaking the door open with a sledge hammer.

A young couple who had never met me came out of their apartment to see what had woken them.

The policewoman's name was Constable Jenny Goldsmith. Apple reluctantly told her the sordid details of my life. They sounded cheap and dirty in the cold quiet of the night.

A life robbed of its music when bared.

An ambulance pulled up about ten minutes later. Red lights flashed in the street, illuminating straggly flowers and a hedge across the road. It was a carnival, out of place in the quiet night street.

An old woman with her candlewick dressing gown pulled tightly around her looked puzzled as she watched the drama unfold.

I lay across the bed peacefully, except for the small pool of green vomit that had dried near my face. All Apple saw was my small shape under the coarse grey blanket. She kept repeating to herself.

'Why? Why? Why?'

At the hospital Apple was told to go home and rest while I slept off the effect of the sleeping pills.

'You know if this had happened a few months ago she wouldn't have been so lucky. We've only had this antidote for a short time,' said a nurse. The hospital staff were pleasant and non-judgemental.

'Look after her,' Apple told a young male nurse.

I slept for three days. I woke with a headache.

I had a drip in my arm, a thick, clear, plastic tube in my urethra, a catheter, and a tube under my nose giving me extra oxygen. I felt weak but otherwise fine.

The nurses checked my blood pressure regularly. I pulled off round plastic plasters from my chest where, I supposed, my heart had been monitored. I felt guilty and stupid, I just wanted to go home and hide my shame.

Apple visited in the afternoons and brought me some clothes to wear home. The ambulance officers had cut off my top.

Apple drove me home from the hospital.

'Don't you ever do that again. That's so selfish,' she said.

'I'm sorry. I won't. I promise. It was stupid,' I said. 'Rosso dumped me. I got busted for working at home. It all just got to me. I think I'm going insane.'

'You always were,' said Apple.

'True, it wasn't far to go,' I said. 'Thank you for being psychic. Thank you for caring about me.'

I was glad I was still alive. I had wanted to die, it seemed like the easy way out, but even as I'd taken the pills I'd hoped someone would save me.

I have looked in the face of death and it was blessed—gentle. At least I will never fear dying. It's only hard for the people who are left behind.

I clung to the germ of hope that maybe one day some wonderful man would come along and make my life better. I couldn't even think about a career. I never really had one.

If I was going to give my children the things they needed I had to earn a lot of money. I sent them every spare dollar. My daughter had a pony, my oldest son went to a private school. I wanted them to have a better childhood than I'd had.

I remembered the squalor—the deprivation of being extremely poor. We were poor even by the standards of an English small town.

It wasn't that my mother was dirty. She was like a child who never grew up. I don't think she understood how to look after herself let alone me.

We never opened the curtains because the house was so run down we were ashamed. It was dark and stale inside.

Even now I can't stand Victorian terraces, they remind me of my childhood.

The only furniture we had was a dusty old divan in a room at the back next to the kitchen and a kitchen table and two chairs. We had a second-hand bed each. I had a second-hand rug that mum had tried to dye purple, that just made it streaky and gave it a musty smell.

Everything in the house cost less than twenty pounds from the Exchange and Mart paper.

I used to climb over the wall at the back of the house. I lived on a street that some of the other kids walked up to get home. I didn't want them to see where I lived. The old house behind the unruly hedge with the closed orange curtains looked shabby.

My parents bought the house after an old person died in it. They didn't have any money to fix it up—God, we didn't even have a fridge. The half-drunk milk used to sit in bottles and go off on the greasy, blue-painted kitchen floor. The paint had worn away in the centre to reveal shiny concrete.

Mum liked to collect stray cats. The downside of that was that the house stank of cat pee and we had fleas.

They landed on my legs when I watched the old television set. I used to hug my knees under my chin and rock back and forth. I wouldn't dare have a friend over.

More than anything in the world I wanted to live in a brand new house like my friends who wore nice clothes and whose parents had shiny new cars. I would have given anything to be like them.

I tried to over-compensate with my own children. I spent ridiculous amounts of money on them.

The winter sun was shining. I savoured it as I walked to the milk bar. I felt the warmth through my jumper, it crept into my breasts. At the same time the breeze chilled my back as though I were naked.

The pavement felt chalky and soft underfoot. I had an urge to lay down on it and drink warmth from the stone.

I was fighting depression, desperate to free my mind from it.

I can't function like this.

My paranoia affected the way I walked.

The eyes of passing people assaulted me. I was sure they were judging me—did they guess my secret?

Why do they look so knowing and disapproving?

A shrivelled old man behind the shop-counter tried to smile as I mis-counted the coins. He grimaced menacingly instead.

My face grew red. I wanted to run out of the shop crying. I steeled myself instead, gripping the loaf of rye bread and soy milk too tightly. Why did I live here with all these sad people, living between their troubled past and death? I walked back quickly.

I learnt one very special lesson at this time. No matter how bad things seem—no matter how bleak and hopeless—there is one constant, and that is change. You do not know what will happen next. This is both a wonderful and a daunting reality. I didn't anticipate what would happen next. I am so glad I was around to experience all of the adventures in store for me.

11
Inebriation:
the drunken miner

'Apple, hi, it's your psychotic, miserable friend. Do you want to meet me at the Dog's bar for a drink?' I said into the receiver.

It was a bar that could have been from any era or any city in the world. Imposing, hand-slumped amber glass light fittings were suspended from the ceiling by black wrought-iron brackets, throwing warm orange light onto glazed concrete walls and floor. Bronze flames from two open fires at each end of the long room shone up the walls.

Three or four lone, middle-aged men sat at a bar made from marble lit from beneath—a long piece of glowing tortoiseshell.

I bought wine at the bar and carried it back to the table. Apple and I looked at each other through garnet fire in the wine.

It was hard to shovel out words like so much snow. I looked into Apple's eyes in the mossy indoor light and thought they were dark lakes. Eyes that had seen sunsets and dawns, the moon.

Her face reflected her gold and copper hair that was the colour of autumn. She wore it wound and twisted at the back in a messy, glam-rock Medusa-wreath. Her voice was dry as leaves as she spoke.

I heard my own voice whose childlike affectation was soft and sweet like the centre of candy, beginning to give way to maturity.

'I'm going to travel for a while, I think,' I said.

'Go to Perth. There's a lot of money there I've heard. The miners work four weeks on and two weeks off and they spend all their money on girls, or Singapore. Asians pay well and they're easy,' Apple said.

'Asians are terrified of me. I think it's my personality. I'm too eccentric or something,' I said.

'They like their women to be obedient. I'm going to Perth in a couple of months,' Apple said. 'Why don't you wait and come to Perth with me? I've got the phone number of the best place to work. The money's really good. I'll give you the details.'

'I'd really appreciate that. I just want to get away from here for a while,' I said.

I wrote the details of the brothel in Perth on a napkin.

'Friends for ever?' I said to Apple.'

'Friends,' Apple replied. We chinked glasses and looked at each other soberly for a moment.

The intense brilliance between us was almost painful.

On the road outside the bar as we left, lay a smattered blackbird, its cold disarrayed feathers torn and stiff. Another stood still at the roadside, perhaps its mate.

'Pray for it, Apple, it's a cruel world!' I said.

A soft chinchilla wind cupped our faces in its cold hands.

'These pavements have so many memories, it's hard not to trip over them,' I said. I was silent and thoughtful as I drove home, full of the richness, texture and tastes of the past that had an elegance the present could merely imitate.

I was relieved to have a plan. I just wanted to forget what had happened—to get on with my life.

I felt anxious. Words like comfort zone, home, familiar, were running around my mind on a loop.

The next day I felt stronger. I had a shower, got dressed, took a deep breath and dialled.

'Hi! I'm a friend of Apple's. She gave me this number. I'm thinking of coming over from Melbourne to work for a while,' I said.

'Have you worked before?' asked the woman.

'Yes, at a brothel here,' I said.

They didn't like girls working privately; it was a crime that banned you for life from the brothels.

'You'll need a doctor's certificate and evening wear, stockings and a suspender belt. We have strict dress regulations,' said the woman.

I put my name down for eight shifts starting in a week, and called to book a flight and accommodation. Apple had given me the number of a lady who rented out small flats for holiday accommodation for two hundred dollars a week.

Fear acted as a panacea, anaesthetising the sense of loss I felt at leaving my belongings. I looked at the things around me with new fondness, tears prickled my eyes.

Adrenaline ran through me like crystal meth, speeding my thought process and giving clarity to my somewhat irrational decision.

The plane soared up into the clouds and away from the only home I had.

I cried silently behind my sunglasses. Cold tears splashed onto my folded hands. I registered the other passengers who sat introspectively. They were mostly older men in suits. Early flights suited their business agenda, they were cheaper but, I thought, more depressing.

Perth is two hours behind Melbourne in the winter, so I arrived two hours earlier, a warp of time. I wished I hadn't had to go. I wished I had found some other solution to my crisis.

As I got off the plane and caught a taxi the morning sun shone too brightly for winter. It cheered me, holding up some heavenly hope of a holiday in a new world. Clean, crisp lines of the city sparkled as the taxi-driver smiled and chatted pleasantly.

Elizabeth, the landlady, gave me a key and showed me to a small but pleasantly furnished apartment. I didn't have to be at work until eight o'clock that evening.

The city was only a five-minute walk away. I could sleep later.

Walking around and looking at the orderly, appealing shop windows soothed me. This city was new and freshly sophisticated.

Clear blue skies defied my attempts to remain unhappy.

I spent hours getting ready, curling my hair in hot rollers, applying fake tan and more make-up than I was used to. I had bought a strapless, long white dress to wear with high-heeled white shoes that I tottered on dangerously. I felt like someone else in the unfamiliar clothes. I hoped I wouldn't have to walk far.

Summer nights are designed by some greater force to drive people into the streets or into the wild, to boil their urges to a fever pitch. Sweat hung in the air with the scent of animals and flowers, an intoxicating perfume that spins even the strongest mind into frenzy.

I fancied I could hear scurrying rodents deep in the parched expansive West Australian desert, communing excitedly in high-pitched mating calls with their city counterparts.

The taxi passed by the large casino to arrive at the brothel's entrance, lit with fairy lights. A white stretch-limo was parked outside. Two glamorous, silver-haired girls got out calling back to the driver and laughing.

I shook inside as I walked through the entrance.

'Hi! I'm new, I just arrived from Melbourne,' I squeaked.

'Are you Ruby?' the receptionist asked.

'Yes,' I said.

'Just sit over there, luv, and I'll get one of the girls to show you round,' she said in a maternal voice.

I sat cross-legged on the edge of the couch. The large lounge area was similar to a hotel lobby. It was full of round tables and upholstered chairs. A number of antique sideboards and reasonably attractive statues broke the sterility of a building that had obviously been originally intended as a factory or warehouse. Exotic fish swam nonchalantly in a large aquarium. Fairy lights ran around the edge of the room, giving it a festive holiday air.

A busty blonde in a tight red suit approached me.

'Hi, I'm Rose,' she said.

She told me that the woman who owned the brothel had worked at the oldest profession for many years in Kalgoorlie, the largest mining town in the desert. She now ran a brothel there as well as this larger, more prestigious one.

I had seen her walk by. She looked mannish, hard-faced and ordinary, not at all like the owner of the brothel I had worked at in Melbourne.

Rose showed me around. There were eleven rooms. Six of them had large spa-baths in the corner. The rooms had names on the doors. 'School-Room' had a blackboard on the wall with chalk and a duster. 'Executive Suite' was one of the better rooms.

Names and themes blurred in my brain, like bubble and squeak, mashed together and fried. I was afraid I wouldn't remember who I was, let alone all the stuff about massage, folding towels, where to put them and where to find new ones.

⌒

I sat in the lounge with the girls. There were around twenty, all well groomed and elegantly dressed. I repeated the prices to myself. Clients paid for the room at the desk on their way in, sixty dollars for a share bathroom, eighty dollars for an en-suite and a hundred dollars for a spa. They paid the girl separately once in the room. They could choose the type of service they required. Most opted for a full service for $150 an hour, or $100 for half an hour. The less-than-full services were confusing and I wondered if I'd have to haggle over the inclusion of a body part.

The other girls weren't delighted to have competition; thankfully some of them knew Apple, which broke the ice. Three or four girls were stunning; they could easily have been models, especially a tall, slim, Russian girl with long black hair and luminous pale skin. I was mesmerised by her beauty. Her resemblance to Walt Disney's cartoon Snow White was uncanny.

Men came in groups and sat talking with girls before choosing. They drank complimentary coffee, tea or coca-cola.

Groups of Asian men sat for hours talking amongst themselves and enjoyed being fawned over. They often left without booking a girl. If they had paid they were given a credit note for next time. Usually only one of them would have paid on the way in. It wasn't necessary to pre-pay, but most men booked in eventually, having been seduced by the skilful tongue of an attractive woman.

Clever conversation was an art form in this business.

⌒

A heavily bearded miner lumbered towards the doorway. His laboured breathing rolled his gut in a sideways motion, giving him balance and against all odds propelling him through the doorway and respectable light of the only establishment that would welcome him with his beery stench and cussing lack of eloquence.

One thing was obvious to me—if he was there at that time, in that condition, he was aware of very little except the base need that gripped his groin tugging him towards tomorrow, lighter by a few hundred dollars.

Silky words from the receptionist spun a web as fine as the silk of rustling stockings on skin. Between the two, they disarmed the last thread of reason from the simple, robust and honest Australian boy. He was about to be preyed upon, as much as he was the predator.

He smiled crookedly as he staggered towards me.

'Whass yourrr name?' he said.

'Ruby,' I said.

'All right, you'll do,' he said.

'Thank you, I'll get us a room, gorgeous, you wait here,' I said, unnecessarily. As he fell into a chair he made a sound like a balloon deflating. He gave me his ticket. This secured him a room with a spa for an hour.

'OK, luv. First on the left upstairs. I'll buzz you at the end of the hour. If you want to extend you'll have to come down in a towel. Make sure you're wearing your shoes though. Have you got condoms and lube?' the receptionist said.

'OK. Yes. Thanks.'

I retrieved my 'date' from his chair and guided him to the stairway by holding firmly onto his waist.

Once in the room I lay two towels on the canopied bed that had a vinyl-covered mattress. I placed my condoms and lube on the bedside table.

Getting him undressed and into the shower that he needed badly, was like wrestling with a retarded barbarian.

I finally removed all of his clothes and helped him into the spa bath, turning on the taps and liberally squeezing in bubble bath from a plain white plastic container on the side.

He sat in the spa. He beamed at me like a huge, oversized gnome, his soft white belly bobbed up and down in the foaming bubbles.

His manner, thankfully, was far more pleasant than his appearance.

I undressed and slid in beside him. Sitting in front of him I moved between his legs and rubbed my breasts over his chest and thighs, rising from the water and whispering in his ear softly, 'Just relax and let me look after you. You feel so nice. I can't wait to get you on that bed and have my way with you.'

I took his foot and massaged the soles firmly in a circular motion and then took his toes one at a time and sucked them.

I calculated that if he sat in the spa for long enough I could stretch this booking into hours of entertainment. He might not get out of here before sun-up. This was obviously the closest he'd been to a woman for weeks, and perhaps the closest he'd been to love in this lifetime. He worked up North in a gold mine, six weeks on and two weeks off, earned about $80 000 a year and spent most of it in bars and brothels.

We sat in the spa for an hour until the skin on our hands and feet was withered and my fake tan floated around us.

The room was named 'Sultan's Tent'. It had a trompe l'oeil on the wall of camels trekking across the desert.

'Would you like me to get you some water? You don't want to dehydrate. You stay there; I'll be back in a sec,' I said.

I jumped out of the spa bath, grabbed a towel and raced out of the room before he had time to respond. I walked through the lounge area, feeling underdressed, to the kitchen. I got some ice and a jug of water and walked very slowly back up the stairs to the room in my virtually-impossible-to-walk-in high-heels.

I'd been gone all of thirty seconds. 'Did you miss me?' I asked him.

I climbed back into the bath and scrubbed his back with the long-handled brush provided for the purpose.

'I think it's time I threw you on the bed and ravaged your body, you gorgeous man.'

I helped him out of the spa. He looked relieved, obviously knowing his limitations and being sensible enough not to attempt anything as dangerous as climbing out himself. I put him on the bed.

'I'd better grab your plastic fantastic and book us in for a bit longer, don't you think? Doesn't time fly when you're having fun?' I said.

He fumbled with his jeans until I took over the search and nimbly extricated the plastic rectangle.

'It's a good job it's only play money, isn't it?' I cracked myself up. *This is easier than I thought it would be.*

I made my way to the front desk. I didn't mind leaving him alone longer this time to amuse himself. He was so drunk that he probably wouldn't have noticed and there was little chance of his drowning accidentally now.

There was a queue at the desk of girls waiting to be allocated rooms and clients waiting to book in. I looked at the clock. It was twelve o'clock already; this was obviously rush hour. I would be working until five in the morning. I knew it.

'Extension please, another hour,' I said to the receptionist, handing her the credit card. I couldn't remember his name. It didn't matter. The price dropped now by thirty dollars, but at one hundred and twenty dollars per hour, this was still better money than I'd earned in Melbourne, because I was going to be doing more bookings.

While I waited for the receptionist to process the payment I watched the large screen in the middle of the lounge showing current music clips that were mesmerising the ten or eleven girls still left in the room, some of whom I hadn't seen earlier. They must have just started. The shifts were staggered, this business never closed, not even at Christmas.

I returned to the room where my 'new boyfriend' was stretched out on his back, waiting expectantly.

'Now tell me all about you, have you ever been married?' I said.

'Na, I lived with a woman once, she got bored 'cos I was away too much and took off with another bloke,' he said.

'Oh! That's no good! Oh well, you've got me now. Turn over and let me massage your back.'

He was trying to stick his callused fingers inside me. I pushed them away firmly and continued my ministrations like a nurse with a naughty patient. I had been far too enthusiastic with the baby oil and I slid around on his back like a seal in an oil slick. Suddenly he slid off the vinyl mattress and hit the wall at the other side of the room forcefully.

I recovered him apologetically and put him securely back on a towel. 'Flat' on his belly again.

The lube I squeezed onto his arse alarmed him a little: 'I'm not a poofter!'

'Trust me. I've fucked a doctor. I'll be gentle,' I said.

He wasn't ecstatic about the finger in his arse, but he liked my tongue and hot breath on the inside of his thighs.

I massaged him slowly, working up the calves to the thighs, over the buttocks to his back, pushing into and around every vertebra; every muscle and contour.

His breathing had relaxed and had now become a snore. His wet bottom lip hung down, exposing his teeth as he dribbled happily in his dreams.

I sat on the edge of the mattress quietly, trying to keep myself awake, techno playing into the room helped. I wasn't wearing a watch but I'd developed an instinct about time.

Minutes ticked by.

I moved my fingers up and down his neck and gently moved the skin over his skull. He awoke, still groggy and compliant. He turned over and rolled off the mattress.

'Whoops a daisy, I haven't finished with you yet, come back here,' I said, pulling his body up from the floor.

I proceeded to massage his chest and arms and slide myself up and down his torso. Oil and scratchy hair swept my breasts and made my skin recoil.

Every step in the seduction was a labour of will, compassion and humour. Sucking at his cock repeatedly had stirred it to a slight erection; it lay cold and flaccid in the uncooperative rubber that was tickling the back of my throat and blowing up into a balloon in my mouth with the energetic sucking.

'Why don't you lick my pussy before I fuck you?' I said.

His beard scratching my thighs disgusted me. I tried to block it out by calculating how much money I could make if he stayed with me for another hour.

Three hours, $430. It was worth it.

I took his card from his trouser pocket and took a towel to wrap myself in.

'Back in a minute, darling. I'm just playing hard to get.' I flashed him a smile and darted out of the room.

'Good girl, another hour?' said the receptionist as I handed her the card.

I was aware of my hair. It was frizzy from the spa and my make-up had washed off. I surveyed the several men waiting in the lounge to meet women.

I returned to the room.

'Here I am, now where were we before I so rudely interrupted us?' I said.

He resumed his position with his head between my legs. Guzzling and slurping noises continued rhythmically.

'Ooh, baby, that feels so good. I like it really gentle. You're turning me on. Oooh, oooh, oooh.'

'Did ya come?' he asked.

'Ooh yes. Couldn't you tell?' I said.

I lay next to him; after all I needed a break after such an emotional experience! His penis opened its eye and looked at my pointedly and said, 'Oi! What about me?'

Oh, all right!

I lubed up his lazy cock, grabbed it aggressively and leaning over it said, 'Come on my face, baby, it's soooooooo sexy,' I said.

The penis smiled at me appreciatively. After rapid and strenuous tugging it spewed its guts over my chest and rapidly retreated for the night. After another massage and shower Johnny boy was out the door, another satisfied customer.

Next!

12
Masturbaton:
the client who was caught

At the end of the night I was exhausted. I fell into the taxi and calculated—$850—wishing I had the energy to feel excited. I was aching all over and felt as though I'd done several rounds with Mike Tyson in a slime bath.

Sleep was weak and evasive during the day. Daytime noises interrupted short sequences of dreaming. Lost hours blended with memories, repeating themselves with confusing details. I was left slow, dull-witted and heavy.

When days are nights and nights are endless, the body doesn't get hungry, there is a sense of unreality, of living in the twilight zone. My soul yearned for the gentle touch and soothing voice of a lover.

Dawn came muddied by the gaudy circus of the night, of a thousand faces and razor sharp words. I felt as though my glitter lay on the soiled floor to be swept away. Layers of innocence dropped away one by one, leaving me vulnerable and without religion.

At the end of four nights I had $3 800 rolled into a bundle in my suitcase. I had lost weight, run out of clean clothes and felt as though I would never get clean. My emotions sat dangerously close to the surface.

I had two days off.

I slept like I had never slept before, nestled deep in the springs and coils of my subconscious. I woke, relieved to be rested, at twelve the next day.

I read magazines and fiddled with my toenails.

I plucked hair from my pubis and eyebrows, sitting on the carpeted floor naked, covered in a layer of fake tan.

Washing was hung all around me, from every tap, chair and doorknob.

I had changed my hours to the graveyard shift: ten pm until seven am, but I thought I would go early and pick up an extra booking.

'Hello!' I said, enthusiastically, as I entered the building.

I felt fresh and young again. The receptionist who I liked was working, a blonde Scottish lady with a genuinely friendly nature.

He was already sitting in the lounge area by himself. I sat down next to him, feeling beautiful in a new dress.

A white silk shirt by Armani hung from his wafer-thin frame with an elegance that belied his youth.

He was mesmerising, surreal, a cool, calm mirage.

I sat face to face with the softly spoken, articulate young man.

'Can we be alone?' he asked. His sincerity was touching, fragile as the flickering light of a candle mirrored in his exotic eyes.

Every external manifestation of him was as pure as a choirboy. His eyes were dark and liquid; they compelled me as though life itself depended upon my acquiescence. He appeared to fear a rebuttal.

I felt as though he had cast a spell on me, as if we danced together in a dream.

'Yes, of course, I'll organise a room. Just wait here,' I said.

I was to find out later shocking truths that left me bemused as contradictions so often do.

Once in the room, he sat surrounded by cushions in the muted lighting.

I held my breath as he spoke. His eyes were locked on mine, receiving my words with an attentiveness that was new to me.

Words tumbled from him in no particular order.

I pieced together a dark, confused tale of need and repression at odds with his exterior calm. He sat still, Pythagorean, and looked into and through me, pinning me with animal eyes.

His every movement was a calculation.

'I want you to show me how to make love, I'm a virgin,' he said.

My mind spun disbelievingly, shocked cold. The words sounded obscene from someone whose every gesture spoke of sophistication and reserve.

The request that he made was shocking because of his retiring nature. I thought that in this place it should have sounded natural that he should find resolution to his repression.

He was only twenty-one and was obviously pre-occupied and obsessional. He claimed to have been seeing a woman for five years without consummating the relationship.

I explained to him my own perception of sexuality, that is, as a natural function. This made no impact on the intensity with which he dwelt on the subject. He referred to being adopted several times as though it was an important detail in his life.

'I'm trying to locate my birth parents. My adoptive parents are very wealthy. I was educated at the best schools, brought up in the country on an estate,' he said.

His frame and features had the fine lines of a European aristocrat. A face that was almost girlish, translucent and beautiful to watch.

I couldn't imagine that he hadn't made many hearts flutter, both male and female. He excused himself to go to the toilet. I pointed him in the direction and waited for him to return. I sat thinking about how I should seduce him.

He returned to the room. Perhaps he sensed my unwillingness to be with him. He did not remove his clothes but paid me. He reddened suddenly, looking flustered, and left.

I sat on the bed bemused before returning to the lounge.

I told the receptionist I'd left the room and sat down with a drink of diet coca-cola. One of the other girls approached me.

'I just had the strangest experience,' I said.

'Was that your client with the white shirt and dark hair?,' she said. 'I caught him pulling himself under the stairs when I went to the toilet.'

'He was going for it. He came when he saw me,' she said, screwing her face up in disgust.

I was shocked. Something of him stayed with me that evening that I couldn't shake. In hindsight, I thought he was either having trouble coming to terms with being gay or that very probably he had been molested. I had a strange feeling that he could be the serial killer who was terrorising Perth at the time.

13
Molestation:
the boy who was molested

The whole city was obsessed by the murder of three young girls who had been abducted from a popular up-market suburb where they had been drinking at a particular bar.

They were all similarly attractive and blonde, well spoken and sensible. It was thought the serial killer was either an attractive young man or a taxidriver, it being improbable that the girls in question would have accepted a lift under other circumstances.

People shunned using taxis and the city taxidrivers had been asked to undergo DNA testing.

The bars and nightclubs were empty for months.

The bodies of the girls had been found horribly mutilated and raped. The details were not released for the purpose of the investigation.

This had led to intense speculation.

I viewed each client suspiciously. I read the paper every day, feeding like a ghoul on the horror and melodrama.

I devoured the details as each murder unfolded deliciously, stimulating a fear in me that was almost sexual. I wondered if I should call the police and tell them about the client I'd seen but I didn't even know his real name. He'd paid cash and, besides, I had no evidence.

I was becoming more confident.

I approached almost every man who sat in the lounge area. I could usually tell within a few minutes of conversation whether they were interested in seeing me or if I wasn't their type.

Sunday night was usually quiet.

I bounced up to a withdrawn young man sitting alone at a table. He was slim and tall with conservatively-styled, sandy hair and neat, casual green pants and a button-up shirt. His face was smooth and fairly attractive.

I sat beside him and beamed my smile into his eyes. My lips were slightly apart.

'Hi, would you like me to get you a drink?' I asked.

'Yes please, a Pepsi,' he said in a strangely featureless voice.

I fetched a glass from the small kitchen that was concealed behind a heavy red curtain. I took a large bottle from the bottom of the glass-fronted fridge next to the coffee machine and filled the glass.

There were only four other girls working tonight. One of them had pro-grammed her music selection into the jukebox.

'Roxanne' began to wail into the room, 'Roxanne, you don't have to put on the red light.' *Very funny*, I thought. The eighties film clip was playing on the big screen mounted high on the wall.

'What's your name?, I'm Ruby,' I said, sitting near him and leaning close to his face intimately.

'I haven't seen you here before. Are you new?' he asked.

'Yes, I'm a virgin. No, seriously, I'm from Melbourne,' I said.

'I'm Paul,' he said.

I cocked my head to one side, analysing the information I was receiving from him.

His nature was diminutive, girly, strange, at odds with his ordinary appear-ance.

'Do you come here often?' I asked.

'Yes, all the girls know me,' he said.

He leant towards me.

'How much do you charge for a fantasy?' he whispered.

'It depends what it is,' I said.

'I like to dress up in women's clothes,' he said.

'Two hundred for an hour,' I said.

I waited while he decided.

'OK,' he said and handed me his ticket. 'I like the Fairy Room,' he said.

'Just wait here, I'll be back in a sec,' I said.

I bounced over to the desk.

'Can I borrow some women's clothes please?'

'Is it for Paul?' the receptionist asked.

'Yes, how did you guess?' I said.

She procured a key from a drawer and led me to the storeroom.

On a long clothes rack, on bent, metal coat hangers, hung a schoolgirl costume, a nurse's outfit and some leather straps. On the floor were some whips and a large black butt-plug.

'It's twenty dollars to hire from the store-room,' the receptionist said.

I selected two large dresses, one of shiny, bright blue polyester, the other had a high white collar. I took a long blonde wig hanging on the end of the rail.

He was going to look like Dame Edna Everidge dragged through a hedge.

The receptionist knew that Paul always had the Fairy Room, it was one of the rooms that shared a bathroom with two others.

I took him by the hand.

In the room he undressed himself and wrapped a towel around his waist. I lay the clothes on the bed for him and readied the room by laying two towels on the mattress.

I went with him to the shower, adjusting the taps for him, feeling the temperature with one hand while he stood next to me, long and pale.

'Don't be long,' I called gaily, leaving him and returning to the room. I undressed to my lingerie and looked idly at the decorations.

Fairy lights were twined through a vase of branches next to the bed and looped through a net over the bed-head. There were large fairies painted on the dark pink walls. A freestanding, large, oval mirror stood in the corner.

I pondered.

There was something missing from Paul's demeanour. Was it masculinity? Intelligence? Humour? Charisma? Personality?

Somehow or other he had been by-passed by all of these qualities.

I looked in the long mirror at my reflection. My face glowed out, pale as a waterlily in a pond. I collected up my stomach muscles so that my tummy was nice and flat, as a precaution against future deterioration.

I was Tinkerbell waiting for Peter Pan.

'Hello, I was getting lonely without you. Here we are, some beautiful dresses for you to put on,' I said, as he re-entered the room.

He put on the silky blue dress and the untidy blonde wig. The dress was elasticised at the waist. It hung off his slim body absurdly, ending at his skinny calves.

He looked like a lanky Miss Piggy.

'Oh, you look beautiful,' I said admiringly. I stroked the silky fabric of the dress.

'You be my big sister,' he said in a baby voice.

He lay on the bed on his back.

'Play with my cock, sister,' he said.

I lay down next to him and stroked his large erect penis.

'What a beautiful big cock my little brother has. Let big sister play with it. You're a good little brother aren't you?' I said.

'Yes,' he simpered.

'Shall sister ask one of her friends to come and play with little brother?' I asked.

I looked at him, he was smiling slightly, his face looked sinister and unmoving, like a clown's death mask.

'No,' he said, 'just sister.'

'I see. Will sister suck little brother's cock? Shall we teach you how to be a good brother?' I ripped open one of the condoms I had left under the pillow with my teeth. I leant over his body and began to suck him slowly. I rolled my mouth around his erection, pushing my mouth as far as possible down his haft without gagging. I ran my tongue around his tip and up and down the shaft, making appreciative noises.

My eyes were watering sightly.

I looked up at him and said, 'Will sister fuck you?'

He didn't reply, he just lay stiffly. His wig had moved to one side of his head, his dress was bunched up around his waist.

I was getting bored with the charade.

I sat over him and lowered myself onto his cock, facing him.

I rode him fast and hard, bouncing up and down vigorously in time with the music that was piped into the room.

'Oh, baby brother,' I said, breathing heavily. 'Such a beautiful cock.'

My thighs were beginning to ache.

It was with relief that I felt him come in little jerky spasms. I dismounted and stood up, wrapping the used condom in tissue as I pulled it off gently and threw it into the small, white flip-top bin next to the bed.

He went by himself to shower, while I cleaned the bed with Windex and a towel and rolled up new towels to place on the bed.

I dressed hurriedly in the long, white slinky skirt and off-the-shoulder top that I wore and put on my high platform shoes.

He returned and dressed himself.

The phone in the room rang to signal that the hour was over.

I led him to the exit door and kissed his cheek.

'See you soon, sexy,' I said. 'Be a good brother until you see sister again.'

Later that evening I was talking to a man in the lounge about the strange experience.

'Poor thing, he must have been molested by his sister as a small boy,' I said.

'It takes all sorts,' said the pleasant man who was an engineer from Port Hedland—a consultant in iron-ore mining.

'What other fantasies do you do?' he asked.

'School-girl, bi-double, anal, nurse, French-maid, bondage, submissive, water-sports, foot-fetish. That's about it,' I said.

'I've never had a fantasy before. I'd like to try something different,' he said.

'Maybe we could invent something new and strange, like sex with an alien life-form in green slime,' I said.

'I think I'll settle for a school-girl fantasy,' he said.

I took his ticket.

'Spa room bath for an hour, and a school-girl outfit to hire,' I said.

'It's certainly your night tonight, isn't it?' said the young, plump, receptionist.

'I'm the fantasy queen. Sounds like an Abba song,' I said.

She unlocked the storeroom for me and I took the outfit from its wire coathanger.

'Asian Suite,' said the receptionist.

I strutted back to collect my client.

I walked in front of him to the top of the stairs and opened the door to the room. The room was cool and dark, with a mahogany bed, Chinese-red walls and tall oriental vases.

'Here we are. This is our home for the next hour. Let's get you into the shower. Are you paying cash or credit?' I asked.

'Credit, how much is it?' he asked.

'Full service is one hundred and fifty dollars, plus a fantasy, fifty dollars extra,' I said.

He nodded, taking his wallet from his pocket and handing me his card.

'You can manage the shower, can't you? I won't be long,' I said.

I took the card downstairs to be processed at reception and returned to find him still in the shower. I opened the glass door, 'You'll dissolve,' I said.

As he got out I handed him a towel.

'While you're getting nice and dry I'm going to get changed in the bathroom on the landing so that I can surprise you,' I said.

The bathroom was next door. I put on the small white shirt that tied under my bra. The pleated plaid skirt was very short with an adjustable waist. I pulled it tightly and fastened the Velcro tabs.

I looked in the mirror. I pulled my hair up in a high ponytail and fastened it with the scrunchy I always kept around my wrist. I went back into the room. He was lying on the bed on his back.

I turned to face the door and bent down so that he could see up my skirt. I smacked my bottom with one hand.

'I've been a very naughty school-girl,' I said in a baby-like voice. 'Would you like to teach me a lesson? I want a nice big cock inside me. I need to be fucked nice and hard,' I said.

'Come here,' he said. I walked over to stand next to him.

He reached up to touch my breasts through the shirt. He had the towel around his waist. His erection pushed it up in a pyramid.

I reached down and touched it.

'What's that?' I asked innocently.

He grabbed my hand and drew it down to hold him.

'Suck it,' he said. His voice was constricted by desire.

I took a handful of condoms from my bag and pulled one open with my teeth and held it in my mouth. I unwrapped the towel from his waist and knelt down to take his cock deep in my mouth.

I rolled my tongue around it slowly, moving down the shaft, sucking the tip hard.

Up.

Down.

Around.

Suck.

Up.

Down.

Around.

Suck.

I chanted in my head rhythmically.

His hands were moving up the inside of my thighs, feeling around the opening to my vagina.

I lifted my head and pushed his chest down on the bed with one hand. I sat over his cock pulling it under my pussy with one hand.

I took his hand and placed it between my legs. Looking into his eyes I ran my tongue slowly over my lips. I undid my shirt buttons and unhooked my bra. I took off my shirt and bra and leant forward holding my breasts one at a time so that he could lick my nipples.

'I've got nice big nipples for you to suck,' I said.

I swivelled around with my arse facing him invitingly and bent forward with my face on the bed. He knelt up behind me and pushed his cock into me as I crouched on all fours.

He was panting with excitement.

'Oooh, ooh, ugh,' he came, shuddering violently.

I removed the full condom with a tissue, quickly and efficiently like a nurse, 'Another donation for the sperm bank,' I said, holding it up.

He looked worried.

'Only joking,' I said. 'There aren't going to be dozens of your children running around Perth.'

'Now, roll over,' I said.

I massaged him for twenty minutes, slapping his arse cheeks to wake him.

'Another shower?' I suggested.

He showered and dressed as I tidied.

I saw him out and returned to the lounge.

'Madeleine, hi. How's your night?' I said.

'Not bad. I've had all regulars,' she said.

'I've had all fantasies.'

Interlude: Deification

Icons

We worship sportsmen. They are symbols of physical perfection and attainment. We aspire to be like them. Children model themselves on them. We expect them to be exemplary. The pressure on them must be immense.

They play hard.

It was quiet for a Friday night. At about one in the morning Rose and I were called to the office.

'We've got an escort job for you both for three hours. Two players from the Pakistani cricket team.' The young plump receptionist gave me a suggestive wink.

I didn't like doing escort jobs, you lost too much time waiting for the driver to bring you back. But at least the Burswood was close by. The Burswood Hotel is in the Perth casino. It's probably the best hotel in Perth.

'Probably have great bodies. They're very well spoken,' the receptionist said.

'Are we paying them or are they paying us?' Rose said.

She must be a cricket fan, I thought. I wasn't particularly star-struck and thought they'd probably be hard work. Big muscles, big egos.

'They're paying in American dollars so I've worked out today's exchange rate for you. This is how much you've got to get,' said the receptionist, handing Rose a piece of paper.

The limo driver was a pleasant man in his thirties who we chatted to comfortably.

'Can you get me an autograph for my kids?' he asked.

'Sure they're for your kids?' said Rose.

'I don't think they'll want to be signing a declaration of guilt,' I said. 'We could go to the tabloids and sell the story.'

'Paranoia will destroya,' Rose said.

Rose looked at the small piece of paper in her hand, it had the room number and names on it.

'Ahmed and Ahmed. That'll make it easy to remember,' she said.

We walked through the large foyer, glancing across the busy gaming rooms and got into one of the six lifts together.

'I hope we don't look like a pair of hookers,' I said.

'Oh well. What the hell? That's what we are,' Rose replied. 'I bet there are plenty of women who'd like to be in our shoes,' Rose said.

'Maybe,' I said.

She knocked at the door. The handsome, dark guy who let us in was very tall. He had a well-defined, muscular body.

'Come in, ladies,' he said pleasantly.

'Well hellooo, tall, dark, handsome stranger,' Rose said, caressing his chest with her hand and pushing her body against his as he stood aside to let us in.

'Would you like some champagne?' he asked.

On the coffee table were two empty champagne bottles and an ashtray full of cigarette butts.

I inspected the green shields on the bottles approvingly. I ran my index finger over the frosty wet label of the bottle sitting in the ice bucket and put my finger into my mouth and sucked it slowly.

'Dom Perignon is my favourite,' I said.

He handed us a flute each, raising his glass in salute.

His friend came through the double door from the adjoining room of the two-bedroom suite. He wore a towel around his waist and was drying himself with another. My eyes travelled over his physique. He looked like a bronze sculpture.

He was a perfect specimen. Handsome face, straight black shiny hair, a long floppy fringe over one eye.

'Hello, big boy. Someone ate all of their dinner when they were growing up,' I said.

They were obviously from a superior race of beings, taller, bigger and more beautiful than mere mortals.

'Do you want a line of cocaine?' the first guy, who Rose had positioned herself next to, asked.

'Yes, thank you, that would be lovely,' I assumed my best English accent to match his.

'Aren't you playing tomorrow?' Rose asked.

'Yes,' they both answered, nodding.

'Naughty boys,' Rose said. She wagged a finger at them.

I giggled and smiled at the topless demi-god who sat next to me on a gold, brocade two-seater couch.

Rose knelt next to the coffee table to inhale one of five white ridges chopped out neatly on the low, glass-topped coffee table.

Rose sat on her new friend's lap, whispering in his ear and laughing. She had discarded her fake-fur jacket on the ground and was kicking her high platform shoes in the air, dangerously near his face. The tops of her tanned thighs peeped from a high split in her long, clinging, pale-blue skirt.

I turned my body to face his friend. I gazed into his black-fringed eyes attentively.

'Where do you live?' I asked, sipping my champagne.

'London,' he said.

'I used to live in London, in Kensington. Bit cold at this time of year,' I said. I got up and took the note from the coffee table and helped myself to a line of cocaine, moving as gracefully as I could. I bent down with my lower back hollowed to show off the curve of my arse.

'Shall we go to my bedroom?' he asked.

'I thought you'd never ask,' I said, assuming a husky drawl.

'Are you married?' I asked, hoping he wasn't. I'd always wanted to marry someone incredibly rich and famous, and still lived in hope.

'Yes,' he said.

'Of course you are,' I said.

He closed the door and lay on the bed. I removed my dress and suspender belt slowly, looking up from under my eye-lashes shyly as I stepped out of my red dress. My virginal, white lace lingerie and lace-top stockings and suspender belt made me look innocent and fresh.

Innocent and fresh as the Whore of Babylon.

I lay over him, brushing the length of him with my pale, scantily-clad body. I brushed his warm flesh with my lips as I moved up to his face and down to his thighs with my breasts resting on him. I had left my open handbag on the bedside table. I reached into it and pulled out two condoms and a tube of edible, strawberry-flavoured lube. I squeezed a large red dollop onto his shaft. Removing my bra, I placed his cock between my breasts, squeezing them together with my hands and moving up and down so that the head of his cock squeezed out of the top of my cleavage.

'I brought the strawberries, you can supply the cream,' I said, laughing at my lame joke. I stopped to apply more gel.

'Your cock's nearly as long as my arm,' I said with admiration, stroking it with both hands.

'It's like a pet python or a baby's arm holding an apple,' I said laughing. I chastised myself.

Rule number one, never, ever, laugh at a man's cock.

I took a condom from its packet and rolled it over his shaft. My mouth was stretched wide. I could only reach half way down. I gagged. My eyes watered. He rolled me over using the force of his body and pinned me under him.

He pushed into me hard. I concentrated on my breathing so as not to tense against the entry. It was like giving birth in reverse.

I felt as though I was being run over by a powerful machine. He knew I loved it because I screamed loudly as he thrust into me, not caring that the entire floor of the hotel could probably hear me.

It helped me to cope; helped me to release my rising resentment.

Working girls hate big cocks, especially when they're attached to strong muscular bodies. I was relieved when he came. I held the full condom up and wiggled it.

'Look! A whole generation of supreme cricketers,' I said, laughing.

He rolled over expectantly for me to massage his body. I began to work his back, his shoulders, strong and wide as the flanks of a race-horse.

I could hear Rose screaming and laughing in the other bedroom.

'I'm nice and sticky, how about you? I feel like a jam donut,' I said. 'Excuse me, I have to take a shower,' I said.

I lifted my legs off the edge of the bed and walked on tiptoes into the en-suite. I turned on the shower and positioned my chest under the water and then bent over holding my arse cheeks open. I dried myself and returned to the bedroom with my stockings and G-string in my hand. He lay on the bed watching me.

'Nearly time for me to go, unless you want me to stay longer,' I said, smiling at him.

'I have to sleep,' he said.

'Good luck tomorrow, I mean today,' I said.

I dressed and wandered into the lounge to check Rose;, she was almost finished dressing. We called the office to let them know we were leaving and let ourselves out.

'He's given us a hundred dollars American as a tip,' she said. 'We'll go and change it in the casino so that we can split it. The driver will be a while. He had to pick up a couple of girls from a job in Dalkeith,' she said.

We stood together in the circular driveway counting our money while we waited for the limo to collect us.

I put on make-up in the girls room at the brothel. I was chatting idly with a pretty blonde girl who I'd found out from Rose was only sixteen. She'd lied about her age to work there and had false ID.

'I can't even get laid in a fucking brothel tonight. I'm going to heal up if I don't get a booking soon,' she moaned.

'Do you miss Melbourne and your family?' I asked her.

'No, I don't get along with my stepfather,' she said. 'Do you know that really tall girl and her three friends?' she asked idly.

'Yes,' I said, 'The tall girl hasn't been here this week.,' I said.

'No, I saw her working in the park. She was out of it. She got the sack 'cos someone caught her shooting up in the toilet. Those girls were all at uni together. They got each other into smack and now they're all fucked,' she said.

'One of them threw up in the hall earlier,' she added.

'Shit, that's terrible. They're really intelligent and pretty,' I said. 'They're so young, with so much going for them,' I added. I felt sick.

I sat in the lounge-room feeling violated by reality. I watched one of the girls nod, she looked like she was falling asleep.

I usually liked to earn at least a thousand dollars on Friday and Saturday nights. The two busiest shifts carried the quieter nights like Sunday, Monday and Tuesday.

I was feeling pressured because I was down on my quota of clients after spending three hours on the round trip to the booking with the cricketers. Two ordinary young guys were sitting at a table together. They were dressed alike in flannel shirts, jeans and Blundstones—the standard attire of miners.

I always thought of the Seven Dwarfs when I thought of miners. A lot of miners had beards and potbellies.

Hi ho, hi ho, with a shovel and a pick.

'Hi, can I sit here? You look like you need some company,' I said with a tilt in my voice that accentuated the 'Hi!' It made me sound enthusiastic.

They were sipping coca-cola.

'Sure, love you to,' said the younger looking of the two, who was slim and attractive. His friend was a little stockier. They were clean-shaven and neat.

'What are you after tonight?' I asked.

The slight guy who was obviously the spokesperson looked a little shy.

'Come on, you can tell me,' I coaxed, giving him a warm smile.

I tilted my head so that my hair fell to one side and put my hand under my chin attentively looking into their eyes.

The young guy lowered his voice. He must have been about twenty.

'Well, we want to try fucking a girl at the same time,' he explained.

I think my head jerked in surprise and my eyes widened. I was a little shocked. I'd never had that suggested to me before. I thought six things at once. Could I handle it? Did they have big cocks? Were they going to be nice and gentle? How much could I charge? Would it be worth it? Would I respect myself in the morning?

'Why not? Live hard, die young, leave a beautiful corpse,' I said. I was surprised at myself, I wasn't usually that adventurous when I wasn't on drugs.

'I'm going to charge you a lot of money,' I said.

'That's cool,' the young guy said.

'How much?' he asked.

'Seven hundred,' I said.

'Ouch,' he said.

'Well, I'm sorry, but you want to play hard, you've got to pay hard. You're welcome to shop around if you like,' I said.

The two guys looked at each other doubtfully.

'No. OK we'll do it. We really want to try it,' the young guy said. I thought they seemed sweet.

'Don't run away, I'll be back to collect you,' I said, marching off purposefully to procure a spa room for an hour for the three of us.

'Are you going in with both of them?' The receptionist looked shocked. I hadn't seen a receptionist look shocked before.

'Yes, aren't I lucky?' I said.

I walked out of the lounge with the two men. I felt eyes following me.

I was vaguely amused.

There weren't many things you could do in a brothel that were *shocking*. I enjoyed the feeling.

This room was larger than the others, especially designed for orgies. The spa was larger. There were two double mattresses next to each other on the floor.

'Shall we have a spa first?' I asked, not waiting for an answer.

I turned on the taps in the deep, free-standing, round, timber tub and squeezed in some bubble bath.

'You two have a shower together first. Do you want to give me credit cards?' I asked.

They looked nervous. I felt sorry for them.

They fumbled in their pockets and each gave me a credit card.

I took the cards to reception and put half of the charge on each.

When I walked back into the room they were both in the shower together.

How cute.

I smiled at them indulgently and handed them towels as they got out of the shower. I placed the condoms and lube next to the mattress. I undressed and sat naked on the timber shelf in the spa waiting as they climbed in either side of me.

I kissed them one at a time and then slid from one lap to the other turning to face them and rubbing my breasts over their chests, I seduced them silently with my come-on look.

I'd perfected this look. It consisted of the following:

Point the chin down

Make a slightly pouty mouth
Smile cheekily
Look up from under the eyelashes
Tilt the face to one side and then
Throw the head back
Widen the eyes, showing the tips of my teeth, biting my bottom lip.
It was a look that said: I want to fuck you; I'm very naughty.

You can communicate a lot by just using your eyes.

With one cock in each hand, I stroked and pulled them.

'Aren't I lucky? Two cocks are much better than one,' I said.

'Shall we get dry?' I suggested, as I daintily climbed out of the spa and stepped gingerly down three steps onto the carpeted floor.

'Don't fall down the steps. We're not insured for broken legs,' I said giggling at the thought of them leaving on crutches.

I dried myself and lay on my back on a towel on the mattress with my legs wide. I played with myself, licking my fingers before inserting them into both holes at once. They were watching me with stupefied expressions as they dried themselves.

'Come on, I shouldn't have to do this myself,' I said.

They joined me on the mattress and began touching my breasts and pussy. Hands ran all over my body. I held their cocks one in each hand.

I reached up and squeezed lubricant liberally on myself. I positioned them side-by-side on their backs and taking two condoms began sucking one cock and then the other. My head went up and down their shafts one at a time while I fondled their balls with my hands.

I looked up at their faces.

They were mesmerised.

I pulled myself up and sat on one, then moving rapidly across to the other, I sat down hard. I turned to face their feet so that I could bend over and finger my arse while they watched, again moving on one cock and then swapping to the other.

'Stand up and fuck me,' I said.

There were mirrors from floor to ceiling on one wall. I stood up and placed both hands above my head on the mirror.

'One of you will have to fuck me from the front and one from the back,' I said.

The smaller guy slid in front of me and facing me, bent his knees so that he could push up into my pussy. I spread my cheeks apart with one hand for the other to enter me from behind.

138

I felt his cock pushing against my arse. The wall of firm muscle resisted the pressure. I pushed out to allow him to push into me. I had never done this before. I was amazed at how easily I accommodated them both. I could feel both cocks fucking me in unison and the sensation was surprisingly pleasant.

The two men were panting from exertion and excitement.

I knew they could feel each other's cock through the wall of membrane and I was sure that was what excited them.

The guy behind me groaned in ecstasy and his friend came shortly afterwards. 'That was great,' the quiet one said. I took their condoms in tissues and we lay together for a few moments.

'Well, that's today's show over guys, let's do it again sometime,' I said.

It's socially unacceptable for two outback, Aussie boys to be latent homosexuals. Their day-to-day life is a long way from Oxford Street. They probably wanted to experience sex with each other and the only way they could do it legitimately was with me sandwiched between them.

As they left I reached up to kiss each of them on the mouth.

I walked back through the lounge area. Three girls sitting together were staring at me. Word had got round.

'I'm a great big slut, and loving it,' I said as I walked by, I laughed at them, at myself.

Perhaps I'm crazy.

I returned to the lounge area and surveyed the room for men.

'Hi, are you sitting all by yourself?' I said to the lone tattooed man in a t-shirt, leather vest and jeans.

He wasn't attractive or presentable and I could see why the other women were reluctant to approach him. He had a patch over one eye. He would have looked like a pirate a hundred years ago. He still looked like a pirate, except there weren't many still in business off the coast of Western Australia.

'Would you like some company?' I asked. He looked me up and down with a suspicious scowl. *Scary.*

'All right, here's me ticket,' he said, showing off a black gap in his front teeth.

'Oh, thank you, I'll organise a room,' I said, smiling appreciatively at his stony face.

I bounced away to reception and bounced back to collect him.

'Come with me, handsome,' I said linking my arm around his.

He walked with a stiff, bandy-legged gait to one of the spa rooms at the top of the stairs.

The room smelt sweet from the perfumed bodies that had heaved and sweated together moments before.

I could feel the cool corners. Wood-coloured shadows grew darker as he entered.

'Let's get these clothes off and pop you in a nice spa bath,' I chirped.

'Yeah,' he said slowly.

'Isn't this romantic?' I said.

He didn't reply. *He obviously thinks I'm an idiot.*

He screwed up his face. It was deeply lined from being screwed up a lot. He looked like a tree trunk, brown and gnarly with a chicken neck and dangerous beady black eyes. He was about thirty but he looked weathered.

'What mysterious eyes you've got,' I said nervously.

I tried to imagine him as a small boy who had been brutalised, in order to feel compassion for him.

He must have had a very hard life.

He finished removing his clothes as I turned on the taps over the spa bath. He handed me three crumpled fifty dollar notes.

'Someone's been here before,' I teased. My sense of humour withered as I looked at his expressionless face.

'Let's have a spa before we get nice and sweaty shall we?' I twittered.

'You look like you've been on holiday in the Caribbean, You're brown all over,' I said. I thought I could see orange flames, camp fires and wolves in his eyes.

'What do you do for a living?' I asked.

'I'm a Coffin Cheater,' he said. There was a full stop at the end of the statement. His tone of voice said, 'shut up, fuckwit.'

My brother-in-law was involved with the Coffin Cheaters bikie gang, he told me some of them were hit men.

'How lovely. Yes, I'm not a nine to five person either.' I sounded cheerful and British like Bridget Jones. 'Lots of good parties and good pills,' I said.

The silence got darker. I could taste coffin wood, funerals and cremation ash.

I had undressed and slipped into the water with him. I took the scrubbing brush and started to scrub his back. He got up suddenly and stepped out. *OK then.*

I followed him hurriedly, rubbing myself with a towel quickly as he finished drying himself and lay on his stomach on the bed. I suspected he was hoping I'd shut up, but when I'm nervous I find it almost impossible to stop talking.

I rubbed his back with cream and slid up and down on my breasts. I reached down to the floor and picked up a condom and slid my index finger into it. As I moved my breasts up to his shoulders I pushed a lubricated finger into his anus. He jerked in surprise.

'It's OK I'm just going to rub your g-spot. Your prostate gland is in your arse and it feels good if I stroke it. You can have a much stronger orgasm if you let me stimulate you,' I purred.

He relaxed. I think he was starting to like me; it must have been the finger up his arse.

Listen mate, I've got to fill in an hour with you, which means I've got to think of new ways to poke and prod and bounce up and down on you.

'Me mate's in hospital. That's why I come down from Bunbury,' he said.

'Poor thing, is he all right?,' I said sweetly.

'Some psycho chick stabbed him in the throat. We was having a party. I had to stick me hand in his neck till the ambulance came. I never seen so much blood, saved his life though,' he said.

'She must have had PMT,' I said.

'She was nuts. One minute they was getting it on, the next she grabs a knife and stabs him. Crazy bitch,' he said. 'The coppers didn't believe me, thought he raped her. Then she attacks them. Can't trust sheilas, mate,' he said.

'Turn over and let me play with that beautiful cock,' I said, lingering over the word cock so that it sounded like a delicious foodstuff.

As he rolled over, a swampy vapour rose from the general direction of his arse.

'Oh,' I gagged and coughed.

'Are you blowing me kisses, you naughty boy,' I said, trying not to breathe in.

'That'll teach ya for sticking things in me arse, dirty bitch,' he laughed, turning around to show me his toothless grin.

Careful, or I'll get my whip.

Or maybe not. He may be a hardened killer, after all.

I decided to try some amateur psychology on him.

Interlude: Violation

Childhood rape

'Have you got kids?' I asked.

'Yeah, one boy,' he said.

'I hope you're kind to him. You obviously had a tough life,' I said.

'Kids have to learn to be tough,' he said.

'I'm sure you'll protect him. All kids need is love,' I said.

His face softened. I felt like I'd made a breakthrough.

He lay silently as I stroked his cock and sucked him. I sat on top of him and pushed myself up and down over his shaft using my knees and ankles.

I worried about RSI in my knees.

He came quietly and I lay next to his side for a moment thinking that even the most hardened killer is still just a little boy inside.

As I worked my mind wandered. I thought a great deal in the long hours between midnight and morning. I relived parts of my life—dreaming is vivid when you're awake.

In his dreams, my father had fits. Sometimes he threw himself down stairs in his sleep. Occasionally he would break one of his legs or an arm. He came home from work unexpectedly one day to find his wife arriving home in a sports car with another man. She had been having an affair for six months or so.

It turned him sour and mad.

Not just that, he was already bitter. A process of amortisation, of the naked life, unembellished by success or propaganda. His truth.

I saw how easy it was to become disillusioned when one grows out of the myths of childhood. They call it depression, but is it that, or just reality, laid up, unadorned?

I didn't understand why he told me to sleep in the spare bedroom but I was too afraid to argue. He was drinking beer out of big brown bottles and chain-smoking. His teeth were stained with nicotine.

One bare window shone out of the bedroom onto the moonlit garden.

There was no lightshade on the single, dusty globe that hung on the end of a frayed striped, black and white cord.

Against one wall stood an old timber wardrobe with short legs. It was full of tumbledown, discarded clothes, mothballs and bent, old wire coat hangers.

I slept under a coarse, old grey blanket and a quilt that I had dragged up the short flight of stairs from my bedroom. I had to sleep on a single divan.

The red fabric of the old divan felt scaly and smelt of dust.

My kitten urinated on my belly so I had to take off my singlet and white cotton knickers.

I fetched a towel to lie over the damp spot.

At twelve there was no sign on my body of the change to womanhood. I was slight and pale.

I was in a disturbed sleep when he lumbered into the room, hitting the doorjamb heavily with his shoulder.

'Dad? What do you want?'

My voice was small and scratchy.

I must have protested, but his weight and the swamp of fear in my brain were immobilising. I could taste the overwhelming smell of his body in the back of my throat—sweat, beer and an animal odour that smelt like meat cooking.

'Put your arms around me,' he said.

His voice was thick and heavy in his throat.

His head went down between my legs.

I struggled a little, but could not break free of the unwanted sensation.

As he rose he thrust into me.

I cried out in pain.

He got up and left the room hurriedly. His shoulder hit the doorjamb again.

I was crying and petrified as I gathered up the quilt and ran to my own bedroom. I locked the door with shaking hands with the old iron key.

Crouching down, I pressed my ear against the door to listen for his movements, breathing hot hammers into my ribs.

He did not return.

The knowledge was like a giant wave, crashing over my head that silenced my voice and the pain.

I cried silently. I curled into a ball, trying to take up as little space as possible.

Revulsion ran through my body, so that the circulation to my legs was cut off, they felt crushed and numb.

I rocked backwards and forwards for comfort, while all the time bells pealed in my head, thankfully preventing me from thinking.

As it began to get light I fell asleep.

The blood in my veins was heavier with the dirt of sin.

I was full of guilt, horrified that I had had sex with my mother's husband, who I could no longer bear to think of as my father.

The man who I'd once loved and trusted.

I was afraid of what my mother would do if she knew.

I knew it was somehow my fault and there was no- one I could tell.

My isolation gave birth to a deep-seated anger.

When confronted by injustice it burst out of me. I learnt to fear people, especially the ones who said they loved me.

I only remembered the rape in dreams.

Dreams remembering themselves in dreams, snippets that woke me—sweating and full of terror in the night.

It would be within me always, an invisible cell or cage that would affect the choices I made in life.

The next morning I walked to Aunt Fern's house where my mother was staying.

I begged my mother to let me stay with her.

14
Defecation:
the fantasy

I couldn't tell her what happened. She knew something was wrong so she let me stay. I sensed she suspected the truth. I also knew she didn't want to acknowledge it.

My father went back to the north of England to live. I never saw him again. The desertion was almost as hard to deal with as the abuse. It was hard to reconcile the fact that I had loved him. It was hard to hate him or feel angry because a part of me *still* loved him.

After four more nights in Perth, my mind was dry like the inside of a cave where fires have burnt to charcoal for a hundred years and dust has gathered from the bones of the witch doctor.

Dry, like the wind of the orient drifting across the Sahara, as the scarab beetle scuttles from the fire in the shadow of the pyramids and the riverbed cracks fill with blood. Dry, like the dark face of an old man sipping mint tea in the heat with a strange light in his deep, black eyes.

A cloud passed across the full moon.

The nights became longer and less real. I sold my arse, my smile, my wisdom—my all.

I felt empty: a brittle, fragile shell.

I sat on the floor of the small, sunny apartment, straightening crumpled notes from my handbag. Most of which were still slimy with lube.

I was glad to see the back of another night. I was weary and bedraggled yet calm.

A volcano of ideas exploded inside me. Thoughts parachuted from my ears and floated down, landing in fluttering bundles next to the money.

I revived and picked up the phone and called Rouge and Jade in Sydney.

'Rouge, hi, I'm sorry, I know it's early! Can you talk?' I said.

'What time is it?' he asked.

'About seven there. I haven't been to bed yet, I wanted to talk to you.'

'What's wrong?' said Rouge.

'Nothing, I've had an idea,' I said.

'What?'

'Can you get me a ticket to the Sleazeball? It's next week isn't it? I can book the flight from here if you get me a ticket,' I said.

'Umm, I don't know if there are any left,' Rouge said.

'Go on, it'll be great. I'd love to see you and Jade,' I coaxed.

'I suppose, I suppose so,' Rouge said sounding confused.

'Yes! Whoohoo!' I screamed and danced around the room.

'By the way, I miss you guys! I'm lonely!' I said.

'I've tried to call you but the mobile's been off,' said Rouge.

'I know, I'm working in Perth. I've been sleeping during the day.'

'Sounds like torture,' Rouge said.

'It's not that bad. I've made lots of money. Have you been behaving?' I asked.

'I've been keeping myself nice.' Rouge's husky voice croaked at me, still comatose from sleep and embedded in some distant plane.

'We'll have to do something about that. I'll have to lead you astray. Love you, I'll call you tomorrow, go back to sleep. Sorry I woke you. Bye. Kisses and hugs to Jade,' I said.

I hung up.

We weren't particularly close but we'd shared a wonderful eccentric exuberance from the first meeting. I'd had dinner with Rouge and Jade in Melbourne several times. I had an easy rapport with gay men.

I counted the days and hours until my departure.

On the last night, a group of girls were booked to perform for the male employees of a health food company in a warehouse/office block at the outer edge of the suburbs on an industrial estate. It was an anniversary of their business.

We were told we would have to improvise when we arrived. We were not all skilled entertainers. One of the girls had been a stripper and seemed confident in a brassy, head-tossing way that denied care.

On our way there in the limousine I quaked inside at the impending exhibitionism. The twenty or so male employees had cleared a space in the middle of the floor and placed chairs in a large circle. The women who worked for the company hadn't been invited.

The men sat expectantly in the empty neutral space that held a vibration of their embarrassment. We all stripped to our lingerie, leaving our clothes near the entrance.

I looked at the other girls for direction. The girls had brought three strap-on dildos with them that belonged to the brothel. We had been told not to have sex with the guys but to try to lure them back to the brothel afterwards.

Under bright, fluorescent, office light, in the sterile interior, it seemed incongruous to be wandering around in lingerie.

A petite brunette was sitting on the photocopier without her knickers and giggling as copies appeared: clear black graphs of her vulva, the sacred heart of her sex.

The motley group of men seemed intimidated and unsure.

A girl called Star had brought a ghetto blaster.

She was about five foot and five inches and underweight, dressed in a dark-blue mini-skirt and bra-top with white fishnet stockings. Her fine, straight blonde hair was pulled neatly back in a ponytail at the nape of her neck.

As she began to dance, her eyes fixed on a point above their heads, her face barely concealed her contempt.

She moved with precise controlled movements. Her perfect body undulated and melted through the music. Her movements made the large partitioned room seem even uglier.

I sat in the lap of one of the men and watched.

All eyes were drawn to her.

A timeless alchemy enlarged her spirit.

She kicked a leg up and stretched it above her ears almost parallel to her body and peeled her stockings from one leg at a time. She discarded the sheer nylon with outstretched arms using her fingertips, revealing delicate pale pink feet with shiny red toenails.

Unclasping her bra-top with a deft flick of one hand and gently throwing it aside, she exposed two plump cushion breasts with nipples as soft and pink as fairy-floss.

The admiration of the men was audible.

Mounting tension caused them to shift their feet and hands in little noisy movements.

Her skirt fell to the ground around her ankles softly, where it was collected on one foot, spun around and kicked upwards. It floated down in a whispering parachute.

She hooked both thumbs into the sides of her virginal, white lace panties, raising and lowering her thumbs with her arse thrust out. She turned her body around provocatively. She bent over slowly and revealed her ripe arse to the eager faces. Looking back over one shoulder, she ran her tongue over glossy bright lips, bending until her chin brushed the floor.

Now stretching upwards on tiptoe, arms straight up and fingers rigid, she posed like a Man- Ray photograph. Slowly her polished fingertips traced the profile of her face, throat and breasts.

She pushed her panties down and stepped out of them daintily.

The high arches of her taut feet flaunted the winking siren polish on her pert toes.

Light shone off the roundness of flesh, bright and unforgiving.

All eyes played around the triangle of shadow; the soft garden of trimmed mouse-gold hair, above neat folds of flesh, concealing her moist, pink vulva.

She rolled her spine backward in a bicycle chain movement, leaning back so far that her fingers made contact with the floor. She pushed up with her hands raising her shoulders high off the floor. Her neck was arched back and her head hung down so that her hair trailed on the floor. Her legs pushed up from the floor arching her stomach into a crab shape. Very slowly she drew her legs over her arched stomach one at a time and pulled her body up into a standing position. If movement were sound, this was Mozart's flute concerto.

The men desired her lithe form now, obsessively. They wanted to possess her, hold her, crush her, penetrate her and own what they would never own.

Her honest, naked body had disempowered their stiff, clothed will.

She was temptress and goddess, mother and child—an incandescent nymph caressing sound.

The other girls and I discarded our lingerie and rolled together on the scratchy, carpeted floor in the centre of the circle of chairs in a pseudo, passionate orgy. We licked, fingered and fucked each other with the vibrators.

It was a scene that Beardsley would have embraced, that should have taken place in a garden bower or Rococo salon. Not on an industrial carpet in a concrete hanger.

The men, full of beer, were delirious with lust. They were provided with three limousines back to the brothel.

On arrival, the owner of the business (who was very drunk) booked me for two hours.

Amidst the confusion to allocate rooms to twenty men the receptionist said, 'You can take the big boss to the Executive Suite.'

He happily sat on the side of the bed telling me his life story.

'I live in Queensland with my wife and baby girl. I've made millions from this business. I bought it two years ago. We make vitamin pills, supplements and natural cosmetics,' he said amiably.

'Well done, aren't you clever,' I said.

I turned on the taps and squirted bubble bath into the water so that the spa could fill while I helped him undress.

He spent forty minutes in the spa being scrubbed and having his toes sucked, while he happily spoke about himself. This was obviously his favourite subject.

I listened as though I was enchanted by every word, smiling sweetly over the bubbles, while my thoughts wandered free, unshackled by the gargantuan male ego.

'Why don't you fly to Queensland?, I'll put you up in the best hotel. I'll pay you two thousands dollars to come up for the weekend if you'll let me push shit up inside you while I fuck you,' he said.

'I want you to shit all over my stomach, rub it all over me, let me push it up inside you, I really mean it,' he said.

'Oh, you sexy man, stop it, you're turning me on,' I said.

'Really? Will you do it?' he asked.

'I'd love to, but not today. It'll give you something to look forward to when I come to Queensland. Now tell me how you're going to fuck me in the arse,' I said.

This guy is up there with the sultans of fucked-upness!
There is not enough money in the world to buy some things.

The urge to roll on the floor laughing hysterically was overwhelming.

I wished I could suddenly remember a prior engagement.

'Why don't I pop down and get us a drink? Don't you move till I get back,' I said in a sweet voice.

I stood on the landing bent double, laughing silently.

I realised the charm of health supplements had gone from for me forever.

I fetched two glasses of coca-cola and returned to the room and began my usual routine. He eventually came, huffing and puffing over me. As happy as a little pig in ...

It was my last night, Thursday. I had been working in Perth for two weeks yet it felt like a lifetime. I was flying out at eight am, at the finish of my shift.

I had brought my bags to work with me and left them in the office. My pregnant luggage, overstuffed with new clothes.

I had survived. Didn't know how. Felt as though I had fucked everyone in Western Australia. The eight thousand dollars I had left didn't seem like much. I had earned nearly ten thousand, but had spent some on clothes and airfares, take-away food and pills for the Sleazeball.

There was a big race in Perth and drivers and mechanics from all over the world were in town, which made it busier than usual.

The girls who worked there were divided into two groups, the ones that spoke to me and the ones who hated me for doing well.

I knew who were junkies and who had kids to support, the basic details of their lives.

The strangest of them were the mother and daughter from Paris who did bookings together. They looked like reflections of each other, separated by age.

Just one big happy family!

I spent six hours in one booking with an amiable drunk. I had tried to persuade him to leave several times but he insisted on staying. At six am I said,

'Fifteen hundred dollars is a *lot* of money, you could go on holiday with that.' I pleaded with him. 'You're going to regret this tomorrow. You won't be able to come again. Mr Alcohol has turned Mr Big and Strong into Mr Sleepy. It's time for bed.' I was exasperated and tired. The conversation had run out hours ago and I was fighting the urge to go to sleep.

'Just another half an hour, I'll be able to come,' he said.

'OK, it's your money.' I hurried to reception and just raised my eyebrows and shrugged my shoulders at the receptionist.

'I hope his wife leaves him,' I said.

I pulled his cock so hard without success during that last half an hour I wouldn't be surprised if he had blisters on it.

At seven am I left in a taxi for the airport. Boarding the plane with caked on make-up and eyes half-closed with exhaustion.

The steward on the flight, a sparse, young gay man, was obviously feeling as lousy as I was.

I asked him for a vegetarian meal. I'd forgotten to order one when I booked my ticket.

'We don't carry spare food, you should have pre-ordered it,' he shouted at me in an unnecessarily harsh, shrill voice.

I felt like I was about to throw up.

Interlude: Illumination

The sleazeball

I sat and cried like an infant, as though every detail of my life had suddenly become a tragedy.

A flood of tears ran down my face in quick succession from a bottomless well of misery.

I trembled.

Another hostess quickly found me a bread-roll, some fruit and an orange juice. She had the offending server removed to the opposite aisle.

I knew I must look terrible I but couldn't find the energy to care. In a few hours I would be in Sydney. I would sleep when I arrived at Rouge's house.

Rouge answered the door and invited me into the hallway. He was around forty-five, slightly built, with very short white hair.

'Welcome to our small mansion, a beautifully appointed stately Victorian edifice—high ceilings, arched windows, decorated with tasteful soft furnishings in yellows and soft reds. With potential for further improvements,' he said. He waved an arm around the lounge dining area.

'There's no point selling it to me. I couldn't even afford a toilet tile,' I said.

I peered into the long lounge and dining room. Warm sun was toasting the glass in the French doors golden.

'It's a feast of expensive fabric. I could get used to living in luxury. You decadent tart! Is this your harem, King Farouk? Where are the houris?' I said, admiring the swags and tails over the windows, the plump button-backed, cushioned folds of upholstery, the pleated cream silk lampshades, the fresh smell of linen and the seductive sheen on crisp chintz. Silk-damasks self-patterned with exotic birds and flowers covered the over-large couches. Little Chinese gentlemen and ladies with parasols paraded in the French toile that covered the high-backed dining-room chairs. Ruffled and piped cushions printed with fuchsia roses with red hearts, softened the couches. A blue and white Chinoiserie vase sat on each side of the two matching mantelpieces at each end of the long room.

'Jade's at work at the Savoy in Double Bay,' he said.

'The swimming pool is going to be built above the dining room so that when we have parties we'll have synchronised swimmers above us while we're eating. Or we can fill it with exotic fish and mermaids,' he said.

'We'll all be naked, except for precious jewels draped over our genitals. We'll have orgies around the pool with beautiful young black boys, and girls,' he added.

'I bet you've seduced plenty of young boys already on your opulent soft furnishings. Is that the flowers I can smell, or come?' I said.

'It's true, it's all true, ha ha,' he laughed excitedly in a shrill voice.

'The house is full of sunshine and flowers, it makes me feel happy,' I said smiling at him.

Yet I felt an indescribable cold air hovering in the hallway, a draught that carried a presence of the death of past inhabitants. I shivered.

Two black and white spaniels bounded towards me.

'Boys, boys, settle down,' chided Rouge.

'I'm exhausted,' I whined. I yawned and stretched out the acid tension in my joints, still feeling stiff from the plane trip.

'I'll make you a nice cup of tea,' Rouge said.

'I'll be mother,' he said as he poured tea from a weathered silver Victorian teapot that gave off a warm tarnished glow.

'I'll be the Queen and you can be Charles,' I said.

'No, he's a bottom. I'll be the secretary who was caught buggering him,' he said.

'We'll make a porn film and we'll call it Gay Royals,' Rouge said.

Jade arrived home as the last McVities biscuit disappeared from the plate. 'You two are such an old married couple, I'm jealous. Most of my relationships only last an hour,' I said.

'We've been together for seventeen years. We're an institution—like a building society. We have our ups and downs and a reliable income, thanks to Rouge,' Jade said in a bourgeois English way that mimicked all he admired: the Queen Mother, Princess Diana and Buckingham Palace.

I wonder if that's why people call them queens.

'I noticed as I walked down the street that the houses were crumbling, in quite a serious state of disrepair, decaying before my eyes. Don't people realise? Are they mad?' Rouge raved.

'I decided to knock on some doors and inform the owners. The first Indian lady shut the door in my face,' said Rouge.

'Dreadful, native people. Should remember the Boer Wars. No manners. Still eating dogs where they come from,' Jade muttered.

Rouge grabbed my hand and we danced around the kitchen chairs to the dulcet strains of Tony Bennett playing from the loungeroom.

'You're English, aren't you?' Jade asked me.

As I was still being the Queen I said, 'Of course, not only that, I am head of the entire Empire. I seem to have found a place where I feel at home, it isn't quite Buckingham Palace, but then, the renovation isn't complete yet,' I said imperiously.

Jade watered his window box of herbs with a small watering can.

'I've been bottling artichoke hearts and fruits for Christmas,' Jade said proudly.

'You always need to keep a few spare fruits in the cupboard,' said Rouge.

'Poor artichokes, having their hearts cut out,' I said.

Rouge ran around the kitchen with two hands poised together against his breast.

'I'm an artichoke running away from artichoke hunters.' He pushed his front teeth forward

'You look more like a mole or badger,' said Jade.

'We're mad, we're all mad, ha ha,' said Rouge.

'Thank God growing up is optional,' I said.

Rouge looked at his watch.

'Two thirty. Time to take the dogs for a walk. Do you want to come?' Rouge said.

'Yes, OK,' I said.

'We take our pills now,' Rouge prompted Jade with a look.

Jade removed seven small bottles from a small shelf in the door of a tall cupboard and placed them next to the sink. He methodically filled two glasses of water and they each swallowed several handfuls of pills.

'I've eaten my body weight several times over,' said Jade. Nobody smiled.

Life, death, living in the shadow of the valley of ...

Centennial Park was only a short drive from the house.

Rouge and I walked through a copse of fir trees on a springy carpet of soft, red-brown, long, thin pine needles.

Snowy white cockatoos lay along the branches of fir trees. With their shiny bone beaks the birds separated seeds from pine cones. The comforting, melodious sound of crackling accompanied us. Occasionally they fell to the ground in a winged flock of feathery confetti.

The dogs ran around ahead, sure of their way.

We came to the edge of the forest, into a clearing that looked down a smooth green escarpment. An imposing, neo-classical sandstone dome stood in the centre of a wide green amphitheatre.

'It's designed to view the stars from inside,' Rouge said, pointing to it.

Suddenly, miraculously, rain came from a clear sky.

A soft, white, uniform, voile curtain fell slowly. Drops fell on the ground in soft little explosions around us. We sheltered under the thick bough of a tall fir tree.

'It sounds like crystal sparkling,' I said.

Three feet in front of us was the most vivid rainbow I had ever seen—a gaspingly colourful performance of water bound in air arched in a perfect unbroken dome across the park. Glowing strips of yellow, orange, red, green, violet, pink and blue stretched high above us.

Rouge walked towards the rainbow with his hands outstretched with a look of wonderment on his face.

As he moved forward, the rainbow also moved, evading his outstretched arms.

'It's a sign from God!' he sighed.

'Especially for us. Thank-you!' I called to the sky.

I felt the sweetness inside me.

I believe in miracles.

'I'm Dorothy in *The Wizard of Oz*. There's no place like home, there's no place like home,' said Rouge.

Rouge behind the wheel of the car was as erratic and irresponsible as an over-excited child. There was a screech of brakes as he narrowly missed hitting a dark blue Ford Fairlane. The driver mouthed the words 'fucking idiot'. I waved to him and wound down the window.

'Happy Sleaze,' I shouted. He mouthed obscenities at us with a red face.

'Oh look, he likes us,' said Rouge waving to the man.

We narrowly avoided several other cars, almost causing a pile-up. We just missed out on the more intimate acquaintance provided by litigation. As we parked in front of the house, sunset was beginning to anoint the horizon with a warm, amber glow, casting a deep, charcoal shadow over the city.

Inside the house Rouge danced around like a little elf.

'Whoooooooo!' he cried out, clapping his hands together and then waving them around his shoulders.

'Oh, Rouge, do behave!'

Jade had been chiding Rouge for years in his particular British manner so that it was more of an endearment.

Jade smiled at me charmingly.

'You remind me of Roger Moore or Sean Connery,' I said. A shadow of youth still lingered on his face and form. Maturity had lent its own appeal to the pair. An aura of happiness shrouded them in light.

'You look tired,' said Jade.

'I know,' I said.

'You've lost weight,' said Rouge.

'I know. It's great,' I said.

'You're too thin,' said Jade.

'A woman can never be too rich or to thin. Didn't Kate Olsen say that?' I said.

'I don't think so. Besides if you're rich you can be fat and ugly,' said Jade.

'It depends on your perspective,' I said.

'So, does absence make the heart grow fonder?' Rouge asked.

'It depends on your perspective,' I said.

I had sharpened my wits on the games of the past two weeks. I realised I had developed the hard cunning of a feral animal. I didn't feel close to anyone anymore. A small wave of self-pity ripped me, inside my ribs where my heart used to be, and the sea of emotion splashed water up into my eyes. I felt prickly. I thought my voice had become falsetto and deceitful. Larger philosophical questions loomed menacingly. *It must be jet lag*, I thought, ironically.

'What are you going to wear?' Rouge asked.

'Aha! Wait and see, remember: less is more,' I teased.

Rouge was twittering like a starling.

'I bought a sailor hat at Gowings and a whistle, I'm wearing Calvin's and long white socks pushed down. Have you got any fake tan?' Rouge asked me.

'Look, I sprayed my hair with glitter,' Rouge moved his head in a circle.

'You look like a Christmas decoration,' I said.

'Or a fairy,' said Jade in a voice tinged with cynicism.

'Do I have time for a sleep before we go?' I said.

'No, Jade's determined to leave at eleven, to catch the show,' Rouge said.

Typical. No rest for the wicked.

'I'll show you down to your room downstairs. We call it the dungeon,' said Rouge, leading me down stairs.

I curled my hair with heated rollers and applied blue-green sparkly eye shadow to my eyelids and silver glitter to my face and breasts.

I put on my stockings and my scant clothing that was barely more than underwear. I put my toiletries in the small adjoining bathroom and hid my vibrator under my pillow to use later.

I clattered back up the short circular wooden stairway to the kitchen.

'You look beautiful. We missed you,' Rouge said, barely touching my cheek with his lips.

'You're looking huge, Jade,' I said. I felt his triceps appreciatively.

'Jade's been working out to look his best for the party,' Rouge said.

'We're all just far too gorgeous,' Rouge said.

'I try,' I said.

'Look at you; they're sitting up nice and high tonight.' Jade cupped my breasts.

'Stop it. You'll turn straight,' Rouge said, pushing his hands away.

'There's no such thing. People are like spaghetti, they all bend when you put them in hot water,' said Jade. 'I'll get you a drink.'

'So I should think,' I said.

'Jade's nickname should be Doctor Death, because he administers drugs in such a serious, professional way,' said Rouge.

Jade smiled wryly.

'Then he can say, trust me I'm a doctor,' I said.

'You *can* trust me, I fucked a doctor once, no, I think it was twice,' said Rouge. Rouge walked up two steps into the dining room with me beside him.

'Jade's got some crystal meth; we're going to inject it,' Rouge said.

I've never injected drugs before. It's like there's a bridge between taking them for fun and taking them seriously.

Rouge and I wandered into the dining-room together.

Jade joined us and immediately became engrossed in elaborate preparations. The atmosphere became charged with religious undertones.

We watched him sterilise a spoon with a cigarette lighter, heating the metal thoroughly. Two plastic bottles sat on the dining table, one yellow for new syringes and a red one for used needles.

I was aware of the texture of the plastic. I could feel the slightly uneven melting surface of it with my mind.

Jade poured innocent looking clear liquid onto the spoon and sucked it up with a syringe.

My emotions about using a needle lay tangled on the floor at my feet.

I watched Jade. The process intrigued me. I felt like road-kill caught in the headlights of the car before the hit. I just suddenly felt my body. I felt how easy it would be to die.

I've formed a new relationship with needles—and with syringes.

'Body of our Lord Jesus Christ,' said Rouge, crossing himself.

'I never got buggered by the priest. Wonder why?' Rouge said, looking up wistfully.

'Because you would have enjoyed it too much. It's supposed to be penance,' said Jade.

'Three Hail Marys and a good buggering,' I said. I should have been a Catholic.

'More tea, vicar?' said Jade, arching his eyebrows. 'Injecting drugs is cleaner,' said Jade.

'It's more efficient,' I said.

'It sounds like an ad for dishwashing liquid,' said Rouge.

'Let me see. What else can we inject? Cocaine, acid, ecstasy, cleaning products, melted down electrical appliances,' Rouge continued in an animated manner.

'If you inject snail pellets you'll spend a lot of time in the garden and you won't eat the plants!' Rouge said, choking on his mirth.

He held his ribs tightly from the pain of laughing.

I watched Jade inject himself. *Is this fucked-up and violent? I want to feel the prick. I want the feeling.*

My heartbeat danced on the old floorboards in time with the hypnotic music.

'Mary Poppins is singing in my head; Just a spoon full of sugar makes the medicine go down,' said Rouge.

He sang out loud, 'La la la la la la la.'

Jade slowly pierced my skin with the needle. I paid careful attention to his instructions.

'Clench and unclench your fist. Put your forefinger firmly on the spot. Feel the needle withdraw under the skin. Breathe deeply,' Jade said.

'What does it feel like?' Rouge asked me.

'Churning in the stomach. A rush. Increased heartbeat. Quickened breath. Like a train riding the tracks, clickety-clack. The old seats are padded with velour. It tastes like metal, steel. The fumes rush through your brain. The blue light on the amplifier looks really bright,' I said.

'Let's go to the party.' Jade was impatient.

'Let's go and make new friends,' I said.

'What, we're not good enough for you now? Miss hoighty-toighty.' Rouge pulled a face at me.

'Have you got my ticket?' I asked.

Jade patted his bum-bag.

'I've got everything,' he said.

I had my ecstasy tucked in my bra.

Rouge locked the door behind us as we left the house.

'Here we are, frolicking towards the night like Puck and the fairy queens under the bright stars,' said Rouge.

Light rain had begun to fall, clip-clopping at first, and then singing through the plane trees.

'The leaves look like golden toasted starfish. You can see their skeletons shining through their papery skin,' I said.

'Praises to the goddess of weather,' Rouge sang. His face was upturned to the droplets, his mouth open rapturously.

We arrived at the show-ground at eleven thirty. Pink light flooded the sky from giant concrete pylons above the show-grounds, bearing rows of oversized coloured light globes. Sulphur in the air mingled with freshly perfumed bodies.

A relentless drumbeat called us like a Pied Piper through the row of turnstiles.

A golden aura of collective energy glowed from the colourful throng.

We belonged to a pleasure sect, sharing the joyful anticipation of children approaching the circus.

A canonisation occurred in these rarefied conditions, especially bestowed by the forces of nature.

Druids formed timeless magical spheres and hovered amongst us, lithe and majestic. Their movements so slow, they were indivisible from the large crowd. Magical beings hung above the ground in a misty substrata between earth and sky.

Unearthly sounds, inaudible to the human ear, pronounced their purpose. Felt rather than heard, as the best conversations always are. Outlines of mystical creatures were without category, neither human nor beast. Their laws far more powerful without technology.

Inside each and everyone lives an inescapable voice, echoing the call, so that the inward ear must heed or sicken to death, fundamentally, for the old ways.

A carpet of sparkling nymphs, with shining skin and eyes, hovered in groups, floating like dragonflies.

Inside, lofty Victorian pavilions were made larger by giant light strobes that accentuated the high ceilings, walls and probed the dark corners. A rainbow shard of silver light illuminated a giant pie of people.

Beautiful faces; biceps, triceps, pecks, abs, tits, pink hair, blue hair, silver hair, cropped leopard-print hair.

A group of young men huddled together, all dressed identically in tartan mini-kilts, thick white socks pushed down on oiled black boots and black studded chokers.

Perfectly sculpted men, strung together with chains and carrying short, black leather riding crops.

We drifted, holding each other tightly. We stopped in one of two giant white canvas tents to watch.

There was a catwalk in front of us. Motionless, expressionless effigies sat on white plastic chairs, like cardboard cut-out people, people somewhat blitzed, left dangling between highs.

A statuesque drag queen held a microphone and introduced and derided competitors in the best costume competition.

Wet, silvery-blue and green sea creatures paraded through Atlantis, the lost city.

One of the competitors nestled like a small exotic bird on the ground in front of me. She sat curved in an arch. The skin of her supple young body hugged the curves of her collarbones, ribs and pelvis: a symmetry of contours—the lines of art. A tiny, perfect bellybutton, ever so slightly recessed, peeped shyly out of the paint.

Her body was painted with garlands of flowers, blue on green. Fresh pink nipples peaked out beneath the paint.

Her only source of warmth was a cap of short black hair that hugged her head. Her little black eyes darted and danced at the conversations around her.

She must have come from the secret woods, from a group of wandering fairies, perhaps she was lost?

She certainly has a lost look on her pixie face.

Two enormously tall gladiators marched by proudly, in exaggerated tall silver headdress and clanging, metal-panelled skirts.

Their breasts and buttocks shone from the dark, gloriously plump and pale.

An Egyptian woman in a bright blue wig clasped the arm of a nurse. The nurse's uniform was a short, white vinyl dress with a large pink cross on the front. Worn with white stockings and a suspender belt.

An occasional fluorescent, sequinned bug with a long, padded tail and some seahorses meandered through the crowd, while already tall drag-queens teetered dangerously on seven-inch platform shoes, holding court to very small young men.

One of the drag-queens wore a bright yellow and navy blue, plastic, spotted mini-dress and matching parasol. She wore a large blonde nylon wig and her eyes were encircled in superbly blue eyeshadow.

There went several Dorothys and a Tin Man—as one would expect in Atlantis.

The air was warm and tense with love.

The batting of false eyelashes beat the air like wings, as strangers murmured together, embraced and parted.

A thousand smiles and kisses hung in the air waiting to be received.

'This is the world of dreams, of wandering minstrels, where the royalty of the night preside,' Rouge said.

'I feel as though my mouth is full of confetti. Words are falling out of me so softly I can't hear them or feel them, as though I'm dreaming,' I said.

'Maybe you are,' said Rouge. 'These are the people you meet in your dreams, who come to dance-parties where they won't be noticed. What is reality?'

'Do you think people in comas come to dance parties as well?' I said, feeling slightly alarmed.

'No. That's different, they're not dream people,' said Rouge.

'How do the dream people get out of dream-land?' I asked.

'They don't. We can see them when we take drugs because we're in a kind of awake dream,' Rouge said.

'Oh! I see. So we can do anything we want to because it's a dream,' I said.

'Yes. Anything,' Rouge said.

As my ecstasy began to peak, warm glow-worms swam through me like sperm. Pleasure was rising in my throat like steam to a crescendo as the song 'Coma' reached climax.

In front of me danced a slim Jamaican girl with classically beautiful features and small, firm, bare breasts, like two plums, with little beads of moisture on and around them.

We moved together.

Her eyes were an inviting pool that sparkled at me, smiled, asked questions, enticed.

A gentle voodoo drew our bodies closer.

Her arms were waving up and down at her sides in an abandoned gesture, floating like the tentacles of a sea anemone.

Silver glittered on her strong, high cheekbones, on her breasts and dark plum glossed lips.

Her skin shone the colour of golden syrup or toffee. I wanted to lick her all over.

Sweet rainforest below her silver-sequined skirt sent up soft perfume.

It seemed natural and innocent to rub my breasts up and down over hers. The sensation of skin on skin filled me. My thoughts melded in a furnace of feeling, freeing trapped emotions.

Volumes of unspoken language passed between us.

'My name's Cherry,' the girl said close to my ear.

'Hi, I'm Lisa,' I said.

Our arms circled each other's waist. I lay my head on her shoulder for a moment.

The stage lit up and the atmosphere in the room became charged with expectation.

Danni Minogue stood frozen on the stage, poised, ready to pounce on the crowd in a long red PVC coat, open to show a red sequinned dress.

She wore red satin horns on her wavy nut-brown hair that hung down her back. Her eyes shone green as a she-wolf.

Behind her, twenty or so dancers were dressed similarly.

'Better the devil you know,' Danni sang and screamed into the night, the power of the words and music swept us up, carrying us above the scene so that we bathed in lights and movement.

Sounds washed through us rapturously.

'Wow!' I half whispered, half sighed, into the air above my head.

I could taste sweat and sex in the smoky grey air.

Underfoot was a satin swamp of shining ash, dirt, booze and human cells, which splashed up onto our legs. *The excrement of sin.*

Outside the pavilion I stumbled slightly, the rocks underfoot were becoming more jagged—the distances longer.

'Darling!' I said, flinging my arms wide as I saw Jade approaching us. I recognised him through a brain-fog.

He stuck burning red amyl so far up my nose that it made contact with my brain, spinning it around, clouding it with a rainbow feeling that rushed through my chest in a post-orgasmic embrace.

His face was alight as he masticated hurriedly, tasting the salt of exertion. He hugged us both and rushed off.

Don't miss the train.

We were all golden-stained passengers on the train ride together.

Impatience tugged me to keep moving and then we found it, Mecca, the tent of shifting sands.

'Can you hear the call of the Muezzin, of the Kasbah? This is the spiritual nucleus of the night, awash with sounds from the collective consciousness, cerebral and beautiful,' I said.

'It's a chill-out tent,' Cherry said.

The crowd inside the tent wore a mantle of lethargy, all seated or leaning, mostly on each other.

An area sectioned off to one side contained three massage tables. In the centre was a large table with candles and burning incense.

The lazy flicker of candles calmed my jittery nerves, reducing the tempo of the night.

Sweet musky scents of incense rose in a spiral of soft charcoal smoke.

Warmth from relaxed flesh emanated a strong musky scent.

Cherry sank into one of the slovenly cream canvas cushion puffs around the edge of the tent. She burrowed in, relishing the comfort. I sat next to her and pushed my head into her lap and closed my eyes. I forgot where I was, enjoying the whirlpool of colour behind my eyelids. In my mind's eye a Darrell Lea shop full of lollies spun frenetically and danced to the music.

I was falling downwards, cradled by tropical warmth around me and softened by a sticky resin in my brain.

'How much is the massage?' Cherry asked someone in the distance.

'Sixty dollars for half an hour,' someone replied.

'Half an eternity, that's OK. Nothing in this world or the next matters,' Cherry said.

'I need some speed,' I said dreamily.

I was vaguely annoyed not to have any. *It would be hard to buy.*

There were more drugs here than anywhere in this hemisphere and you couldn't buy them for love or money. What was that? Fucking stupid system!

I consoled myself that I might get some from Jade when I saw him, or from Rouge. *Someone must have some.*

The thought thrashed around in me for too long.

Cherry lay down on a massage table with her face uncomfortably thrust through a hole, as though she was partially decapitated.

I was placed beside her on another table.

Fingers sank into my spine and flesh. I drifted into a zone where I existed as a giant pulsating jellyfish, a receptor to pleasure and sound.

Music poured through the atmosphere, a current ripping through my heart into my essence and pumping through my blood stream, which was fairly congested from the other excess passengers.

This is heaven.

I fell in love with the soft rounded tones of the girl's melodic, tranquil voice: a lake or summer dawn.

Chattering by small groups of people around me sounded like cockatoos squawking—a raw creaking sound.

I was economising with speech, trying to conserve my energy. My thoughts came slowly, succinctly.

The massage ended. I slipped my lace top back on sleepily.

Cherry had finished before me and was sitting on a beanbag nearby, with her eyes closed, smiling to herself.

'Come on, sleeping beauty!' I said.

She jerked and opened her eyes.

She stood up and leant towards my ear and meowed.

'Come to the toilet.' The question held more innuendo than the simple request.

15
Urination:
my fantasy comes true

It was momentarily quiet in the tiled, prison-cell—it's fetid stench softened by its femininity. Lust had lit Cherry's face. I looked into her luminous hazel eyes that swam with the vast liquidity of the open sea.

A drag queen came into the room. Leaning close to the mirror, he began to draw with bright orange lipstick all over his face.

'What do you think of this colour?' he asked.

'It's great,' we lied.

I watched him with wide eyes.

'I would have thought he would have shaved,' I whispered into Cherry's ear. 'Look at his regrowth. That's the worst make-up I've ever seen on a trannie,' I said.

He looked glazed and tragic and although standing still, he seemed to be staggering.

His purring South-American accent redeemed him a little as he lisped through an ongoing critique of his make-up.

I looked at myself in the mirror. My face was glowing. Hugely dilated pupils made my eyes deep emeralds.

Cherry stroked my skin with admiration.

'You're so soft. Your skin is soft porcelain, it feels like bird's eggs,' Cherry said.

She was biting her lip obsessively.

'Darling, I love your feathers, can I feel them?' asked the drag queen.

'Sure,' I said, allowing him to rub my chest.

He wriggled his shoulders backwards and forwards in an elastic, shimmying motion, with his head thrown back. His eyes rolled up to the oily peeling paint on the ceiling.

'He seems to be celebrating,' Cherry said.

'That's his mating dance,' I said.

Cherry pushed open the black, gloss-painted door of a cubicle, pushing me in front of her aggressively. Our heavy breathing was indistinguishable one from the other.

She pinned me against the locked door with her mouth.

My head was pressed hard against the door. My back arched, every atom of my being stretched and tensed with desire.

Cherry's body was forced against mine. Her hands moved over my breasts. Her pubis was pressed hard against my own.

She thrust her hand into my knickers, easily pushing three fingers into the wet opening. As she pushed her tongue in and out of my mouth I could feel her small predatory, porcelain teeth. The slightly sour taste of stale chemicals melted in our saliva.

'I'm drowning in you,' I said.

As we fused into one, mossy, liquid, golden rays shot through my brain, lighting up pleasure centres. We were tangled together like plants or tentacled sea-creatures, one organism, natural, part of the universe. Cherry's fingers struggled inside my knickers to stroke the crack of hair and flesh that opened around my pearly clit.

I felt as though I would come at the touch. I clenched my teeth with desire and gripped her shoulders tightly.

Her fingers were fine and delicate as they played me like the strings of a cello. Music built inside me to a crescendo and then an explosion of joy.

The door in my mind opened and filled with light as I relinquished myself. Warm wet milk ran through my body and onto the inside of my thighs.

The frigid must find solace in classical music.

A rusty metal box on the door, holding crisp, single sheets of toilet paper, bit

166

into my arse, reminding me of the world that existed outside my body.

'Piss in my mouth,' Cherry said. I was shocked, yet excited.

She knelt down level with my groin, and eased my knickers down. She crouched in front of me, waiting. I closed my eyes and frowned with concentration, trying to ignore the warmth of breath on my genitals and the heat and wet slick of Cherry's mouth as it latched onto my vulval lips.

I could only squeeze out a tiny amount of urine. The feeling of release into the burning hearth of a warm mouth was exquisite.

I was shaken by the head rush of sensation.

I felt like letting out an inhuman high scream of delight.

Cherry spat into the toilet.

'That felt amazing. What did it taste like?' I asked.

'Sour, like lemon juice,' Cherry said.

I fondled her milky warm breasts with my hands, drinking their softness through the touch. I could taste warm milk in my throat.

Cherry extracted some 'goey' in a ratty bit of plastic from her pocket.

As I squatted and peed a long tinkling yellow note, Cherry made a line on the plastic cistern behind my head, rolling a five-dollar note as tightly as she could into a straw.

She gestured with her hand for me to have some. I dried myself and pulled my knickers up.

Holding the straw delicately between two fingers, I cleaned up the last crumbs of lumpy powder. The snorting roared like a wave in my ears. I threw my head back to inhale every particle.

'What the fuck is yous doing in there?'

There was a loud bang on the door.

'Great, a female truck driver, ignore it,' I said. I looked into her eyes, holding them with mine. 'I'm so glad you found me. I've been waiting for you,' I said. I was chewing myself furiously. My jaw felt tight. My mouth made little wet kitten noises.

I was suddenly aware of the people beyond the door as if their stares could burn through. For a moment I felt shamed by my lack of decorum.

'Come on, let's get out of here,' I said.

'Yes, I'm getting bored with the décor,' Cherry said.

Outside the rain had stopped and the air was crystal clear, electric and sharp. Lights danced on the tarmac paths.

'Black lights on a wet street. Tracks leading straight to the moon. Can you feel the heart of the city beating with ours?' I said. The lights around us were transformed into a starry-scape as we watched a threesome of boys. Under the yellow streetlights their pretty features were clear. The tall thin one in the centre wore a sailor outfit and hat. He was wearing red glitter around his eyes, bright red lipstick and black heavily pencilled eyebrows. A fantastical cabaret creature flanked by two bookend European boys dressed in regulation black. They were laughing and murmuring together with the solicitous tones of old friends.

'Very Pierre et Gils,' I said.

'It would seem natural if they stopped and turned dramatically and performed a song and dance routine,' Cherry said, as they passed by us disinterested.

Holding hands tightly we hurried towards the thumping drum and bass and the huddle of humanity.

Just inside the door, seated on a high bench, were Rouge and Jade, side-by-side, unaware of each other's presence, nodding their heads in synchronic time to the beat.

'They look like the velvet dogs with sprung heads that you used to see in the back of cars,' I said.

'If someone asked you to describe ecstasy, what would you say?' Cherry asked.

'I'd say it's a glowing, warm inner sun shining through your eyes. Being stroked by an opalescent moon. Tingling, pink blood vessels excitedly stirring beneath the skin. The white dawn of the mind nudged into consciousness. Buried truth, intense feeling. Being awake for the first time. Truly spiritually connected,' I said.

Around us a lake of faces danced in and out of the rhythm of the drums. We wandered the fairground, caught in a web of music, watching the procession, smiling serenely, until I could no longer ignore the insistent pain in my feet.

I sat down in a doorway—a small person pile, with a ladder in my stockings. My posture suggested an actress after the crowd has left, a kind of post-performance sagging. Mine, and the faces of the people ambling past in the cold pale dawn light, wore a vacant look—white parchment waiting for the script to be written on it.

Rouge and Jade found us there.

'Let's go back to our place,' said Jade

'We'll have a nice cup of tea,' Jade said, placing his arm around my waist as we left the showground.

'How about gratuitous sex?' I said.

'Oh, you can do that too if you have to, just don't leave any snail trails around the place,' Jade said.

We walked together arm in arm.

The car was parked in a side street. I could feel my hipbones shining through my parched skin.

My recessed eyes had died in their bruised sockets.

A group of sun-tanned Muscle-Marys walked huddled together in front of us. The wispy blond hair of the prettiest of them fell across his high cheek-bones, framing pale chestnut eyes and cheekbones. *So beautiful they must have been sculpted by an artist.*

Powder blue larkspur fell forward over the mantelpiece, scattering a talcum of orange yellow pollen on the glossy cream paint.

Large, white, star-shaped, Christmas lilies with dark red veins, sent out a strong scent, almost an affectation by the subtle standards of the hedgerow and field.

Rouge brought in a tray and sat it down on the coffee table.

I sank into voluminous, duck-down-filled, pink damask sofa cushions that yielded beneath me.

On the glass-topped coffee table sat a pile of carefully placed glossy art books. The warm, red, Persian rug on the floor was of the inflexibly tradi-tional kind.

Chandeliers danced gently in the light. My senses were lulled into sleepy interest as I drank the symphony of visual gratification.

The walls were painted the sharp yellow of early-spring crocus.

Floral chintz, festooned curtains held sprigs of wild red roses in their folds.

Sydney was nice and sunny, these people were nice. The world was friend-lier here.

I felt comfortable with the two men. They were long past the age when they had to prove themselves, or raise their voices to be the centre of attention. I liked that.

They listened attentively to each other and laughed gently and easily at themselves.

I helped Jade carry in teacups from the kitchen. The cups chinked pleasingly to each other, happy to be in the lounge-room, out of the cold, drafty kitchen cupboard.

Rouge had brought a bottle of red wine and was struggling with the cork-screw. The cork was liberated from the bottle with a satisfying rush of air.

Dull ruby liquid swirled into balloon glasses;, syrupy, heavy, velvet.

Smoky liquid ran down my throat. Drugs had corrupted my tastebuds.

The wine tasted like funeral ash. I relished it more from memory.

The speed in my blood would annul the intoxication and vice versa.

The wine felt nourishing as it anti-oxidised some of the venomous chemicals. Rouge read my mind.

'Do you think money corrupts?' asked Rouge, whom money and drugs had corrupted years ago.

'No,' I said, 'but I think people make money their goal to mask their inadequacy. Happiness doesn't come from materialism. Money can give power to people that shouldn't have any.'

'I like having money.' Rouge looked gleeful.

'But is that because there are other things missing from your life?' I said, being a patronising bitch.

'No. I just like art and beautiful things. There's nothing wrong with that!' Rouge said.

'No. But that's different to wanting money for the wrong reasons,' I said.

My argument was running out of steam and conviction. I just couldn't be bothered, frankly, with Rouge or his endless self-indulgence. I looked down at the spaniels, which I suddenly found infinitely more interesting. They had raised hell when we arrived and had now sunk into two corners of the room to lick their genitals with long sleazy strokes of the tongue. Cocker spaniels, I thought, how apt that they would be Rouge's dogs. Smells of tannin and sugar from tea, of wine and stale sweat soaked bodies, mingled with fermented mouldy dog-smell.

Jade asked me, 'Are you coming to recovery?'

'I don't know why they call it recovery, it's just a way of trashing yourself more,' I said. Cherry and I smiled at each other.

I took her hand and led her to the room at the back of the house that had been made respectable for me with fresh sheets and towels.

The renovation hadn't reached this part of the house. The walls were damp, painted with yellow-green gloss paint that had been popular in the fifties in lower middle-class Australian homes. The paint shone with condensation and wore the patina of a thousand cigarettes and the breath of old people.

We sat on the bed together.

'The corners feel like sadness,' Cherry said.

'Tell me about your childhood,' I said, leaning forward and resting my chin in my hands.

'I left home when I was fifteen and came to Sydney on the bus. I got a job washing dishes and lived with another girl who'd runaway,' she said.

'Were you lovers?' I asked.

'No, just friends. She died,' Cherry said.

I looked at her sadly.

'How?' I asked.

'We were both working as go-go dancers at a nightclub. One night she didn't come home. We lived in a loft above a shop across the road from the club. When I got home a few days later the police stopped me at the bottom of the ladder that led up to our room. They took me to the police station and threw pictures of her in front of me. She'd been raped and strangled. They thought she'd been killed by a ring who were making snuff movies. They never solved the murder but every time I see the guy who owns the club it freaks me out,' she said.

'That's awful. Let's promise to be friends forever,' I said, hugging her quickly.

'What's always? I mean who knows? The world could end tomorrow,' Cherry said. She looked down sadly.

'Don't be so fucking pessimistic. You sound like the voice of doom,' I said lightly, adding,

'Do you know Nana Mouskouri?' I laughed.

'That's obscure,' she said.

'It's what I say when the conversation needs direction,' I said. 'Give me more drugs!' I screamed into the silent corners of the room and then waited, as if expecting a reply.

Cherry fished out a sad pouch of plastic that looked as though it had been savaged by something ferocious. There was a little bit of speed left.

'All we need now is a red check tablecloth and some plastic cutlery. Remember those little china tea sets you used to have when you were a kid?' I said. 'I feel like I'm doing the moon walk, suspended in egg white,' I added.

'That would make you a yolk,' said Cherry.

I lay back on the bed, with my head on the pillow, eyes closed, surveying the vistas of mountains and villages of unbounded beauty with my third eye.

My vagina filled with milk. I glowed, iridescent; blood vessels visible through my skin. My genitals formed a giant incandescent lotus blossom; peach glowing into orange, lit by a fire of mystical energy, licked by flames of desire.

It was hard to anchor myself to this planet. I was longing for the touch of lips on flesh, the taste, and the searing pleasure.

I reached up my arms to the shores of physical touch that I longed for, offering myself up for gratification.

My lips were wet, my organs and passages open.

Cherry came to me quietly, moving over me slowly, although not heavily.

'Your skin makes silk seem as coarse as hessian,' I said stroking her arms.

The light framed our silhouettes, as, joined at the hipbones, we undulated together.

'You're a goddess. You shine like a candle in my heart,' Cherry spoke the words softly.

I sighed, unaware of why I should sigh, or what I should say that did not come to my mind or lips.

We talked to each other without words. From the corner of our eyes we saw the shadow of our conversation.

'Let's curl up together and hibernate like wombats,' I said.

'Do wombats hibernate?' asked Cherry.

'If they don't they should. We'd be setting a good example, there should be more hibernation,' I said.

'But it's spring,' said Cherry.

'So? You should be able to hibernate any time you feel like it. We'll be the people for the independent hibernation movement,' I said.

'Are there any other animal movements we have to pioneer?' Cherry asked.

'Nope, only that one at the moment,' I said.

'Thank God, I couldn't be fagged,' said Cherry.

I took off my clothes and slipped under the doona. Cherry slid in beside me.

I got up and put on the soundtrack from *Betty Blue*. It played hauntingly into the room.

I stroked Cherry's skin, enchanted by its melting softness.

Cherry lay on her stomach, quietly serene, with the sheen of light on her body making her look like the Virgin Mary in the painting of the Naked Maja by Goya.

Her dark eyes shone guileless and relaxed. Her pixie cheeks hinted at mischief. The mole above her lip moved as she opened her mouth, showing perfect pearly teeth.

Her hard nipples rested on the crumpled white sheet. Her rounded buttocks ended at two dimples at each side of the hollow of her back.

Her skin was flawless and downy with the light giving it a surreal grey tinge.

I lay on top of her, looking at my hair fall in mingled tones of red and chestnut as it brushed the top of her shoulders.

She felt as soft and warm as sand in summer that rolls away under you.

Her small dark, dimpled fingers twisted the sheet around in imaginary knots. I moved off her. She rolled onto her back, folding her hands behind her head. My hands cupped her full breasts, feeling them warm and satin like proving bread.

My open mouth began under her chin and moved down her throat hungrily, my tongue lingered in the hollow at the nape of her neck, moving over the tender flesh of her breast to the nipple. Her belly was a gentle, rolling hill that drew me gently downwards to a leafy glade, a cool ravine: moist, verdant, fertile.

I touched her labia gently with my fingertip. Her clitoris nestled like a small, shy animal, burrowed away. It retreated slightly at the intrusion. She relaxed, receiving my fingers. I felt her clitoris harden.

Cherry pulled my face up to hers, kissing my eyelids, cheeks, mouth and the bridge of my nose. I lay over her, feeling her breasts crushed beneath mine.

We rolled over together so that I was beneath her. She held my hands firmly above my head as she pushed me back onto the cool cotton pillows, easing my shoulders from my t-shirt. She kissed my luminous flesh as it sprang free.

Cherry's lips moved over the plump cushions of my breasts, licking the edges of the areolae, her tongue making a flicking sound and pulling blood to the area. I sighed with relief when Cherry finally took my nipples deeply into the heat of her mouth.

I called to the spirits in the room using sounds that were primal and familiar: low moans, high nasal screams and growling noises from my chest and throat. Cherry's hands were controlled and hesitant as they stroked my ankles, shins, knees and thighs, touching the skin barely at all. Little currents of air followed the movement of her fingers, forming tiny mountain ranges of goose bumps on my legs.

I gripped the sheets as though I would tear them, petrified with anticipation. Cherry's fingers now sat on the lips at the edge of my vagina, searching for the secret place there. Her warm tongue moved slightly above my clitoris, skirting the edge of the swelling tirelessly. Clear vaginal fluid flooded from me; rivers that ran sweet and clean.

Our mouths moved together anticipating changes of tempo, a tango of synchronicity, entering each other.

Cherry suckled the silver flesh of my stomach lovingly.

The air was full of the musky sweet scents of sex.

I felt for the vibrator with one hand, and finding it under the pillow, I flicked the switch and pushed up into Cherry's waiting flesh, harder than I'd meant to. Cherry withdrew slightly, shocked by the violence of the penetration, but then relaxed warming to the sensation.

The feeling of electricity sparking released spurts of ejaculation at the height of every movement. Her vagina consumed us both.

'Fuck you, bitch!' Cherry said in a husky voice.

She pulled the back of my hair, forcing my head back. I bit my lip tasting metallic blood. The shot of adrenaline moved through me.

Our bodies threw shadows up the wall that looked like two monsters killing one another as our flesh and bone married one another.

Cherry's hair curled damply around her face as she thrashed on the bed.

Her hands still gripped my hair so that I felt the pull and relished the gnawing pain at the roots of my scalp.

Cherry moaned like a bear, deep in her belly. I covered her mouth with my burning lips.

I lay still, curled against her side, luxuriating in the nearness of her body.

'Drugs have been described as a golden butterfly flapping its wings in your chest. This is butterfly time,' I said dreamily.

Cherry nodded.

Eerie stark light was creeping into the room, making it feel colder, as the light in the fridge does when you open it at night. Our faces had a blue tinge and our features were hollowed like a constructivist painting. We barely slept, spooned together, but rather travelled in and out of a communion of dreaming, while our bodies rested.

Rain had oiled the foliage framed by the small window, so that it winked and sparkled in a lively breeze. I shivered and buried myself deep in the doona.

I was still magnetised to consciousness, if a little unfocussed. I was barely within my physicality, lethargic and short of breath. A dull circle of pain at the base of my neck rose and fell from consciousness.

In another room, jazz from a bygone era bounced off the walls. A fly buzzed itself to a lonely death.

Life was a distant orchestra to my trackless mind that clung, fragile and sensitive, to the vibratory atmosphere. Day and night had become one, golden, dewy dusk, a reverie and memory of day.

My mind was aware of things that were not there. Vivid fantasies that comprised a production line of disjointed halting sequences.

A black and white 1920s Charlie Chaplin movie played in my head.

Women dressed in scarlet satin petticoats, black on the old film, their cheeks stained red with the blood of innocence cast their eyes upward melodramatically, waiting to be saved.

My mind was a disused bomb shelter or a barn where the unfettered fowl have left their tattered and torn feathers of reason and flown.

My body had gone soft like white-mould-cheese.

Opposite in the park, two water lilies swayed on a lake peacefully, between sleeping swans, whose heads were tucked into downy wing feathers. Young light touched the hearts of the flowers delicately as they opened, as if lit from beneath, melting yellow stamens into pink so that it glowed an iridescent peach: the colour of love. Outside, the air was full of the fragrance of baking bread and crisp newspapers.

We woke at nine. We showered together giggling at each other.

I packed my things hurriedly. Rouge appeared in the hallway wearing fresh clothes but looking tired.

'Have you been to bed?' I asked Rouge.

'No, in Sydney we don't sleep, we just take drugs,' Rouge laughed, hunching his shoulders in a child-like way.

'I've ordered you a taxi,' said Rouge.

'Oh, so you can't wait to get rid of me,' I said. I raised an eyebrow.

'Yes, you're ugly and you smell,' he said.

'I knew it, no-one's ever told me the truth before,' I said laughing.

'If I was straight I'd marry you,' he said. He kissed me on the lips.

I threw my head back and let out a scream.

'If only I had a dollar for every time a gay guy has said that to me I'd be rich,' I said.

Cherry and I exchanged phone numbers and left the house together.

The sun bleached the street pale. Leaves lacked the energy to dapple the pavements.

Rouge and Jade already stood on the path outside the house to see me off.

The skin on my arms shone sallow and white, like a thin crust of uncooked pastry on a sun-starved child.

I smelt the head-spinning, whorish, sweetness of tumbling jasmine, my own body oils cooking in the sun. The faint scent of garbage mingled with the smoky aroma of the city. Somewhere at the base of my skull was a reluctance to revisit the moribund frigidity of Melbourne.

A tepid eighteen-degree breeze livened the passages to my brain.

I felt free of shackles. Something twinkled in the eyes of my friends that promised lights and sunshine and ease of living. As I kissed them one by one, I felt like clinging.

'Goodbye, and thank you for letting me stay!' I said.

'It was our pleasure,' Jade replied.

Jade's clipped accent purred with the fake warmth and sincerity that he had acquired from his expensive private school education.

Rouge almost jumped from the pavement with enthusiasm as his energy spilled from him.

'Will you come to Sydney again soon?' Cherry asked me.

'I don't know but I'll call you. I promise.' I hugged her tightly and kissed her full mouth and got into the taxi.

The pinched, grey face of the middle-aged taxi-driver had seen me embrace Cherry. He stared back at me knowingly, his eyes were the colour of white-edged smoke. His eyelids were partially lowered. Red freckling on his polished scalp, shone through a spinney of sparse ginger and grey hair as he threw my bags into the dirty metal boot unfeelingly.

They fell with the dull thud of corpses.

'Goodbye! I hope I'll see you soon!' I said, waving to them.

A bright neon sign blazed, 'Gaming Palace' as I sped to the airport.

When I got home I rang Apple.

'Perth was great, I made a thousand dollars a night easily,' I said.

'I have to go over. I can't work here at the moment. I'm burnt out. I hate the clients. I had one yesterday and I couldn't do it. I screamed at him and threw him out,' she said.

'Shit, are you OK?' I asked.

'I've been working for too long, more than ten years. I'm going to pack up my stuff and move over to WA. I might even move to Thailand after,' she said.

'You're taking the girls?' I said.

'Of course. Their father doesn't want them. He doesn't even call them on their birthday,' she said.

'Heh, if anyone asks, don't tell them where I've gone. I took out a bank loan for twenty thousand dollars and I'm taking the rented fridge and washing machine. I can't pay the bills,' she said.

'Of course,' I said. 'I forgot how depressing Melbourne is, I think I've got itchy feet,' I said.

'Well, as long as you haven't got any nasty little rashes,' she said.

'I'm going to have to go away again as well, I just can't be here,' I said.

'Where are you going?' Apple asked.

16
Asian Nation:
working in Singapore

'I don't know. To hell probably. Anywhere. Everywhere. I'm going to follow my fanny.'

Apple laughed.

'You're mad,' she said.

'I know,' I said.

'A friend of mine is working in Singapore. She said you get a thousand dollars for one booking there, I'll give you her number,' Apple said.

'Asian men don't like me but I might just go anyway. You never know,' I said. 'They might change their minds.'

Singapore is clean and orderly. The people are demure, quiet, and industrious. Penalties for theft or drug dealing include death or amputation. Consequently there is very little crime.

Commerce in Singapore is conducted around one long road called Orchard

Road. Almost all of the five-star hotel chains and international designers of clothes, accessories and jewellery are represented there. The prices for designer goods are cheaper here than elsewhere.

Malaysians love to shop. They love designer labels.

Leading off Orchard Road is a short paved walkway where expatriates drink at a fashionable bar, a cosy, timber-lined room with a lofty ceiling and oriental decorations.

Opposite are the bustling night markets where you can shop and eat local dishes such as nasi goreng until dawn at cheap outdoor cafes.

In the middle of Orchard Road in a modern office building, on the first floor is the largest escort agency in Singapore, run by a curt, toad-plump, Indian man with black moles on his pock-marked face and his haughty, plump wife.

The girls sitting in the two-room office are divided into two groups: the Europeans and the illegal immigrants from the Philippines who are considered to be second-class citizens because of the poverty in their country and are treated as such by the Indian couple.

The pale-skinned Asian girls earn very little money comparatively, about one hundred Singaporean dollars compared to the six hundred dollars or more that Europeans earn for a short-time booking.

A short-time booking can last up to four hours. An all-night booking is negotiable but at least a thousand dollars for a European girl and about three or four hundred for a Filipino or a local girl.

The Asian girls are sweet but keep to themselves.

The bulk of the clientele are Indian or Asian, they are usually generous and extremely wealthy. European men pass through on business. A few work in Singapore on contract.

The Sultan of Brunei and his relatives visit Singapore or have women flown to them. There are princes, diplomats, millionaires and billionaires.

There is a lot of money to be made if the owner of the agency likes you.

Apple's friend Olive was making two thousand dollars a night. She was a twenty-year-old, petite, Spanish girl with straight black hair and almond eyes. Olive and I were sharing a flat not far from Orchard Road with a French girl and an English girl. The French girl had been working in Singapore for five years. She was about to marry a prince from Jakarta who she'd fallen in love with.

The English girl was tall, slim and blonde and had her boyfriend from England living with her. He had a job in a local hotel.

They were saving to buy a business together. They already had fifty thousand dollars saved after working there for six months.

Olive took me to the agency and introduced me to the owner. I could tell he didn't like me. Come to think of it, I didn't like him either.

I was sent on a group booking to a karaoke bar. It's traditional for Asian men to entertain with prostitutes. They drink top-shelf whisky neat from tumblers and sing karaoke.

I was with two Filipino girls and four Europeans. We sat drinking with five Asian businessmen who laughed amongst themselves in clipped squawks with heads nodding like cockatoos. They were a small army of manicured, miniature soldiers. Their implacable faces had all the warmth of executioners.

Olive and I chatted about the basic details of our lives to pass the time.

'It's my life's mission to marry a wealthy man and live in luxury. I'm travelling around the world looking for a suitable candidate,' she said.

'If he has a friend when you meet him, remember me,' I said.

The microphone was passed to me but I declined. Singing badly and out of tune would make me look far less attractive than I was already feeling.

The other girls sang and cooed together like seagulls and talked amongst themselves. We were ignored by the men until the end of the evening when it was decided which girl each man would like to take to their hotel room.

Asian men generally like very young women, especially blondes.

As I'd expected they hadn't warmed to me. I was ignored and dismissed at the end of the evening.

On my second night I arrived at the agency to wait for a booking. The favourite girls of the owner had all been telephoned earlier and sent out on bookings. These four or five girls seldom sat in the office. Usually they were sent out all night, sometimes booked for days or sent to neighbouring countries.

An Australian girl had just arrived from Sydney.

Scarlet was big boned, very tall with curly dark hair. She wasn't beautiful but she had personality. She infected the space around her.

We liked each other immediately.

Her laughter came often and sparkled like fairy dust, brightening the atmosphere in the office that was dull and flat, weighed down with the heaviness of our desperation.

I slipped into Scarlet as though I was walking into the moving circles of light that dance in shallow water.

She gave off positive ions like the seaside. Her voice had a similar lullaby quality to waves lapping a sandy shoreline.

Neither of us was booked for the next two days. We sat around the pool at the Hyatt during the day sunbathing, pretending to be guests of the hotel. We had lunch in Little India at a well-known restaurant called the Banana Leaf Apollo, where, for a set price, the waiters drop assorted curries onto a banana leaf on the table in front of you.

You eat in the traditional manner using three fingers of your right hand.

We emerged into the bright sunlight and looked at each other. I laughed hysterically, bending double, with my face close to the ground. Tears rolled down my cheeks. We had wide yellow circles of dye from the curry around our mouths. No matter how hard we rubbed the stain wouldn't come off.

'Yogi Bear and Booboo,' I screamed, holding my sides.

'Who would have thought you need practise practice to eat with your fingers?' Scarlet said.

We caught a bus back to Orchard Road laughing at each other all the way. Scarlet was staying with a friend of hers in a cheap apartment near mine.

That evening an attractive Australian man in his early thirties came into the office and chose Scarlet and I.

Australian men have a particular look:, light hair, short necks, wide shoulders, thick arms, blue eyes, long eye-lashes and a particular hunch to the shoulders that causes their knees to bow forwards slightly.

We went with 'Lee' in a taxi to the Shangri-La Hotel where he was staying.

It was one of the most expensive hotels in Singapore.

We passed through the impressively spacious foyer, from where I could see a large kidney-shaped swimming pool surrounded by tropical foliage.

'You must be loaded,' said Scarlet.

'I just made millions from an invention I patented,' he said.

'What did you do before?' Scarlet asked.

'I was a football reporter on a TV show,' he said.

'I thought I recognised you,' Scarlet said.

'I'm on my way home from England. I just pitched an idea for a new game to an English company,' he said.

Once in the room Scarlet asked, 'Can we order room service?' She was jumping up and down on his king- size bed.

'Sure anything you want. Knock yourself out,' he said.

'You're so nice,' I said, happily.

'Can we have a bottle of Dom Perignon and a bowl of French fries please?' Scarlet spoke into the black phone next to the bed. She hung up the phone.

'Let's go for a swim,' Scarlet said.

Lee put his bathers on. Scarlet and I stripped to our bras and panties.

We wrapped ourselves in large white bath towels and took the lift downstairs. There was no-one else around.

The nights are seductively balmy in Singapore, thick with the scent of frangipani and humming with crickets. The air was divinely still, existentially peaceful, so that the trill of a small bird sounded clearer. The warm air moulded itself around my cheeks. The fresh, minty scent from leaves and shrubs greeted us.

We lowered ourselves into the steaming turquoise water, soft and silk as poppy petals. Lee butterflied the length of the pool powerfully. He swam over to me wiping his hair back from his face.

'You're a good swimmer,' I said.

'My mother wanted me to be a professional,' he said bitterly.

'Did you rebel?' I asked.

'Nothing I do is good enough for her now,' he said.

'Is that why you're such a high achiever?' I asked.

'Probably,' he said, resting next to me at the side of the pool where I held onto the edge with both arms making little sharp splashes with my feet.

I smiled at him provocatively.

'I'm so happy to have someone I can talk to in English,' I said.

'Asian men are different. You can't tell what they're thinking,' Scarlet said from the other side of the pool.

'Be careful, the thought police will get you. You can't have independent ideas here,' I said.

'Or chewing gum,' said Lee.

'Heh, do you guys know if we can get some cocaine?' Lee whispered.

'Shhhh. Are you *crazy*. It's the death penalty. They *hang* you,' said Scarlet.

'Yeah, but you could still get some from a club or something. Don't you guys know anyone?' Lee persisted.

'We've only been in Singapore for a couple of days,' I said, splashing up little white-diamond sprays of water with my feet.

Lee pressed his body closer to mine.

'I like you, I'm not really interested in the other girl. She's nice though. Will you stay the night?' he whispered.

'I'd love to,' I said.

Lee pulled himself to sit on the side of the pool.

'Let's go upstairs,' he said.

We pattered along the terracotta tiles with bare feet, wrapped in our towels. We went through the foyer and up in the lift. A Japanese man was already in the lift.

'Koneechi waaa,' Scarlet said, bowing her head with her hands pressed together to her chest.

We ran up the corridor to the room screaming and laughing. Lee opened the door.

'The chips are getting cold,' Scarlet said, helping herself to a handful and dipping them into a small jar of tomato sauce.

Lee took the champagne from the ice bucket and dislodged the cork pointing it at the ceiling. It flew out dramatically and hit the plaster, bouncing to the ground ending up in the corner behind the rubbish bin.

He poured the foaming liquid into three flutes and handed one to both of us.

'Here's to life,' he said.

We chinked glasses.

Scarlet went to take a shower. I took off my wet underwear and hung it over a chair to dry.

I sat on the bed with Lee who was wearing a giant fluffy bathrobe. I snuggled against him.

'You feel like a teddy bear,' I said.

Lee flicked the switch on the remote control turning the channel to MTV.

Scarlet appeared from the shower in a towel, her black curls were glistening wet, her face shone fresh and pink. She sat with us on the bed.

'Ruby's going to stay with me,' Lee said.

'That's fine,' said Scarlet good-naturedly. Lee got up and gave her seven hundred Singapore dollars. He'd paid the agency separately.

Scarlet dressed and kissed us both goodbye. She left with a little wave.

Lee leant over and kissed me.

'Stay there,' I said.

I got up and took my condoms and lube from my bag and put them on the table beside the bed.

'Now, where were we?' I said.

We lost ourselves in the liquid sensation of tongues and mouths tangoing together. With my eyes closed I felt as though I was flowing down stream.

I fondled his hard cock with one hand. It was hot and hard like a stone heated in the sun. He pushed and pulled at my breasts.

The alcohol had made me slightly drowsy.

I rolled a condom onto him with my mouth. He let me suck him for a while and then he lay on top of me and fucked me until he came.

I removed the condom and wrapped it and put it next to the bed. We fell asleep together comfortably as though we knew each other well.

A trolley moving past the room in the hallway heralded morning. My eyes itched with tiredness. My face was slightly raw, unaccustomed to so much kissing.

He was still asleep. I jumped up, went to the toilet and splashed my face with cold water in the bathroom and put on make-up. I wanted to look my best when he woke.

As I walked back to the bed he yawned and stretched out his arms.

'Hi, sleepy head,' I said.

'Hello, gorgeous,' he replied.

I laughed.

'Are we having brekkie together?' I said.

'Sure, order me coffee and fried eggs and bacon,' he said.

'Do you want extra cholesterol with that?' I asked.

'No, that'll do,' he said.

I ordered breakfast using the room service button on the phone.

'Now then, let me rub your back,' I said.

He rolled over onto his stomach and spread his arms wide on the bed.

I gazed into the distance as I moved over his back and buttocks rhythmically in circular movements with my fingers; I then rotated my chin over his shoulders, back and buttocks. I repeated the same movement with my elbows. I poured myself over him like warm custard letting the skin on my breasts meld with his as I moved them up and down his back.

'That's nice,' he mumbled into the bed. His mouth had relaxed into a rubbery purse.

'Do you think we remember the future, that we know what's going to happen to us?' I asked with a far-away feeling.

'Anything's possible,' he said.

'I think we do,' I said.

He rolled over; his erection was hard and red.

I ripped open a condom packet and sucked him for a moment before mounting him. I writhed on top of him, holding my breasts in my hands with my head thrown back. He came quickly.

'That was wonderful,' I said, 'better than callisthenics by the pool.'

'Just in time too,' he said, as room service knocked at the door.

A young Indian man wheeled in the trolley with silver cutlery and a white orchid in a silver vase on a crisp white cloth.

The waiter took out the hot plates from the compartment underneath the trolley and laid the food out for us.

Lee signed the docket.

'Enjoy, sir, madam. Good morning,' said the waiter, nodding and bowing out graciously.

I ate scrambled eggs and toast and drank tea.

'Do you know, this is the best tea I've ever had. See, the British did some good by colonising these countries,' I said as I dressed in my slightly damp underwear and the short black and white cocktail dress I'd worn the night before.

'I'm not sure about raping and pillaging and robbing other countries,' said Lee.

'You're probably right,' I said. 'I suppose I'd better leave you in peace.'

Lee walked to the bureau and took his wallet out. He handed me a thousand Singapore dollars and thanked me.

We kissed.

'I might see you in Sydney one day,' I said.

'Sure,' he said.

I was sad as I left. He'd been good company. I would have liked to have seen him again.

Scarlet and I sat from six until eleven in the office for the next two nights without doing a booking.

'This is fun. It's been a nice holiday but I'm not earning enough money to stay here,' I said.

'I'm going to work for one of the smaller agencies,' Scarlet said. 'I might get more work. I want to stay for two more weeks. I've been working for five years. Before I get married and have kids I want to have the Asian experience, I'm nearly thirty,' she said.

'Do you have a boyfriend?' I asked.

'Yes. He's a computer programmer. He's a bit square. He has no idea I work. At home I take a train to Newcastle on the weekends and stay at a brothel there. He thinks I go and visit my mother,' she said.

'Isn't it stressful living a double life?' I asked.

'No, I love it. I know I'm not young and gorgeous but my mother always told me you can do anything you want if you believe in yourself. I've paid off my house. I could never have done that on my wage as a receptionist. I still work part-time as a cover. I enjoy my day job,' she said.

'I've always wanted to work a corner near William Street. I'm sure those girls clean up. I'd take a discreet corner in a back street. I don't think anyone would recognise me,' she said.

'I've never met anyone who really enjoys working,' I said.

'I love it. Sometimes I have great sex. If you get a guy who knows what he's doing you can have great orgasms,' she said. Her face was alight as she remembered.

'I could never find a client attractive, it's hard work,' I said.

'Plenty of girls marry clients,' she said.

'I suppose. I had a couple of interesting regulars in Melbourne who I liked as friends. One or two of them were spunks but mainly I call them the piggy men,' I said.

Scarlet laughed.

'They all look like piggies. They're fat and white from working indoors. Too much money and no idea how to make themselves happy. They eat and drink too much to try to satisfy themselves. They have too much of everything including sex. Nothing satisfies them,' I said.

'Sad, isn't it. You'd think if you had all that money you'd be happy,' she said.

'I would be,' I said.

'We should try and pick up clients in a hotel bar. I know heaps of girls who work in bars,' she said.

I hesitated.

'What if we get caught?' I said.

'We'll just have to be careful,' she said.

The next evening we walked down Orchard Road to the Hyatt and sat in the bar sipping vodka and limes. I looked around at the men in the bar nervously, trying to catch their eyes. I was dressed in a short black skirt with a silver chain belt swinging around my hips and a white blouse. I crossed my stockinged legs and smiled at a middle-aged man flirtatiously.

He walked up to me.

'Would you like a drink?' he asked.

'I thought you'd never ask,' I said. 'Are you here on business?'

'Yes. I'm an engineer,' he said.

'You're English,' I said. Trying to think of some scintillating conversation to impress him with, but got stuck on the obvious.

'What part of England are you from?' I asked.

'Manchester,' he said.

'Lovely part of the world,' I said, thrashing around in the banal. I had no idea what Manchester was like but I suspected it was just a big ugly city.

'How long are you here for?' I asked.

'I'm leaving tomorrow,' he said.

'Oh, what a shame,' I pouted. I really didn't care if he stayed or went and it probably wasn't a shame for him either.

'Are you staying here?' I asked.

'Yes, the company pays for it,' he said.

'I'd love to see your room,' I said looking at him seductively. I turned and gave Scarlet a wink, she was engrossed in conversation with an old Asian man.

'Sure,' he said. He looked confused.

I hooked my arm through his and we walked to the lift together.

Once in his room I sat on the edge of his bed.

'I didn't like to tell you downstairs but I'm working,' I said.

He looked shocked and puzzled.

'What do you mean?' he asked.

'I'm looking for someone to pay me for sex,' I said. There were probably much more diplomatic and enticing ways to approach the situation but I wasn't sure what to do and I felt embarrassed for him and for myself. I hoped I hadn't offended him.

I had.

'I'm not interested in paying you. I thought you liked me,' he said stiffly.

I repressed the urge to snort derisively. He was extremely unattractive.

'I'm sorry,' I said, 'my mistake.' I was worried that he might call security. I smiled at him sweetly.

'You have a nice night,' I said, backing towards the door.

I hurried down the hall and took the lift down. Scarlet was sitting alone at the bar.

'How did you go?' she asked.

'I think we should go somewhere else in case he reports us to security,' I said.

She got up and we walked out quickly together.

'I didn't pull it off,' I said. 'It's too hard. He thought I was attracted to him. He didn't want to pay for it,' I said.

We walked to a small local bar and drank three or four vodka and limes quickly, looking around to see if there were any potential clients. Scarlet tried to pick up unsuccessfully. 'Let's go,' she said.

We meandered down Orchard Road together. In front of us a small Malaysian man who must have been about fifty zigzagged across the pavement. He had a shrunken dark face and wore the scruffy clothes of a workingman.

'He's pissed,' Scarlet whispered. 'I dare you to pick him up,' she said.

'Where would I take him?' I asked.

'There's a house across the road where you can rent rooms by the hour. I'll show you.' She pointed to the right, down a street that ran off Orchard Road.

'See the one with the fairy lights across the front? Go on, I dare you,' she whispered.

I hurried my step until I was walking next to the man.

'Hello, do you speak English?' I asked.

He looked confused.

'Ingleesh?' he asked, screwing up his face so that he looked even more like a monkey than he had before.

'Yes. You sexy man. You and me fuck,' I said, deciding to get straight to the point. I moved my index finger in and out of a circle made by curling the thumb on my other hand over to touch my finger.

He grasped my meaning with a look of surprise.

'Four hundred dollar,' I said, putting four fingers up in front of his face.

He put his hands out with the palms facing up and hunched his shoulders.

'Much money,' he said.

'Three fifty,' I said. 'That's it.' I moved my hands sideways in a cutting motion.

'OK,' he acceded reluctantly.

'Over there,' I said, pointing to the house.

I linked my arm in his and crossed the road. I was almost a head taller than him and although I was slim, his waist was smaller than mine. For a moment I felt guilty. I was probably taking a whole week's wage from a drunk who looked like he couldn't afford to eat. *Oh well.*

I looked back at Scarlet. She gave me a thumbs-up and waved.

I walked up a short flight of stone steps with my 'boyfriend' who I had now nicknamed 'Monkey Magic'.

I rang the doorbell of the house and hoped Scarlet was right and they did have rooms to rent. It was about eleven pm. A shuffle moved towards us down a hallway.

A short plump Asian woman held the door open. She looked as though she had been sleeping.

'How much for room—one hour?' I asked, opening my mouth wide to form the words clearly.

'Fifty dollar la,' she said. In Singapore the local women end their sentences with la in the way that Australians use 'but'.

'OK,' I said.

She showed us to a room off the hallway.

The small one-storey house was decorated in an offbeat, European, kitsch, 1950s-style with decorations that made it look like Christmas. The walls were papered with bold-patterned red and silver flock wallpaper and the blue and gold carpets had busy designs on them that didn't match.

I was feeling quite drunk. I put my hand out and pointed to my palm. He gave me my money slowly. I took it quickly and tucked it into my bag taking out condoms and lube.

I took off his clothes. His body had a strong odour of sweat, fried food and unwashed clothes.

I pushed him towards the glass-encased shower in the corner of the room. He showered quickly as I undressed. I gave him a perfunctory back massage on the high, soft, bed that was covered with a gold chenille bed-spread. I rolled him over and pushed a condom onto his small erection with my mouth. I only had regular size condoms on me, his cock was about the size of my thumb. The wrinkled rubber tickled my throat and mouth as I sucked him.

I changed the condom for a fresh one and let him lie on top of me and fuck me. I held onto the edge of the condom carefully to make sure it didn't slide off inside me.

He laboured over me. I moaned with less conviction than usual, barely able to feel his cock. This was so obviously a charade I was surprised he came easily. We dressed hurriedly, hardly looking at each other.

I paid the woman who was sitting on a chair at the front door with her head nodding on her chest.

I believe all people are equal, but I was acutely aware of the social inequality between this man and I. Ironic, considering I was the prostitute who had picked *him* up in the street. I felt he was beneath me, part of an underclass of poorly paid labourers.

At the bottom of the steps I kissed his cheek and walked off quickly.

The next day Scarlet rang me. She thought my adventure exciting. I wasn't so sure.

'I'm finding this hard, I'm going to see if Hong Kong is better for me,' I said.

We exchanged our home phone numbers in Australia.

'We'll catch up again one day. Good luck,' I said.

The next day I flew to Hong Kong and booked into a youth hostel on Kowloon Island. I called from my room in the hostel and gave my details to an agency I found in the phone book. I couldn't read the writing but the pictures of girls were self-explanatory.

The Asian woman who answered the phone took a description and said she would call me if there was any work.

I walked through the pallid smoke left behind by the debauched night, down the main road to buy fruit from the market. It was humid and steam rose from the roads. Small men spat on the wide, overcrowded pavement in front of them. I repressed my disgust and the urge to smack them on the top of the head for their bad manners. The city smelt of diesel smoke, citrus and body oils.

I was enjoying the blazing signs: stamen yellow and fire engine red graphics, a mumbo-jumbo of unintelligible words.

The street was full of canvas-topped open trucks: mostly vegetable and fruit deliveries.

Names of businesses said Shanghai, Hong Kong, Beijing. The narrow side streets bustled with lively snakes of people, all hurrying, important and serious, going about their business.

The tempo and energy of big cities excited me.

I took a ferry to Hong Kong city and caught the tram that runs on an almost perpendicular track up the side of the mountain, to the museum.

That night the agency rang my room.

'You go to hotel on Hong-Kong mainland. He's English man. He live in Hong-Kong for many years. He pay you cash,' she said. She gave me his name, the address of the hotel and his room number.

I dressed and went to the front of the hostel. Reception called a taxi for me. It was a reasonably long drive through the tunnel under the harbour. I paid the taxi and found my way to his room. It was a small, shabby hotel. A man of about sixty with thin black hair answered the door, fully dressed in a business suit. He smelt strongly of alcohol.

I put my arms around him.

'You're a nice cuddly teddy bear,' I said.

His ruddy face hardened, deepening the ruts that ran from his nose to the sides of his mouth. He reminded me of a giant turtle that lives in a hard crusty grey shell. Perhaps it wasn't tactful to draw attention to his bulging belly that hung over his belt.

'Less go out,' he said.

'Oh, really, wouldn't you rather get nice and cosy with me here?' I said patting the bed.

'No,' he said.

'OK. I'd love to go out with you,' I chirped.

I held his leathery hand as we walked down the street down the road to a small wooden door that he seemed familiar with. He pressed the bell. An angular Asian woman, with black hair scraped severely back from her face into a tight bun, admitted us to the club. Her eyes smouldered at us. She wore a traditional Chinese midnight-blue silk dress, embroidered with gold dragons. Her body was a flat, thin frame that the fabric must have been woven onto, so tightly stretched over her pelvis was the dress.

I looked around; there were a few European men in the room.

About ten scantily-clad, caramel-skinned, young Asian girls in shiny platform shoes danced on a circular stage in the centre of the small black room to Asian pop music.

Yellow light danced on their firm, brassy thighs as they moved. They reminded me of a rack of assorted spices.

One wore only a see-through, white, lacy-knitted top, edged with white feathers that stopped short of her firm brown arse-cheeks. Her large nipples looked black against her dark skin. She smiled at my client with a dull sparkle, cheap, like diamante.

He watched her entranced.

'Aren't they beautiful?' he asked. I was sure I saw a gobbet of spittle roll down his chin. His forehead shone with a fine film of perspiration. His beady eyes made him look like a frog. I looked up at the Asian girls; I saw leopards watching us with amber, almond eyes and feline cunning.

Two acorn-skinned girls slinked towards us and wound themselves around both of his arms like ribbons. They melted into his sides, sweet as two toffees, yet I suspected, with the bite of chilli.

What am I; chopped liver? I stood in front of him trying to catch his eye to no avail.

'You can go now,' he said curtly, waving me away with his hand. My jaw fell open disbelievingly.

'But, I don't have enough money to get home,' I said.

17
Destination:
working in London

He rifled through his pocket and handed me five hundred Hong-Kong dollars. It was the equivalent of just over a hundred Australian.

'Here.' He turned away from me rudely.

My heart leapt into my eyes for a moment. I told myself it wasn't anything personal.

I heard one of the girls giggle as I left. I was humiliated.

I suspected this might be his usual routine—to impress the Asian girls that he seemed so fond of, so they could watch him dismiss the white women in favour of them. The agency probably deliberately sent unsuspecting new girls to him for a fee.

I sat in my room for two more evenings, waiting for the phone to ring, feeling isolated and panicky. I plucked the hairs from my bikini-line and painted my nails. I was eating fruit and very little else to save money.

Emptiness is a place like hell—desolate, sickly, burning.

I booked a flight to London to leave the next day.

⌒

At Heathrow airport I exchanged my money. I only had two hundred pounds. I took a train to the West End of London and a tube to Kensington.

I remembered a boarding house that I lived in when I was eighteen. I thought there might be somewhere cheap to rent in the area.

I ended up at the exact same four-storey terrace house that I had lived in, in a street called Lexham Gardens.

I rented a small room at the top of the house with a single bed for seventy pounds a week from a Middle-Eastern man.

The house had been modernised; you no longer had to put coins in a machine on the wall to get measured amounts of hot water. The bathrooms were new, the walls freshly painted. If it had been cleaner it would have been pleasant.

There was a pay phone on the first floor landing. I took the directory to my room and found the escort section. I called several numbers. Two agencies told me they weren't busy enough to have any more girls working for them. I eventually found an escort service that was interested and was given an address near Baker Street tube station.

On my way to the station I saw a phone box with hundreds of phone numbers stuck on the walls and ceiling advertising private erotic massage and escorts.

The office was in a large, white-painted terrace with black wrought-iron palings. The Victorians didn't have a lot of imagination and reproduced the same house to populate most of central London. I read the list of tenants next to the heavy, black- painted door and pressed the button.

A polite, syrupy, woman's voice answered 'come in'.

The door clicked open.

A short, battle-scarred stairway took me to the door on the first floor landing.

The neutral office was sparsely furnished with an unremarkable desk with one empty chair in front of it.

Behind the desk sat a blonde woman. She wore a cream blouse and tweed skirt. She had bloomed into comfortable middle-age, especially around the middle. She would have been beautiful ten years ago.

She looked me up and down. I felt inadequate.

'Are you going to start today?' she asked. She had a Scandinavian accent.

'Yes, thank you,' I was relieved.

'What's your name?' she asked, writing notes on a book in front of her.

'Ruby,' I said, a little tremulously.

'Nationality?' she asked.

'I'm English but I live in Australia,' I said.

'We'll say Australian. About twenty-eight. Thirty-four, twenty-four, thirty-four,' she said, as she wrote.

'Yes, sure,' I said, having been reduced to a group of numbers that didn't quite add up. Maths didn't matter, just illusion.

'What hours are you open?' I asked.

'Three till twelve, or one on busy nights,' she said.

It was three thirty in the afternoon.

'What are the rates?' I asked.

'We charge seventy-five pounds. You get the same. You're not to charge any extra,' she said.

'If they pay by credit card you get your money the following day,' she said.

She showed me through a door leading into a small adjoining room. There were chairs around the walls and a television mounted on the wall.

'It's quiet at the moment. The bathroom's down the hall,' she said.

I helped myself to a dog-eared magazine from a stack on one of the chairs and sat down. There were three other women sitting around the room. I summed up the competition.

'Hello, I'm Ruby,' I said.

'Hello,' one of the women responded in an Irish accent. 'Where are you from?'

'Australia,' I said. 'I'm travelling. I'm from Devon originally. I've lived in Australia for ten years, since I was nineteen, I married an Australian tourist who I met in London, so that I could live with him in Australia. We only knew each other briefly.' I looked at her. She had a pretty face. She was curvaceous, which is another way of saying plump. Ripe and round as a cantaloupe.

'It's funny,' I said, 'I've never seen a blonde Irish woman. I suppose I thought Irish people were all dark-haired.'

'It's just like any other country. There are all sorts,' she said.

I felt a bit silly.

'Of course,' I said.

Neighbours was playing on the television. In the background a familiar song played. Russet was singing their number-one hit. My heart somersaulted. I felt homesick. I wondered when I'd have enough money to go home.

Two young girls, pretty as peacocks, chatted together happily. One had opulent raven hair and striking blue eyes. She wore a black leather jacket and knee-high black boots. She was talking about her up-coming nineteenth birthday in a voice, thin and brittle as sea-shell.

'Are you going home to Bristol?' her friend asked her.

'Just for the weekend,' she said.

'I'm still in love with my ex-boyfriend. He's a black African. I love black guys. His mate just got shot in a drive-by shooting. He was into crack,' she continued.

'Shit,' said her friend in a cultured voice.

'How's uni?' the dark-haired girl asked.

'I've got exams next week,' said her friend.

I watched them interact, enviously. Aware of my aloneness.

The taller girl was very attractive, slim, with long legs and straight, shoulder-length, honey-coloured hair.

The Irish woman smiled at me.

'I'm just working here while I'm studying law,' she said. 'I was working as an exotic dancer.'

'That would be fun. Why did you stop?' I asked, grateful to have someone to talk to.

'My head lecturer came in. I don't think he saw me. If he did he never said anything. I can't afford to get thrown out of my course,' she said.

'Would they do that?' I asked.

'Yes. Do you know if you're picked up in the street on suspicion of prostitution three times you get a criminal conviction. Even if they have no proof. My friend got picked up walking home one night. Luckily she didn't have condoms in her bag. If you go into a five-star hotel for a drink with another woman you have to leave your passports at the reception in case you're soliciting,' she said passionately.

'How archaic. Hypocrisy and repression,' I said, feeling the weight of the British establishment.

Ding-dong. The bell went. The receptionist called out.

'Customer!'

The girls lined up at the door, I stood up behind them, straightening my skirt and hair. One at a time I heard them introduce themselves.

'Hi, I'm Lucy, are you having a nice day?'

'Hi, I'm Samantha.'

'Hi, I'm Belle.'

'Hi, I'm Ruby, pleased to meet you.' I shook his hand shyly and then returned to the waiting room. The receptionist poked her head around the door.

'Ruby, the gentleman would like to see you.'

I was thrilled.

'This gentleman is taking you to his apartment for an hour. It's not far. You can get a taxi back. He's paid by credit card,' she said. I smiled at him gratefully.

We walked to his car that was parked nearby. It was a black Porsche. I was impressed.

'What do you do?' I asked him. I looked at him as he spoke. He was attractive, not tall, but fit, with light brown hair and blue eyes. I wondered why he was paying for sex.

'I'm an accountant,' he said.

If he'd asked me to marry him at that moment I would have said yes. Suddenly I wished I'd gone to university and got a good job so that I could marry a respectable man. I felt the class divide that English people are so aware of.

We parked in his car park, beneath a modern apartment block and caught the lift up.

It was a pleasant two-bedroom apartment with new furniture. He showed me into the bedroom.

'I'll take a shower,' he said.

I took out my condoms and lubricant and undressed to my lingerie and sat on the edge of the bed.

I looked at the photographs on the bedside table and the male memorabilia: a golf trophy, beer stein and football jersey.

He came into the bedroom wrapped in a towel.

'You've got a tan,' I said.

'I've just got back from Spain,' he said.

'Was it amazing?' I asked.

'Relaxing,' he said.

I wanted to talk to him. I wanted to stay in his apartment, not just for one hour. We made love. I didn't feel as though I was working. We had normal, enjoyable sex. As I rode him hard, I screamed and moaned. I released myself into the sensation. I wondered if he thought I was a good actress.

I eased myself off of him, holding on to the edge of the condom with my fingers. I was embarrassed to see blood on the condom as I wrapped it in tissues. I excused myself to the bathroom with my handbag, luckily I had a tampon. I showered quickly and put on lipstick.

'You don't mind if I don't see you out. I think I'll have a nap,' he said, still lying in bed as I dressed. I kissed him on the forehead.

'See you soon,' I said hopefully.

I hailed a black cab in the street outside his building.

It was still early, just before seven when I got back to the office. I sat in the waiting room for the remainder of the night. Two more girls had arrived: a very tall Cockney with long bleached hair and a young Australian girl.

The two attractive young girls were sent out together to party with a wealthy Arab. There were very few customers.

I chatted with the young Australian girl, she was from Canberra.

'I heard there's a lot of money to be made in Denmark and Switzerland. They like girls with dark hair because all the women are blonde. But I heard it's very expensive to live in Switzerland. I'm thinking of going there next. I've got a guide to youth hostels,' she said.

I left at eleven and caught the tube back to Kensington. I bought a chocolate bar from a vending machine at the station.

The next day I had fish and chips at McDonalds. I bought a pleated mini-skirt from Marks and Spencers and a see-through blouse from Top Shop.

I returned to the agency in my new clothes.

The first three clients didn't choose me. By eleven pm I had read all of the magazines.

He was around sixty, tall and grey-haired in a long, black wool coat.

There were only two of us left in the waiting room, the Australian girl and myself.

He chose me.

I took his arm affectionately.

'His name's Michael. He's going to pay you at the end of the night because he's not sure how long he'll see you for,' said the receptionist.

'Hello, dear,' he said jovially in a thick Irish accent. His voice was heavy with drink. He squeezed my waist.

As we left together arm in arm, I regaled him with my family tree.

'My mother's half-Irish. Her family are from Larne in Northern Ireland. My great grandfather sank the Larne ferry,' I said. 'Where are you from?'

He laughed drunkenly.

'County Cork,' he said.

'What are you doing in London?' I asked.

'Business. I've got a law firm,' he said.

We caught a cab to Piccadilly, to a small private hotel.

'They know me here,' he confided. 'Let's be having a night-cap in the bar first shall we?' he said, linking my arm in his.

The bar was painted black with gold-framed hunting prints and oil paintings hung on the walls. It was dark, glowing seductively with amber warmth. Bars come alive at night and are burnt out, smoke-dulled, shells during the day. Not unlike myself.

It's embarrassing walking arm in arm with a man old enough to be your father, but I smiled at him adoringly.

The pleasant young barman smiled at him in recognition.

'Pint of Guinness and a white wine,' said my date.

We sat at a small round table. I played with the drink coaster.

'Do you have children?' I asked.

'Yes, to be sure. They're grown up. My son works with me,' he said proudly.

'How interesting,' I said, feeling bored and wishing the night was over.

Upstairs in the small but tidy room I coaxed him into the shower.

'You have a nice shower for me so that I can lick you all over, you scrumptious man. Off with your trousers, that's it, good boy,' I said.

'You're a naughty girl, aren't you,' he said.

'Ooh yes. I can't wait to be naughty with you. Let's be very bad,' I said.

He slapped me hard on the arse, falling sideways and hitting the wall.

'Oops a daisy,' I held onto his arm and guided him. I waited with a towel to help him out of the small shower.

'Let's get you to bed, sexy,' I said drying his white belly and doughy thighs. I held him firmly as we staggered towards the bed.

'Come here, you,' he rolled over and lunged at me clumsily.

'Just lay back, sweetie, that's right, let me do all the work,' I said.

He lay on his back while I rolled a condom onto his flaccid cock with my mouth and began to suck furiously. I removed the condom and squeezed lube onto him and began pulling at the reluctant member, stirring it to a slight erection. Sitting on his shaft I rubbed my arse backwards and forwards vigorously while working his cock with my hands.

He was almost erect so I rolled on another condom and sat on top of him while holding his cock firmly at the base. I squatted with my knees wide, singing to myself.

'Oooh, aaah, ooooh.'

'I don't like the condom. Take it off,' he barked.

'Oh, you are naughty. We don't want to give your wife any diseases, do we?' I said sweetly.

It must have been the repressed rage he felt towards his wife that caused his erection to shrivel rapidly.

'You dirty slut,' he yelled.

'Hey, don't be mean, we're having such a nice time,' I said.

He reached up to slap me but missed.

'Cunt, you cunt,' he shouted.

I grabbed my clothes from the floor and ran at the door as he pulled himself off the bed. I dressed as I ran up the corridor, shaking.

Downstairs at reception I pulled myself together.

'Hello, I'm so sorry to bother you. I'm terribly embarrassed. I've just been with a business colleague in room 14, Michael, and I can't for the life of me remember his surname. I have to send him an email in the morning. I wonder if you can help me?' I said to the pleasant young man.

'Oh, Mr Hennessy.'

'Yes, that's right.' I sighed with mock relief.

I went home feeling sick with shock. I had been with him for two and a half hours and he hadn't paid me.

I remembered hearing two of the girls talking about an escort who was raped and murdered when she was sent to a bogus private address in the suburbs. This wasn't Australia. I realised it wasn't as safe. The agency wouldn't care what happened to me; they had their money.

I slept badly and woke early.

I rang directory assistance from the pay phone on the landing.

'Hello, County Cork, Michael Hennessy Solicitors,' I said.

'M J Hennessy and Son?' she asked.

'Yes, that's it. Thank you,' I said.

'Hold for the number.'

I wrote it down and dialled. I held my breath. 'Hello is Michael Hennessy available please?' I said.

'No, I'm sorry he's in London on business,' said the girl.

'Could I ask your name?' I asked.

'Fiona,' she said pleasantly.

'Thank you, Fiona,' I said.

I rang the hotel in Piccadilly.

'Michael Hennessy, room fourteen please,' I said in my business voice.

'Michael, I just rang your practicse in County Cork and had a nice chat with Fiona. She sends her love. Before I ring your wife I'd like to give you an the opportunity to pay me. You owe me two hundred pounds,' I said.

'What do you mean?' he said in a groggy voice.

'After you got violent last night, it must have escaped your memory that you were paying me for sex,' I said.

'OK. Come and pick up your money,' he said.

Although he tried to sound tough, I could tell by the tremor in his voice that he was terrified.

I ran downstairs and up to the corner and hailed a taxi to Piccadilly.

I read the driver the address from a card I had taken from the hotel.

I paid the taxi and dashed into the hotel and up the flight of stairs. I remembered the way. I knocked on his door firmly.

'Michael, it's Ruby,' I called in a voice without its usual charm or softness.

He opened the door slightly and pushed the money at me.

I went home on the tube relieved but drained. I began to pack my things. I was over London. I walked up to Kensington High Street and found a travel agent.

'Hi, I'd like to book a flight to Denmark tomorrow please,' I said to the girl.

I organised a flight for seven am the next morning.

It was only seventy pounds one way. I didn't have much money left.

I went for a walk to Buckingham Palace and on the way back to my room bought crispbreads, yoghurt and some salad from a supermarket.

After flying to Copenhagen I checked into a youth hostel and caught a bus to the city centre.

I found a tasteful, glossy, display ad in a tourist magazine. It was one of only four ads, discreetly placed on the back page. This was how I had found the agency in Hong Kong.

I had some lunch in a cafe and walked around the small, gothic city until evening. I asked directions from passers-by. The bar was easy to find.

18
Flirtation:
at the Cockatoo Bar

The Kakadu Bar was down from Webers Hotel. Known as the 'Cockatoo bar', it was an institution that belonged to the spoilt days when Denmark was an economic hub. Denmark had once been the most successful economy in Europe—a porcine economy.

Chemically aided farming on reclaimed land was a modern miracle and meant high yields from a small area.

Along with every conceivable body part of the pig, pickled herrings were a big export.

In the seventies famous stars from all over the world came to perform at Wintergarden, a funfair for adults and children alike. Wintergarden is built in the centre of Copenhagen. It was much quieter now.

I walked into the bar from the icy street.

I immediately felt at home.

The smell of fermented wine, wool carpet and smoke was the smell of my mother's house.

Comprising two spacious storeys of deep, blood-red, carpeted comfort, with heavy, traditional, wooden, carved furniture and serious woven upholstery, the bar felt plush in a way that was designed to flatter the clientele and help ease money from their pockets.

The faces of the eight or nine women who worked there were reflected out of the gleaming, curved brass edges of the bar. In the soft light the women had animated red lips, sparkling eyes and flashing metallic hair.

Most of them were over forty. They seemed to match the solid furniture.

They glared at me with looking-glass eyes, reflecting mild hatred, thinly disguised as boredom.

A layer of muddy make-up concealed their true homely identity.

Only one attractive young woman was friendly to me.

I later found out that a client had bought the business for a young woman called Lisle. Her doorman, Bent, her right-hand man, was the unofficial manager. He was a stout, firm-minded, kindly father-figure with oiled, black hair at the sides of his head. He carefully combed the few remaining long hairs over his smooth dome.

The Italian architect, Bruneleski, had engineered the first unsupported dome on the cathedral in Florence. It was used as a model all over the world. Bruneleski would have been impressed by Bent's pate.

Bent showed me around and told me the women were to have their clients spend a minimum of seven hundred kroner at the bar before they were allowed to leave to visit the hotel.

This was the only legal way they could provide escort services. I had found out on my travels that prostitution is illegal in most countries, although tolerated by authorities, who are well oiled by vice.

By the time my date had spent his money at the bar, it was supposed to be: a) easier to extract money from him and b) likely he would be in a deep alcoholic slumber by the time I removed my clothes.

This enabled the lady to flee the hotel and catch the last bus home.

I sat in the upstairs bar near the entrance.

Burnished light fell in tennis balls from rows of downlights that trammelled the long, low ceiling. The light volleyed through potbelly glasses that were suspended in rows, upside down above the dark timber bar. The light fell onto the rounded brass edges and dripped amber into the blood-red carpet.

Night pressed its hearty chest against three low, small-paned windows, hung at the sides with short tapestry curtains.

A rich stew of grapes fermented with dust, from countless litres of deliberately spilled wine on carpet, filled my head and hung inside my nostrils heavily.

The women had learnt to surreptitiously throw their wine onto the carpet under their chairs, to remain sober while drinking with the clients—although some did not.

A single plume of smoke wound slowly up to the black ceiling, from a slim cigarette, joined, yet held elegantly aloft from, a stout woman with short, dark-blonde curled hair. She wore a resigned, cunning expression.

It was her poise that separated her from the kitchen and homely duties.

I drank in the familiar dank atmosphere.

Weary though I was, a wire of adventure tweaked my nerves. It was eight o'clock or so, resting, dark. There was no chatter amongst the women. Waiting like a tigress, I felt the huntress stir inside me, a dormant anger frustrated at waiting.

The heavy wooden doors swung heavily on squealing hinges.

I heard Bent's consolatory tones rising over the swift inward draught.

'Good evening, sirs, may I take your jackets?'

I could hear two male English voices respond, mature, yet falteringly unsure.

I immediately sat taller on my haunches, igniting the amber spark in my animal eyes.

I looked at the other women, well aware that they were definitely not my friends, but rather arch rivals.

I looked at the end of the bar, to where a young woman leant in a halo beneath a down light.

She wore a low-backed, scarlet dress, with a matching fake hibiscus pinned securely behind one ear into straight, shimmering, coal-black hair that hung in a waterfall to her elbows.

Her full lips were painted bright red, a colour few women can wear well. Her face was coldly expressionless—a mask that could have killed with one look.

An Asian transsexual, she was not beautiful or even pretty, but striking.

She looked straight into the rows of bottles behind the bar that the barman was polishing methodically, making a soft swoosh with his cloth and ignoring the girls.

She downed a shot of neat vodka.

The sound wafted up from a trio of string musicians in their fifties, who played covers on a small dais downstairs.

Two English girls sitting at a table together were giggling together nervously.

The woman in red clenched her small, perfectly white, translucent teeth, looking as though she wanted to slap them.

Business had slowed down lately, there was barely enough work without new girls.

I saw her brush her left breast with one hand. It was sore from a manhandling the night before. The silicone needed replacing with saline. Another operation.

I had heard her talking in the bathroom when I was getting ready.

Many transsexuals commit suicide.

'Not this little yellow duck, not me, baby, I'm a survivor. Fuck you all!' she had said.

I thought that after working there for years she probably ached as though she had.

I drew my sabre.

Words of strategy readied themselves in armies of thought.

I was versed in current affairs: the Dow Jones, the price of gold, impending wars. Around forty-seven were being fought at any time in various locations.

This was a world in which one should always be armed.

The two men walked straight up to the bar, as men tended to do, having a relationship with bars that women merely imitated.

The barman stood with his legs apart, his small, keen dark eyes fixed on the customers. His expression was serious but not deferential as he waited for their order.

'Two beers please,' said the taller of the two men.

The wine list would tear the lining from their pockets, I mused, as I walked slowly towards them in a short, grey pleated skirt, my maroon shirt open to the gentle curve of a full breast, as white as the side of the moon, shining up to them.

Were you expecting someone shorter? I quipped to myself, smiling with amusement as their eyes rested on my chest and stayed low.

'Hello, my name is Ruby.' I said, extending a slim pale hand, curving my arm shyly.

It's the beginning of a love story.

I smiled upwards to the smaller of the two men from beneath a fringe of dark lashes, with a full mouth that suggested deliverance.

I observed him as he stood like the white rabbit in still indecision. The cogs of his brain were whirring behind a blank canvas that waited for the artist to paint on some small sign of emotion.

I thought of barren cliffs and moors. This was not Heathcliffe, although there was a peacock elegance about his shiny grey suit.

His colleague was broader and tall with a wealthy paunch. He wore dark blue, one-hundred and twenty gram Bryony superfine that hung like water from his thick frame.

He resented the rejection of him as my first choice of suitor, showing it with the set of his shoulders, eyes and chin, as though he had been halved somehow.

He turned away from us, grazed the room with cold blue eyes, gesturing to two seasoned whores, sure of a good time.

It was unlikely the women would get more than one client within their grasp each evening and money made them unscrupulous, as money tends to. They responded enthusiastically and quickly moved to the table where the men had sat down.

I was vaguely aware of my stocking that had a small run slowly itching down my thigh. I tried not to move my leg as I sat down.

My man had a serious face, the kind that liked to say no. It would be a challenge to dislodge his inner accountant and bring him over the line of resistance, not to my charms of course, but to parting with a large amount of money.

I sat with my spine stiff and tall, thrusting my breasts forward.

'You must buy us wine to drink or we are not allowed to sit with you. The bar has to make money,' I explained.

'I see, which one do you want?' my new friend asked.

I handed him the menu. He huffed a little like the wolf from the Three Little Pigs, wrestling with his inner adversary. He reached into his pocket for a pair of small gold-rimmed spectacles.

I was supposed to order champagne but I didn't have the hide and ordered a moderately priced red wine instead.

The two older women cajoled the other man in silver tones, sweeping aside the issue with a sophisticated wave of long painted fingers.

I knew from speaking with one of the women briefly that she had a retarded son to look after. Her name was Elsa, a cultured woman of at least forty. She had wide, forget-me-not blue eyes and silver hair that shone unnaturally bright against her chocolate tan. Her manner was genuinely sympathetic.

The other woman, although a little younger, was as solid as a round cheese. She wore a tailored tan skirt-suit with beige stockings that shone with a pearly gleam. Both of the women wore plentiful gold jewellery.

I liked Elsa, she reminded me of my Aunt Fern.

They sat across the table from me in the upholstered booth, spilling jovial banter onto the waxy, cherry-wood tabletop.

The larger man rested two large arms around each of the laughing women.

I probed 'George's' life, poking around the way you rifle through old clothes in your wardrobe, pulling out this or that old jumper.

I was wandering through his modest garden. A lawn mower hummed somewhere nearby. A bee rested on a full white dog rose. A plane flew low overhead to land at Gatwick. And then I seemed to take a boat at Henley Regatta with him. He, wearing a ribbon-trimmed straw boater, dark blazer and neat white trousers. Just down from Oxford to watch the racing on trailing green water. I, wearing a floaty white dress.

He looked slightly like a crow with a sharp, long nose and pinched features. He was strapped tightly, bandaged and constricted.

Had he ever abandoned himself to laughter from the belly, lost control to passion, rage, excess?

I often had the urge to run barefoot through a spinney, twirling in a flurry of pine needles and moss with wind on my face, in my ears and flowing through my hair. I had read *Lady Chatterley's Lover.*

Did George have moments of wild abandon?

I thought not.

'You're a nice man. Your wife is very lucky,' I said.

'I'm not so sure she would agree with you,' he replied.

He laughed, a small discreet sound like a cough.

'Well then, she's foolish. Sometimes we don't realise how lucky we are. You know what they say, a good man is hard to find, or is it, a hard man is good to find?' I said.

I laughed modestly and looked sideways seductively, flashing my teeth and a sly-eye smile.

Obviously George was not one to succumb to the folly of wasted words.

'I have a meeting in the morning, how much do you charge?' he asked.

'I have two prices: one thousand kroner for all night and six hundred for a short time.'

'How long is a short time?' he asked.

'About an hour,' I said.

'Do you kiss?' he asked.

'Not everyone, but maybe for you. I'll make you happy, you'll see.'

'Shall we take the bottle with us? It's easier to talk at the hotel,' I added.

I trapped him in my eyes and smiled deeply, letting him swim in the pool of my light. My voice slowed coaxingly, spread itself like honey over bread.

I liked him, not just because he was going to pay me a lot of money, but also because he was mild-mannered and sober.

He seemed lonely. Maybe he just wanted someone to listen and understand the pressure of his work. Maybe he was afraid of being alone in the sterile hotel room that mocked the futility of his existence and his blind lust.

I wasn't really listening but I heard his words and smiled sympathetically. That was all he needed.

I thought that the wives of these men must fail them.

The other two women were whispering in his friend's ear. I watched as he leant forward, a little drunk already.

I had seen the women tipping their drinks under the seat deftly, frequently filling his glass. He was now on his second bottle of champagne.

He allowed them to stroke his thighs and back, flattering him.

'Why don't we have a foursome with these two girls?' His voice slurred slightly as he leant across to his friend.

'No, thank you, I'm happy here,' my gallant friend said.

This game has no rules. I smiled at George thankfully.

As the night got deeper the frequency of the music and talk in the bar was rising.

I quickly went to order a Cabernet Sauvignon.

The barman looked at me sternly. The other women had ordered champagne: I was in trouble.

It was a sore point with him when a woman hadn't sold enough drinks.

'Could we take it away?' I asked.

'The other girls don't like you taking it out. They have to drink here, why shouldn't you?' the barman said crossly.

'What difference does it make?' I looked at him, exasperated.

'I hate rules. If I wanted to live with politics I would have worked in a bank. They're just jealous, besides, doesn't the customer come first?' I put my hands on my hips defiantly.

'It's not my rule, they've been here a long time. Do what you like.'

'They've been here too long. They're like stuffed animals,' I said.

I felt surreptitious eyes watching me.

Suddenly the room felt humid and stale like the armpit of an ape.

The barman reluctantly wrapped the bottle in brown paper and handed it to me.

'We have to tip the doorman one hundred kroner,' I explained to George, as I held onto his thin arm.

Bent fetched the man's coat, tipping his head in a bow that showed his broad, white, shining scalp in stark contrast with the stern black suit that he wore. Bent held the door open respectfully for us, pocketing his tip. Taxis waited outside on the mirrored road that glistened from lightly falling rain.

It was a charming small hotel, not far from the palace.

The hotel foyer seemed to recognise me, with its harsh cream floor tiles, carpeted in the centre, and cream marble counter that spun light onto our faces in a glare of shame.

Three staff: one young woman and two attractive young men in uniform, saw me enter.

They seemed pleasant, not speaking, yet recognising me with a friendly smile. Perhaps knowing I would tip them one hundred kroner, as I had been warned to do by Bent.

A long silent corridor led to George's room.

'I have a collection of these plastic keys at home, they're useless things,' he said as he pushed the card into the slot.

'Playing cards perhaps?' I suggested.

'You see the chair with the swan's head? That was Josephine's emblem. Napoleon was the eagle. It's called Empire style. Romantic isn't it?' I said. I brushed the polished mahogany antique chair with my hand.

'I would be a snow leopard, and you?' I said.

'I don't know, maybe a fox,' he said and laughed.

'No, they're hunted,' I said, as I laughed indignantly.

'Doesn't that make it more exciting?' he asked.

'You don't seem like the sort of man who would want to live dangerously,' I said.

'I'm here aren't I?' he said.

'Am I dangerous?' I asked.

'You're expensive,' he said and grimaced slightly.

'All the best things are,' I quipped. 'Aren't you going to offer me a drink?' I said.

He gestured to the mini-bar with a wave of his hand.

'I'll have a brandy, thank you.' I looked coquettishly at him, and waited for him to pour the small bottle into a glass.

I perched on the edge of the couch with crossed legs. He handed me the glass. The ethanol swelled in my nostrils as I sipped.

I rustled in my handbag for massage oil, condoms and lubricant and placed them beside the neat bed with its crisp white sheet folded down like the corner of a page.

'Shall I pay you now?' he asked.

'I suppose we should get the business out of the way so we can get on with enjoying the pleasure,' I said gratefully.

'Would you like me to have a shower first?' he said.

'Thank you, you're so sweet,' I said.

As he showered I tucked the notes into my bag.

I knew he would only pay me for one hour—he was too sober. Non-drinkers were far too sensible.

I felt a pang of regret. I could have tolerated him for longer.

I waited in the still room that smelt of soap and polish.

The walls were lemon with a fresh white ceiling and dark blue carpet with a gold fleur-de-lys pattern.

A neat writing bureau stood in the corner. The Victorian-style couch I was perched on was covered with expensive dark gold fabric embroidered with small black bees. I fingered them appreciatively.

He walked out of the white tiled bathroom with an ample bath towel around his waist that hugged his china-white skin. His back still sported small droplets of water.

Slim though he was, his flesh hung from his ribs dejectedly. A fold down the centre of his ruddy throat made him look as though he needed ironing.

He had the suntan of a man who has never taken his shirt off when he mows the lawn on Sundays with his sleeves rolled up.

He sat on the bed.

I undressed slowly, sliding my skirt down over my thighs. I looked into his face with a smile full of sex. I was a naughty schoolgirl, gleamingly innocent; a young cat with cream on its chin, sure of itself; completely and unashamedly wicked.

I pulled my shirt over my head in one movement that exposed the sharp outline of my ribs, stretched over with thick, creamy, oyster skin. Tossing my hair back from my forehead, I stood before him in my lingerie.

I ran both hands over my small firm breasts, pushing them up and together.

I slid my hands slowly down to my hips, stomach and thighs to draw his attention to my body. I knelt down with my knees wide apart, pushing my fingers into my black satin panties and licking my finger-tips slowly.

I laughed, at him, at myself, a little crazy, a little drunk, revelling in the luxuriant feeling of my own warm soft flesh.

I was a Babushka doll, so many layers to shed and then, in the centre, a tiny vulnerable baby, with the same painted face as the outer shell.

He sat mesmerised on the edge of the bed, wearing the face I had seen so many times, a little stupid and greedy. He looked like a combination of the Seven Dwarfves. I, Snow White, was maternal and completely in control. I stood up quickly, turned my back to him and bent forward with legs astride. I ran my hands up the inside of my thighs and drew aside the fabric of my panties, to reveal the shaved folds of my labia.

I rubbed at the skin that I've always thought looks similar to plucked chicken, feigning pleasure at my own touch.

He must have been hungry. Perhaps the thought of chicken was making him salivate.

I felt like reminding him to breathe, as he sat petrified.

Perhaps he was afraid of the crazed chicken woman who looked very tall as he sat on the edge of the bed.

Maybe he was worried that I might overwhelm him completely.

My stockings rasped against my thighs as I unpeeled them one at a time. I worried about the slight bulge of flesh at the top of my thighs. I was contemplating liposuction.

As I caught sight of myself in the mirror on the wardrobe door, a quick flash of green illuminated my eyes.

Nina Simone was singing inside me: 'Celine Woman, for a thousand dollars she wail and she moan'. Another more serious song about pain and apartheid came to mind, sung in the characteristic deep throaty voice of the singer, 'Dead men hanging from trees like exotic fruits'.

The fleur-de-lyis pattern on the carpet was pulling me downwards.

'Turn over, George, let me massage your back. You are in good shape. Is that too rough? Tell me if I'm hurting you.' My voice pattered.

He lay on his stomach breathing hot short breaths against the white pillow.

'Relax, let go of your tension, that's better,' I coaxed.

I moved my breasts over him slowly, moulding his skeleton with my hands. My thoughts rolled thickly in a swamp, a sensual warm mud bath, barely registering feelings.

I was in danger of putting myself to sleep.

I wondered why I had no guilt with these strangers, no matter how dirty I got. I felt nothing except tolerant amusement.

Yet, with my few serious lovers, I was caged and tormented by doubts and insecurity.

Memories of passion consumed me in a long sigh of pleasure, of two anxious mouths devouring one another.

There was guilt, always guilt, on my shoulders.

He moaned with pleasure beneath me as I worked his legs and buttocks with the palms of my hands.

I turned him over, sucked his flaccid cock to a short, stiff erection.

I straddled him, riding noisily until the spasm beneath me signalled to finish.

I felt nothing. I was focused on the acting, on keeping my facial expressions sincere, emitting believable sounds.

I lived instead in my mind, entirely separate from my body.

'Goodnight darling, sweet dreams,' I said softly, as I dressed myself quickly.

He lay on the bed with his eyes closed.

He didn't move as I shut the door quietly behind me.

As I walked quickly from the foyer, my body felt as light as a guitar string.

I slid a hundred kroner note onto the end of the reception desk.

It was a relief to emerge from the sheer, white light of the hotel that bared me, into welcome dark that swallowed me into part of the whole movement of life. 'Damn!' I shouted out as I watched the last bus rumble away in a bath of warm light.

It was a stiff walk to the hostel at the edge of town.

I walked home, half on my knees or falling against every upright surface I could aim for so many times in the weeks to follow. I would have virtually walked every square inch of the earth by the time I left Denmark—in high heels.

The sky was hung with rain clouds the colour of foreboding. A very attractive blonde girl squatted to piss on the cobblestones in front of me. She was obviously drunk. I had to move away to avoid the steaming stream.

The action contrasted sharply with her beauty. Sharp pain bit into my ankles, as the back of my new shoes pinched me. I would have worried about it, if not for the liquor-fuelled furnace in my belly.

This is the life that chose me. I don't feel I had a choice.

Mary Magdalene was said to be a whore. We give our love, but we are ostracised from the flock. It takes courage to live this life. It shouldn't be a crime. Hypocrites carry secret desires suppressed within the sacred bed of holy matrimony.

My stigmata bled tiny translucent drops into a dull pewter chalice as I muted my pain to the throbbing veins of life.

What's going to happen to me? Is this all there is? Can I bear it any longer?

Interlude

Foundation

I relived my childhood.

I had grown up in the English countryside.

It was the bells ringing on Sunday morning that prevailed in my memory over and above every other detail.

Soft gauze hung over the grass and the shroud of yellow daffodils that grew around my church, rendering the mornings soft and new. God carefully orchestrated it all, as I believed, to ease the shock of waking to a harsh world.

The ever-present awareness of God buffered me against fear and loneliness. His gentle forgiving face accompanied me in my imaginings.

On Sundays I got up early, dressed carefully in my one good dress, faded and too small for me, and walked the long walk to church. I sang in the choir, or rather mouthed the words, being shy of the sound of my own voice.

With my round face shining, I turned to the sky, thinking good thoughts and smiling unconsciously. I had one friend, Jill, who was also in the choir; this was where our common ground ended.

This was the high point of the week, away from the stench of cigarette smoke, alcohol and dirt: from the rasping voices raised in accusation that twisted my gut with fear.

The Beatles had glamorised working class England. The lyrics of their songs spoke of love. I was obsessed with love and happy endings.

I pored through mail order catalogues wishing I could buy the smart clothes, flowered china tea sets and bright plastic toys. My mother told mey I was spoilt, being an only child.

Everyone knew that only children were spoilt.

I had a birthday party once. I sat ready for three hours before the children arrived, sick with anticipation. I had been so nervous and shy that afterwards I couldn't remember the details, just a blur of conflicting emotions.

My mother had a showy beauty that people admired. She prided herself on her modesty, that is, in not taking pride in anything, especially her daughter. She said that I made her realise she wasn't cut out for motherhood. Especially since her only memory of her own parents was of two lacquered black coffins side by side in stately, cold silence.

My grandmother had brought up my mother. The old woman's ideas were deeply rooted in the days of the drawing-room-parlour and constricting traditions. A young woman should wear her liberty bodice to keep her back stiff and she should hold her cutlery correctly—these were the important things in life.

Devon is the furthest point south of progressive thought in the Western world. The rules that govern life in rural England are essentially pagan. Superstition, witchcraft and smuggling are probably still a way of life along the windy, jagged coastline.

Bad judgement was a tradition in our family.

One of the worst choices my mother made was her husband.

Once they had been a glamorous couple. He, a raven-haired rocker, tall and fit, with rugged gypsy good looks, from a family of thirteen who came from the nearby city of Exeter.

She, tall, willowy and classically beautiful, with long shining black hair that hung down her back and rippled with blue lights as she walked.

The unwritten laws that governed the small lives of these country folk decreed that success was measured by marriage and childbirth.

If a woman was left on the shelf after twenty-four she was an old maid, gathering dust at family parties; the subject of rumour and pity.

Some small display of finery, in dress, or home decoration further improved one's post-coital social status.

In this village atmosphere the only entertainment was gossip, vicious and crippling.

I was born perfect and pretty in the first year of my parents' marriage. My mother dressed me in little kilts and woollen tights.

I learnt early to smile and cajole my way into the hearts of adults. I would perch on the knees of the men, my hair curled prettily, and gaze shyly from translucent eyes, a plump pink knuckle held between my teeth.

The smoky rooms were full of witty adult banter and Frank Sinatra's slow seductive crooning. It was 1964. My father joined the army and was posted to Germany, where we enjoyed the camaraderie of other expatriates and the hospitality of a generous culture. Even though we were the occupying invaders the locals appeared to bear us no grudge.

These were innocent years. The Germans were new-found friends, kind and hearty. The skies were no longer dark with bomber planes, the roar of fear.

My parent's generation benefited from the war. With the deprivation of rationing and lost loved ones over, new freedoms created an atmosphere of gaiety and revelling. Even simple pleasures like butter and fresh eggs, stockings and chocolate seemed heavenly.

On the army base, vital young couples were thrust together, sharing the intimacy of pleasure-seeking.

Music played long into the nights. My parents laughed together, swung each other round to 'The Twist' and 'Rock Around The Clock', sharing their youthful love of fun and adventure.

They didn't dream of growing old and serious. My parents didn't realise that life would change and that they would later grow bitter, bloated and full of self-hatred.

Farmers around the air-force camp pragmatically conducted their business as usual, digging potatoes and downing giant steins of beer.

I spoke conspiratorially, in mock German, to the many stray cats who which wantonly populated the cellar of our unprepossessing red brick house. They were my friends.

I made them cakes out of mud and chastised them when they were bad, for not doing as they were told.

I knew early that I irritated my mother. She preferred the company of her friends or a good book. My mother was particularly inconvenienced by displays of emotion.

It was summer. I was bundled into our little white Volkswagen. There was an air of tremendous excitement in the house as we packed. The adults said we were going 'abroad'. I had no idea what a holiday was but I knew it was going to be good.

We formed a humble convoy with two groups of my parent's friends in their cars. We set off through Holland, Austria, Switzerland and France to Spain.

I stared from the back window, feeling sick from motion and the thick, acrid, grey cigarette smoke that filled the car.

My eyes feasted on the vision of wildflowers: sometimes fields of red poppies, wildflowers or edelweiss growing from rocky mountain crags. In Holland there were cultivated fields of red and yellow, tiger-striped tulips. Spain was a miracle of burning golden beaches.

In the bars, there were beautiful dancing ladies with jet-black hair scraped back tightly into tortoiseshell combs. They wore long vivid dresses with wide skirts, layered with black lace—pulled up to show the seductive curve of an ankle and calf. At night I went to restaurants with the adults.

I sat low in a big bentwood chair, reaching up into a large dish of paella, fascinated by the timeless, intensely sensual gyrations of the taut woman dancing in front of me. I sensed the animal, the lust.

The male dancer wore a black small-brimmed hat perched squarely upon the crown of his head and tied tightly under his chin. An impossibly crisp starched shirt, decorated with frills down the front, was tucked with anal care into his tight black trousers. The controlled movement of his muscular body caused the tightly fitted fabric to mimic the golden skin beneath it.

I caught a glimpse of the velvet softness of his stomach through the fine cotton of his shirt, the line of black hair leading downwards from his navel. As he pulled his head up, the veins on his neck protruded. His angular chin and nose pointed over the crowd with the arrogance of an aristocrat.

His muscular shoulders were pulled back and his chest was thrust forward, pressing against the air with feeling. He emanated the power of a stallion. The woman's body shuddered dramatically, as though repressing her need for him within her arched body. I knew that she longed for him.

Her vermilion taffeta dress, fitted tightly at the waist, flared into a full skirt that was longer at the back, forming a train.

The two beautiful young adults were seemingly thrown around the centre of the crowded room by their passion, barely touching each other. Their intimacy caught the breath of the onlookers and held it in their chests with anticipation of each movement, the way you hold your breath in suspense before reaching orgasm.

They were perfectly in unison as they moved toward their own climax of feeling. The swish of the wide skirt, and snapping castanets, provided the only musical accompaniment. The sound rose and quickened in intensity.

Years later I would finger my little plastic doll with the red dress, almost identical to the dancing woman, and remember the taste of paella. I vowed I would have my own red dresses. I would inhabit womanly sensuality—passion and holidays were linked in my mind. Sunshine and sexuality. It was the happiest time in my life.

The life that my parents led during these years must have exhausted their entitlement to happiness. They returned to England and the dreary deprivation they were used to.

My father's athletic frame thickened, his intelligent good humour vanished, replaced by anger and misplaced idealism.

He railed against the government, at things that could not be changed. He became unrecognisable not only in his manner; his outward features mimicked the growing bloated internal ugliness.

This in turn, caused my mother to harden like brittle toffee, syrupy yet unyielding.

She withdrew her body and her emotions further, until her presence in the house had the substance of a subdued, brooding shadow. In the mother country, in our seaside hometown, the economy grew hopelessly bleak. Strikes became so common that it was unusual to have electricity at the same time as gas and collected garbage.

Jobs were scarce, luxuries, such as meat, hair conditioner or household appliances even scarcer. My father went to work at the northern end of the country, leaving my mother to bring me up alone. The fairytale of youth was over for us both.

Hopelessness bred dirt and ugliness.

We barely had enough money for food. I wore my great-aunt's cast-off clothes to school. They were old lady's clothes and hung off my skinny body. There wasn't any money to buy the extras that I needed like coloured pencils and gym clothes.

We never had a holiday again.

Children at school sensed my weakness and chanted cruel rhymes when I walked past, about my poverty and my flat chest.

My nickname was BO because my jumpers smelt musty. I wasn't good at washing my clothes and Mum didn't have time.

I can still feel the shame.

I huddled over a candle in the cold in our dilapidated house and dreamt of becoming a princess one day, or a famous actress. I would have beautiful clothes. I would be a beautiful, rich lady. I watched old black and white films. I liked the Audrey Hepburn movies. I was going to be like Gigi. I was convinced I would marry a wonderful rich man. Be careful what you wish for.

19
Salvation:
the start of the end

There are no hills and dales or mountains in Denmark. It is a flat and feature-less country, except for practical waterways that barely move.

In winter it is minus two degrees in the middle of the day in Copenhagen. It is so cold you would think the sun would never shine again. The cold reaches right down to the cellar of your stomach, the well of your being and through the windy corridors of your chest and lungs.

Winter is made for dark thoughts. The sorrow I had been feeling was for all of mankind.

The bar seemed darker and more lifeless than ever as I dragged my chains to work that evening.

I sat in the corner alone sipping coca-cola.

I heard the door open.

It was early, all of the women hadn't arrived yet. There were a group of three, and two others by the bar. As he walked into the bar, he seemed to fill it with his size and spirit that was far larger than his six-foot-three frame and heavily muscled shoulders.

He looked straight at me with powerful, blue-steel eyes and a steady gaze that hinted at the strength of his will. Not once did he glance at anyone else in the room.

He walked straight up to me with loose swinging limbs and sat down. He lay his coat over the back of the empty chair next to him. Bent hadn't been at the door to take it.

'You're with me,' he said. I was flattered and relieved that my night was a success so early.

He looks dreadful. What is he wearing tracksuit pants for? You don't dress like that in Europe, you idiot.

'You have such big arms,' I said, feigning awe.

'Here, feel,' he said. He drew my hand to touch his triceps.

As he flexed, I felt the thick, wide, blue, veins on the iron ball of muscle.

Sun seems to shine from the small golden hairs on his wrists—from his eyes.

Fixing me with a look, he asked, 'Are you English?'

'Yes, but I've lived in Melbourne since I was twenty,' I said.

'I'm from Sydney. My name's Red,' he said.

He leant close to me and whispered in my ear. 'I've just dropped two pills.'

'You're mad. This isn't Holland,' I whispered back. I looked around anxiously.

I wonder if he's a gangster or a drug dealer?

'The people here are very conservative. They don't take drugs. They wouldn't approve,' I hissed.

'Relax Max,' he said. I watched with horror as he put his foot up on the edge of the table. Involuntarily I moved my arm to push his foot down and then checked myself.

I smiled at him encouragingly.

'I miss Australia. It's so immense you could be lost forever, even from yourself. The sun is so strong; it toasts people dark golden-brown all over. The vast, red desert and fields of crisp wheat,' he said. 'I don't know why but I felt compelled to come here tonight. We're obviously meant to meet. It must be destiny that brought me here. I've never been to a place like this. I never pay for sex. I don't enjoy the idea of a woman pretending. It doesn't turn me on,' he told me.

I melted a little. *If only.* I had lived for so long in a comfortable, clover-bed of habitual untruths—I was suspicious.

As he continued speaking with his pleasant manly voice, sparkling lights slipped over and through me. *I'm being hypnotised.*

I noticed his stylish gold Philippe Patek watch.

He might have some credibility in the business world, even though he's obviously a crazy drug addict.

'I'll take you home for a visit. Imagine this. Close your eyes, let it fill you,' he said.

'In a cool gully a pair of ragged kookaburras sit on a branch, preening their clotted cream feathers with funny long beaks. They look down enquiringly at the humans passing beneath the gum tree. Their long tail feathers, spotted with iridescent turquoise, wag up and down.

'They have wide heads with low brows and small beady eyes. They call out to each other in the loudest cries, cackling and yodelling into a sleepy fern gully, beside a stream whose s-bends snake over ripple-patterned sand-beds.

'Sunlight falls through palm trees in halos of light, catching plant -life in spotlights. The chiaroscuro carves the vivid colours: green, teal, yellow, plum, orange, purple. Palmate frilly layers of luxuriant vegetation, tumble in green waterfalls. Frothy streams run over stones, soft with moss, mint and lime green. Here and there a clump of pink lilies or vivid blue morning glories mingle with vines bearing wild honeysuckle flowers. Clumps of white lilies shine like angels resting on the cool slopes. Butterflies couple and float, landing on shrubs covered with flowers that look like handfuls of buttercups, as bright as the flesh of sunshine.

'The smell of wild violets and soot, fungi and water fill the air like the smell of sugared almonds. Orb spiders spin giant silver webs.

'An oasis away from the scorching sun,' Red said.

'It sounds beautiful,' I said.

'It's the most incredible country, isn't it?' he said.

'You've succeeded in making me home sick,' I said.

He's a worry but he's very romantic. Iridescent.

He got up and moved behind me. He threw his arms around my back with a bold movement. I stood up unsteadily and held his arms firmly.

'I don't want you to be thrown out.' I laughed to disguise my embarrassment.

In Denmark I've only encountered very sophisticated mature men. I've forgotten the Aussie larrikins and drunks I used to see in Perth.

Red said, 'You know, you'll fall in love with me. I'm a good guy. You'll be my girl. I'll take care of you. You can still work if you want to. I'll never tell you what to do, but I don't think it's healthy. Why don't you have a holiday for a while? Come back with me. I'm rich enough to look after you and we can have a lot of fun together,' he said. His eyes were overbright and his teeth were grinding. His jaw was tense and he was hugging himself and fidgeting.

He's obviously very high. I have to get him out of here before he embarrasses me to death.

I still thrilled inside at his words. They sounded like freedom to my thirsty ears, they murmured the sweetest brook over parched land. It sounded unbelievable but a big part of me longed for a more fertile life.

It's hard to trust someone you don't know, to believe in fairy tales and happy endings. I'll play along for now.

The coincidence of bumping into him so far from home could be destiny.

He's probably lying. It's just the drugs talking. It's still too good to ignore. After all, I haven't got anything to lose.

I sooooo want to believe him.

When you really want to believe in something badly, your misgivings can be packed away.

'You will still have to pay me for tonight. If you marry me I'll give you back your money. Let's split this joint,' I said lightly.

'It's a deal,' he said. We shook hands.

We went to his hotel in a taxi. It wasn't far. He insisted on lying down on the back seat.

'He's a bit drunk,' I told the taxi driver as I helped him out.

I steadied him as we walked through the foyer. I was worried that he might stop and chat with the reception staff so I propelled him up the corridor.

The wallpaper in the hallway was striped a welcoming butter colour. The carpets were dark blue.

It was the same hotel I had been to many times, my favourite.

Once in the room I felt a little nervous and less in control than usual.

'I'll have to get the money from you first. I charge seven thousand kroner for the night,' I said.

He was surprised.

'I only have six thousand, is that OK?' he said.

'Sure, that's fine. Just for you.' I tried to sound light-hearted.

'I don't want to have sex. I don't pay for it. I couldn't stand to think of you doing it just for the money,' Red said.

I hadn't met many men who didn't want to fuck me. I was filled with relief. To show my gratitude I wanted to give him a good time. This was different. I wanted it to be different: to melt my cynicism like the snow melts in spring.

We lay together, stiffly.

'Take off your underwear,' he said in a childlike voice.

I hated to take off my black lace suspender belt, lace-top stockings and satin push-up bra. It was my shield, the costume of an actress.

He felt big and strong, the way my father had used to feel when I was a very little girl. I lay naked and vulnerable in his arms, spooned against his large frame.

Outside is a sky full of stars.

He's not just big like winter. His size is impressive, a monarch, or conqueror, like Alexander the Great.

He's a combine harvester, I'm the mouse. Having the chance to run, I give myself up, to be engulfed in the power of the machine, in a giant field of his presence.

I felt uncomfortable not to be working. I wanted to chatter meaninglessly to him the way I did to my clients but he pressed his finger against my mouth to silence the nervous ramblings of my mind.

'Alone we are exclusive, together divine,' he said.

I feel like a soldier on foreign soils, not sure which way to advance, still full of adrenaline but not faced with an enemy, just sweeping peaceful views of the countryside.

I've been engaged in battle for so long it's hard to accept that the war is over.

I lay down my armour, disarm my sworded tongue.

Eventually I slept, still half alert. I woke cradled in his arms surprised at how comfortable it felt, like laying in a giant armchair.

I feel as though I know the feeling of my body imprinted on his.

We made love still half asleep, our flesh hot against the cool of the room. Inside each other's skin. I felt drunk with a sensation that made me want to sing hosannas.

We lay conjoined in the after-bright, a warm, blue glow similar to ultra violet.

Minutes before our genitals had been locked together by the horns, as bulls fighting, tearing away what we needed. Two bodies swelled hard and angry, and after, we fell back exhausted.

My vaginal muscles still gripped his wilting penis as though chewing the last of a feast.

I've gone soft as butter in the sun, with a sharp yellow sheen, smelling of daisies.

We lay on soft cotton sheets.

Melted together in the warmth the way dumplings soften at the edge in a stew.

As I breathed in and out to the rhythm of him, as our skin kissed,

I thought, he knows the twists and turns of the world better than I. The funfair, the tunnel of horrors, the ride.

I sighed.

I came to slowly. I felt fragile—an orchid.

In the first few moments of consciousness I could hear birds and seagulls calling, earnest, urgent, pure sounds in the square outside the hotel.

The church bells were ringing in the 'plads',' or squares, outside, reverberations of traditional values in the ancient dust of crumbling churches.

I felt his body warmth and measured my joy and contentment against the fear of change.

He woke and rolled towards me, scooping me to him with his big arms.

'Hi, did you sleep well?' he asked,

'Yes, thank-you. You?' I said.

'A bit,' he said.

He kissed me gently, nibbling my bottom lip gently.

I moved my mouth to speak, but he silenced me by pressing his finger over my lips.

He deftly flipped my body around so that I was facing away from him, lying on my side, seated against his lap. He pushed my torso forward slightly, away from him, as he entered me from behind.

I was completely possessed, overwhelmed by his size and the power of his body. I screamed with every thrust, dizzy and breathless, with closed eyes, letting the sensation take hold of me.

I had never felt so consumed.

I screamed as the feeling inside me grew to unbearable tension. I wasn't sure if it was pleasure or pain.

He moved me under him and pulled my knees to the sides of my face.

I braced my muscles against the strengthening thrusts. His face reddened and contorted in climax.

I lay with my head on his chest quietly and then asked in a small voice,

'Would you really like me to come to Sydney with you?'

'Did you think that was just a line to get you into bed?' he said.

He looked down at me smiling slightly.

'No, actually, you didn't need to try that hard to get me into bed,' I said.

'Of course I do. I expect you to come with me or I want my money back. I've bought you for life. Wasn't that the deal?' he said.

'Am I your slave?' I asked.

'Of course. You know what Australian men are like. We like our women barefoot, pregnant and in the kitchen,' he said.

'But I can't cook,' I said.

'Then I'll have to keep you in the bedroom. That works better for me anyway,' he said. 'Do you want to order some room service?'

'Can I?' I asked, gleefully.

'What do you want?' he asked.

'Fruit and English breakfast tea,' I said.

He rolled over and picked up the phone. Ordering the same for himself.

'I've got a meeting today. You should go home and get your things ready. We'll be leaving on Friday.'

'That's in three days.' My eyes widened.

'I'll take you out for dinner tonight. Meet me back here at seven-thirty. We'll have a drink first. Have you got a mobile phone?' he said.

I was thankful I had hired one. He punched my phone-number into his handset as I gave him the numbers.

I bathed in the wide porcelain bath, enjoying the luxurious feeling. I could hear the breakfast-trolley arrive in the bedroom.

Wrapped in an enormous white towelling robe that dragged on the ground, I ate, feeling small and shy.

'You look like a child. I'm going to call you my baby-girl,' he said.

'Shall I call you daddy?' I asked.

'No. That's a bit sick. Just call me Red, or handsome or God if you feel like it,' he said.

I laughed. I was glad he was still high.

I feel beautiful when he looks at me. I hope he is genuine. Maybe he'll disappear and it's all just bullshit. I'm prepared for that. My flawed, drug-fucked knight in shining armour.

He was in the shower as I left.

As I walked down the corridor, I felt conspicuous, although I didn't pass anyone.

For the first time, I left a hotel without feeling guilty or paying money to the reception staff. I smiled and lifted my head slightly.

I've come to believe in money, independence and struggle. The struggle is inside me, most of it is probably imaginary.

I think I know my worth and don't need a man. Or do I?

I've been working for five years. Time has spun, flown past; the essence of speed has constricted my heart. Unnamed fears and past pain have made it hard to breath at times.

It's like being in a car driving towards a wall, screaming stop but unable to control the motion or the vehicle.

That night I went back to the hotel to meet him. I knocked at his door timidly. He opened the door and let me in. He was on the phone. It was obviously a business call. I watched him speaking.

He's impressive when he's being serious.

He took me to a very expensive restaurant for dinner. We drank Dom Perignon as casually as though it was water.

The waiter's impressed. He's falling over himself to be helpful. He looks as though he's dipped himself in the soup and risen, dripping obsequiously. His small dark eyes are gleaming fanatically. It must be the candle-light or maybe the big tip he thinks he's going to get. His black hair is oily. He looks like a herring.

I pinched myself.

I'm living in a fairy tale.

I just might be a princess after all.

Or am I just enchanted by the relief of being rescued and having him provide a brighter future for my children and I? No, I really want to love him. He makes me feel special.

The next day—the first day of my new life.

Autumn had begun to lay down her honey mattress thick and low, fermenting the air with amber perfume that reminded me of old brandy. As the day died, the moist, warm, breath of afternoon was swilled into an early sunset; a crisp, cool dusk.

It was a good time to leave, a natural exit.

I rang the bar to say I was going home. I knew I was burning my bridges and needn't have bothered.

Bent will be angry if he finds out I've 'stolen' a client.

I packed my things into my suitcase. My life doesn't seem so bad any more.

There's a decadent seductive charm in moral twilight. I have a choice—I can feel guilty and wrong for being unconventional, or I can embrace it. I can throw myself into the memory of a life of colour and richness that amounts to art. This is a sacred moment.

Who knows? Perhaps at this very moment all people will see their lives with clarity, and accept themselves.

High above the clouds, between continents, between lives, on the route of a unique personal journey.

A kind of mass apotheosis.

It's not about right or wrong. We are just who we are.

I am so grateful for the things that have been and the things that have not. The journey wasn't always easy, but you know, I wouldn't change a thing.

On my last night in Denmark, Red and I ordered dinner in the room. We watched *Pretty Woman* on the in-house video in the hotel room. I lay with my head on his chest listening to his heartbeat.

'You're my Pretty Woman,' he said. I smiled up at him.

At the end of the film a small cynical voice in my head said: I wonder if he will continue to cheat on her with hookers, both male and female. Will he call her a prostitute every time they argue? Will their kids grow up to become drug addicts because he never learnt to be a loving father? Will she become rich and bored and eventually leave him for a more seductive younger man? Such is life!

Suddenly, I wondered with gut-dropping deadness, were there really happy endings or was that just a little bit naïve? Do the princess and prince in fairytales grow old and fat and die of debilitating illnesses? Don't be silly.

I've been everywhere and seen it all. I've had sex with a large proportion of the world's population in every conceivable circumstance, manner and position. At least nothing can shock or surprise me in the future.

When will I learn? Never throw out a challenge like that to the universe!

There are no endings just new beginnings.